THE VICTORIANS AND
SOCIAL PROTEST

THE VICTORIANS
AND SOCIAL
PROTEST

A Symposium

Edited by
J. BUTT and I. F. CLARKE

DAVID & CHARLES
ARCHON BOOKS 1973

This edition first published in 1973 in Great Britain
by David & Charles (Holdings) Limited Newton Abbot Devon
and in the United States as an Archon Book
by The Shoe String Press, Inc., Hamden Connecticut 06514
ISBN 0 7153 5776 X
ISBN 0 208 01329 6

Printed in Great Britain
by W J Holman Limited Dawlish Devon

CONTENTS

INTRODUCTION
J. Butt and I. F. Clarke

THE VICTORIANS have too readily been dismissed for their bland complacency. These inter-disciplinary essays are partly intended to expose the assault on some established notions which was proceeding during the Victorian period. We were also intent on taking into account differing attitudes to ideas like utilitarianism, progress, self-help, *laisser-faire* and socialism. Thirdly, movements like Chartism or Land Reform were possibly more immediately important to Victorians than one might gather from treatment of them in general books on the period. Finally, we thought it appropriate to balance Robert Owen's millennialist vision with a contribution relating to that most original of European pessimistic writers, Dostoevsky; his *cri de coeur* against the uncritical acceptance of ideas of progress or scientific advancement for its own sake is the subject of Dr Noble's essay. Despite Dostoevsky's anti-utopianism, he was essentially prophetic about the future both of Russian liberalism and of the western capitalistic form of industrialisation based on *laisser-faire* economics. He shared with Robert Owen a recognition of the potentialities of modern science and technology and a fear that the aggressive egotistic liberalism of his day would never blend these with a humane ethical system. Owen, ever the optimist, believed that a 'rational' educational system could eliminate the worst excesses of individualism. Dostoevsky's forecast was one of doom, of European political, social and military catastrophe.

In his essay, Dr Treble challenges the commonly accepted and superficially attractive view that Irish immigrants stiffened the sinews of working-class radicalism. Before 1848, at any rate, the evidence from the North of England suggests that Irishmen fought Ireland's battles on English soil and were by no means assimilated into indigenous radicalism. O'Connell rather than O'Connor led the way! The irrevocable breach between these two in 1836 made Chartism a victim of Irish party politics, a process in sharp contrast to events at the end of the nineteenth century. Revival of interest in Chartism is becoming widespread, partly because of the increasing revelation of regional and local differences in the movement which makes it an attractive topic of post-graduate theses and partly also because of the general development of Social History as a discipline. As social historians concern themselves with exploring and explaining the militancy of some groups of the working classes and the relative apathy or reluctant conformity of others, it seems possible that a new reassessment of British working-class movements in the late 1830s and the 1840s may emerge. The links with Owen and the Owenites, so brilliantly expounded by John Harrison in *Robert Owen and the Owenites in Britain and America* (1969), could be taken still further into the century in the hope that the connections between socialism and political radicalism could be uncovered.

A revival of interest in John Stuart Mill in recent years has revealed no typical complacent Victorian second-rate thinker to be readily dismissed. Rather, as Mr Gordon shows, the complexity of life, experience and thought was very apparent to Mill, so much so that he was unable to produce a synthesis because he did not believe it likely to be either possible or valid. His attack on Bentham's philosophical radicalism with all its false certainties was exceedingly wide-ranging and profound. In several respects J. S. Mill began the fundamental questioning of Victorian commonplaces which more recent philosophers have continued.

Our own age can rarely find sympathy with perhaps the most under-rated Victorian idea, 'Self-help'. Dr Gilmour rightly emphasises its meritocratic implications which allowed attacks to be made on possibly more objectionable notions such as 'birth' and 'station'. The attitude of Dickens to the idea of 'Self-help' was bound to be ambivalent, if only because he had too massive an imaginative conscience to be content with posing as an example of it. His alienation from such traditional Victorian ideas took the form of literary protest. Middle-class life with its conventions and security mocked bitterly the experience of most working-class families. Gentility, so important to the commercial classes, often tended to stratify imagination beneath apathy and deadened conscience, two elements essential to social protest movements.

The hypocritical cast in much 'Self-help' was immortalised in Uriah Heep, and the advice purportedly given by Uriah's father, 'Be 'umble...and you'll get on', was no doubt an accurate assessment of the motivation of much of Victorian lower middle-class conformity. But Dickens indicates in *David Copperfield* that self-made men did not need to lack basic decency or dignity—nor did they need to possess them as though by law of nature. This could equally be said of aristocrats. The Dickens of the early works expected self-made men to change Britain and the world for the better; the Dickens of *Hard Times* and *Little Dorrit* was much more pessimistic. It was as though experience had convinced him that 'Self-help' generally destroyed any feeling of humanity.

The intellectual rejuvenation of socialism in the 1880s and 1890s owes a great deal to William Morris and George Bernard Shaw. Mr Redmond finds the similarities between the intellectual positions of the two men far less significant than their differences and in the process convincingly demonstrates the subjectivity of many socialist attitudes. Both Morris and Shaw harked back to the experience and ideas of Robert

Owen; both respected him for his attempts to reform British society and both, like Owen, abandoned Christianity and used sectarian language to describe and to enunciate their socialism. It was as though socialism was a doctrinal compensation for their having abandoned a chilly, class-ridden established faith; indeed, as if it were a new religion, which once generally accepted, would lead to a new heaven-upon-earth.

Although the shadow of Marx had intervened between Owenism and the socialism of Shaw and Morris, utopianism survived. Shaw, however, concerned himself with a vision of the triumph of the meritocracy; Morris, on the other hand, was intent on the victory of the idea of equality. Mr Redmond shows the full spectrum of Victorian socialism, with Shaw and Morris at opposite ends of it. Shaw's utopia was a denial of the senses; that of Morris represented the fulfilment of natural and good instincts. Shaw's ideal human being was not an individualist in any sense; he was community-orientated in exactly the same way as Owen's 'villagers' of co-operation.

The challenge to Liberalism by the newly emergent Labour Party is a common enough account of Edwardian politics. Professor Perkin's analysis of the land reform agitation significantly redates the origins of the decay of the Liberal Party. The land question, normally discussed as part of Irish politics, was of fundamental importance in the evolution of the Lib-Lab ethic—or the moral approach to politics, which Professor Perkin associates with the growing importance of professional men in the power structure of the Liberal Party. The movement of the Whigs out of the Liberal into the Conservative Party was a continuing process—but was greatly quickened by the land-reform agitation. Intra-party tensions made it difficult for the Liberal Party to retain the whole of their 'business' support, and radical solutions to the land question increasingly alienated all defenders of the untrammelled rights of property. This was ironic, since it was the concepts of free trade and free markets which had harnessed so many businessmen to the chariot of Liberalism.

The thorough-going transformation of the Liberal Party into a vehicle for the achievement of working-class objectives was never really practicable. An eclectic adaptation of Owenite ideas in the 1850s and 1860s by working-class organisations such as the co-operative movement made this unlikely; in the 1880s and 1890s the socialist revival among the lower middle classes as well as among trade unionists made the creation of a separate working-class party almost inevitable. The Liberal Party could never kick away the feet from under this infant protest movement, because it was not able to shed its Whig and business wings fast enough. And so Liberalism began its progress towards the position of a relatively 'precious' political philosophy, unrelated to clear class or economic interests and confused, but constantly moralising, about its future and objectives.

ACKNOWLEDGEMENTS

As editors, we are most grateful for all the patient work of our secretaries, Miss Helen Watterson, Mrs Georgina Buchanan and Miss Ann Hewitt. The Conference, held in the spring of 1971 to commemorate the bi-centenary of the birth of Robert Owen, from which this symposium of essays has gradually evolved, was supported by the Court and the Vice-Chancellor of the University of Strathclyde; we are glad to have this opportunity to acknowledge their help formally. To our colleagues and to the participants at that conference we are most grateful for their enthusiastic support.

ROBERT OWEN OF NEW LANARK: HIS CRITIQUE OF BRITISH SOCIETY
J. Butt

Public attention has long been directed to a reform in Parliament as a panacea for all political evils in which the expectants will be sadly disappointed, for it can effect no good or evil. Parliament elected by manhood suffrage, things remaining as they are, would make little or no change for the better to the working classes, but would waste perhaps more useless debates on subjects little understood by the new debaters. It would, however, be wisdom in the government to bring in and pass a bill for reform on the most liberal conditions— however liberal it will be harmless and it will prevent more waste of invaluable time.[1]

SO RAN part of the Memorial of Robert Owen 'late of New Lanark' to the Right Honourable the Lords of Her Majesty's Treasury, presented in January 1858 and dismissing irrefragably the foremost agitations of early Victorian Britain as so many political irrelevancies. It was this disregard for political change which made Owen the despair of many radicals. Yet his recognition of the limitations of political reform in producing social and economic change contained an important truth: given the vote and secret ballot, it did not necessarily follow that the standard of living or the quality of life of the working classes would improve.

However, Owen's position in 1858 marked an advance on

his views of 1819 or 1832.[2] Then he was in outright opposition
to the idea of universal suffrage or vote by ballot. His experience in America (1825-7) confirmed him in his rejection of
political agitation.[3] But the real origins of his political conservatism are to be found in his experience in Manchester
during the early 1790s when anti-Jacobin riots in a number
of towns forced dissenters like Joseph Priestley to leave the
country or to take refuge with friends. Owen's association
with Unitarians in Manchester is well known; less comment
has been made on the fact that he signed a Unitarian message
of loyalty to the Crown in 1793 and allied himself openly
with those merchants and manufacturers who publicly dis-
owned the revolutionary sentiments of 1789.[4]

Owen's career had been that of the lower-class cosmopoli-
tan. Obeying his own precepts about the importance of childhood and adolescence in the formation of character, we should
note that his varied experience in retailing probably contributed a great deal to his later capacity to charm all sorts
and conditions of men and women. In Stamford, as a shop
boy, he served the grand customers of his master, James
McGuffog, a linen draper, and acquired that due deference
and mock gentility which enabled him later to mix with the
lairds of Lanarkshire, princes of the blood-royal and aristocratic cabinet ministers. When he moved to London to the
firm of Flint & Palmer, whose working-class clientele bought at
cut prices for cash only, he acquired a wider business experience in a harsher environment. No doubt, he also acquired a
deeper understanding of humanity. Later, he gravitated to
Manchester and for the princely sum of £40 a year sold bon-
nets to middle-class ladies for Satterfield, who was from 1791
bonnet-maker by appointment to royalty.[5] Commonly, successful human relationships are dismissed as part of 'good luck';
Owen's virtually indefinable ability to persuade groups of
people to joint action—and often failure—probably owes
much to his early career as a salesman.

Certainly, Robert Owen's success as a cottonmaster depended upon more than his ability to be 'a shoe-shine with a smile'. In his autobiography he claimed that when he went to Manchester, he was nothing more than an awkward retiring youth. This may have been true. Yet Owen's upward progress was soon clear. He formed a partnership with another young Welshman, John Jones, a skilled mechanic, and began machine-making for the cotton industry. Their initial capital was very slight—£100 which Owen raised from his brother, William, a successful London saddler who had married his master's widow—their premises were rented, and their raw materials they obtained on credit. Jones soon recruited forty men, some of whom were employed on spinning and making rovings, while Owen attended to commercial transactions. Their activities were highly specialised and involved virtually no co-ordination. Considering their lack of experience and slender capital resources, this may have been just as well.[6]

After a short time Owen left Jones—ostensibly for fear that the latter might ruin him—and became manager of Peter Drinkwater's Bank Top Mill, the first cotton factory in Manchester to be powered by a Boulton & Watt rotary steam engine. Drinkwater, as Dr Chaloner has shown, was a man of considerable practical ability and knowledge, with a reputation for technical innovation, and well able to instruct Owen in the details of enlightened management.[7] Owen proved a diligent and conscientious learner and when he left Drinkwater (probably in 1794), his upward mobility continued. He became the managing partner for a very large concern, the Chorlton Twist Company, which was heavily dependent on nonconformist funds—initially the money of Henry Marsland was privately available to Owen and his friends.[8] In the late 1790s Owen extended his experience from mill management to purchasing cotton wool and marketing his firm's fine yarns. One of the best markets for Manchester fine yarns was the Glasgow area, a main centre of fine muslin weaving.

Among the yarn dealers of Glasgow, David Dale was outstanding, with mills at New Lanark, Catrine, Newton Stewart
and Spinningdale. Yet Owen's initial contact with Dale was
apparently a matter of chance—through Dale's eldest daugh-
ter Ann Caroline whom he eventually married on 30 September 1799.

From Dale, Owen and his partners bought New Lanark for
£60,000. This purchase price was to be paid over 20 years at
£3,000 pa with 5 per cent interest, and this method of settlement should be seen as a generous gesture on Dale's part,
since he must have been exceedingly doubtful about whether
he would live until 1819 to receive the final instalment. In
practice Owen gained a great deal from his association with
the Dale family. At the time of his marriage he received a
dowry of £3,000 and doubled his capital, according to his own
calculations. In addition, since David Dale was cashier of the
Royal Bank's Glasgow branch and an influential shareholder,
Owen's marriage had the effect of giving him possible access
to extensive trading capital. Alex Robertson has shown that
Dale's connections with the influential Campbell clan through
marriage provided Owen with other financial advantages
such as access to the surplus funds of Archibald Campbell of
Jura from whom by May 1812 Owen had borrowed £25,624
18s 8d. This money, Owen used, to finance his own sharehold-
ing in New Lanark.[9]

After his marriage it was natural that Owen should have
become one of David Dale's trustees. When Dale died in 1806
—he had been ill for a considerable time—he left Owen
£2,000, but at that time Owen owed his estate £11,007 2s 6d.[10]
Thus the funds of David Dale had become an important
source of Owen's capital—and they remained so, for in the
period 1812-13 when Owen was in considerable financial difficulties, it was David Dale's daughters who underwrote his
debts and saved him from bankruptcy.[11]

According to his autobiography, Owen's relationships with

his two sets of partners at New Lanark (that of 1799-1810 and that of 1811-14) were bedevilled by their opposition to his schemes for the community of New Lanark.[12] This was by no means the full story, since they agreed to the spending of considerable sums on the mills and village. Owen's financial difficulties—and the general problems of the Scottish cotton trade in the period 1809-12—caused Owen's partners to desire retrenchment and to fear the possible effects of his bankruptcy. Both these responses were perfectly natural in an age of tightening bankruptcy laws and unlimited liability.

Owen's capacity for effective human relations is commonly demonstrated by reference to the enlightened personnel management that he practised at New Lanark. Equally, it could be argued that his dexterity in obtaining partners and mobilising his personal credit revealed this skill. Despite his difficulty in retaining partners, he never lost on the process of 'take-over'.[13] Indeed, at revaluations of New Lanark, instigated in consequence of changes in partnerships in 1810 and 1814, he made considerable capital gains. His business efficiency can be ultimately assessed by his profit-making ability:[14]

1799-1810	£90,000. 0. 0.	average 15% per annum on capital	
1810-1814	£109,871. 12. 3.	„ 46%	„
1814-1825	£192,915. 11. 4.	„ 15%	„
1825-1828	£6,558. 16. 0.		

Total	£399,345. 19. 7.

It is certainly possible that, with Owen's advantages, other men might have made more money at New Lanark. Equally, they might have made less! Yet Owen's fame ultimately depended less upon profit-making but more on his humane methods of management of mills and paternalistic government of the village. These have been examined intensively but, I think, should be regarded as part of a much larger attempt by factory-owners to increase productivity by improving the quality of the labour force, by establishing quantity and stock controls over output and by modifying the environ-

B

ment.[15] Owen was the most famous but not the only exponent of scientific management during the Industrial Revolution and he achieved his fame very largely because he publicised his views more effectively than other enlightened employers and applied his theories in a more doctrinaire and ultimately more humane fashion.

He reduced physical effort in the mills by systematic planning of work flows and the introduction of hoists. He attacked theft, embezzlement, dirtiness, immorality and drunkenness. He costed labour in all the processes—even in repairs and maintenance. On the machines hung 'silent monitors' to offset the need for corporal punishment by supervisors—or swearing. These were small four-sided pieces of wood, with each side a different colour. The colour set to the front indicated the previous day's standard of behaviour and work effort. Black denoted sloth, blue idleness, yellow that more industry was still required, and white excellence. Owen noted in his *Life* that he 'passed daily through all the rooms and the workers observed me always to look at these telegraphs—and when black I merely looked at the person and then at the colour'. He could inspect the past performance of each of his workers from the book in which a numerical record of the colours earned was made. The instinct of social competition was clearly being exploited to raise individual levels of performance. But significantly, Owen's numbers to equate with the colours made excellent one and sloth four. Thus, the higher the total, the worse the past behaviour.[16]

Concern for general improvement of environment and particularly for community planning is prominent in many of Owen's writings. This had its origins in his experience in Manchester where he was one of the members of Dr Thomas Percival's Board of Health along with his partners, John Barton and John Atkinson.[17] His later attention to individual cleanliness and public health at New Lanark—his insistence that dunghills should be removed from the streets and his competition for bug-free houses (prize: a pot-plant from Mrs Owen) could be matched by many parallel instances among the master-builders of factory communities. Individual responses of this kind by factory-masters gradually established the social environment for the development of a public health movement. In Scotland, as Professor Smout has recently shown, there was a tradition of village planning and a growing *corpus* of theory developing from this, for example, Robert Rennie's 'Plan of an Inland Village', one of the prize essays of the Highland Society (1803).[18]

Attempts to improve living and working conditions, in Owen's case, had a classical and pantheist flavour. He was similar to any enlightened despot of the eighteenth century in tolerating all religions and then producing a distillate from them which he called the religion of charity; this was to be the agency for a rapid change of heart, 'the thief in the night' which could at first change the social attitudes of the population of New Lanark and then later overtake the hearts and minds of all humanity. Civic virtue and loyalty to New Lanark was created by a range of policies. Highlanders were encouraged to retain the kilt because Owen believed that like the toga it was a sign of ancient goodness. He allowed them to play shinty and provided a clergyman to preach in Gaelic. Dancing, drilling and community singing were all part of a collectivist training for a return to ancient purity which industrialisation had threatened.

Yet considerable were the economic advantages to a factory-owner of a labour force prepared to believe in the philosophy of self-improvement. Despite his disregard for conventional religions, Owen believed that the inner discipline created by the working class for themselves had a respectable religious base. The 'rootlessness' of a new industrial labour force, what Durkheim was later to designate as 'anomie', could be offset by a commonly accepted ethical code and an aggressively practical policy of social improvements.

Owen did not court popularity to implement his social policies at New Lanark. It is well known how his reluctance to abandon his ideas contributed to his quarrels with successive groups of partners and ultimately led him across the Atlantic to New Harmony. The resistance of the labour force to his schemes has received less attention. In 1807 John Marshall, the Leeds flax-spinner, noted: 'Mr Owen is said to be a very strict man and is not popular in the neighbourhood'.[19] Owen himself in his *Life* and in *Essay Second of A New View of Society* certainly exaggerated the poor state of the population of the village before he went to New Lanark, possibly because of the initial local resistance to his new management, and in the process denigrated the role of David Dale. When the Scottish cotton-spinners began to collect information in 1816 for their case against Owen's Factory Bill, which the elder Peel had introduced in the Commons, it is well known that they secured the support of the Lanark minister, the Rev William Menzies. What was previously not known was that they also obtained testimony about New Lanark from a Mr Mitchell, one of the teachers appointed by Dale. His answers to set questions posed by the masters' association also indicate the nature of the questions: [20]

Answer to Q1

I resided at the cotton-works of New Lanark for twenty-three years, and held the office of teacher during that period. The works belonged to Mr Dale for the first ten years of that time, and after that to Messrs. Owen and Company. . .

Answer to Q2

Mr Dale gave education free of expense to the children of all the people employed at his works. Those too young for the works attended school during the day and those employed at the works, in the evening. The number of children and young people who attended was about 180 at the day school, and often from 600 to 700 at the evening school. . .

Answer to Q3

The progress of the young people was very considerable, and the plan adopted seemed to answer the benevolent intentions of the proprietor, in giving useful, moral and religious instruction to the youth at his employment. Indeed the greatest attention was always paid to the school both by Mr Dale and his managers. The children and young people were publicly examined every six months, and premiums were distributed to those scholars who had made the greatest progress...

Answer to Q4

The people first employed by Mr Dale were remarkable for sobriety, virtuous dispositions, and propriety of conduct. As the village became more populous, some characters not quite so correct got in amongst them; but the morals of the whole village were certainly equal to those of other villages of the same population...

Answer to Q5

The children who had parents in the village attended worship with them; but Mr Dale employed a number of children who had no parents in the village. These regularly attended the church meeting-house at Lanark, along with the teacher, and one of his assistants...

Answer to Q6

Before Mr Owen came to these mills, the working hours were from six in the morning to seven in the evening, and the workers were allowed half-an-hour for breakfast and an hour for dinner. Mr Owen lengthened the hours of labour to eight in the evening. After several years they were again reduced to the former hours; and I am informed they now work only to six in the evening. With regard to provision for educating the youth, Mr Owen also gave free education to all who chose to attend; and the day school was well-attended, but the night school fell greatly off. For ten years Mr Owen paid no attention to the school. In place of being examined once in six months as in Mr Dale's time, we had only three examinations in the course of thirteen years. During the two or three last years I was at the mills Mr Owen paid attention enough to the school; but I did not think it productive of an advantage. He was always introducing new plans, and particularly a new system of morals, of which he claims the sole invention; but this system was not introduced while I was there...

Answer to Q7

The people are rather improved in cleanliness, and the houses and streets are kept cleaner. Their circumstances, comforts and appearance are much the same as in Mr Dale's time. Their morals

are certainly not improved. As an instance there were few illegitimate children born in the village while it belonged to Mr Dale.
For the first seven years it is said there was only one; and during
some of the last years that I resided in the place there were from
ten to fourteen illegitimate births annually in the village. I left
Lanark mills in September 1814, and I understand I have had
many successors since that time.

Thus, it seems possible that it was primarily after 1810 that
Owen became concerned with the schools in the village, and
this was exactly the period in which Lanarkshire and other
parts of industrial Scotland were faced with fears of a radical
rising led by 'workmen's combinations'. Thus, Owen's support for a national, non-sectarian system of education may
have been rooted in his belief that this would help to prevent
social disorder.

The parish system of schools survived in Scotland, although
under considerable pressure in the industrial towns. Yet many
industrialists founded schools as Dale had done at New Lanark. What was novel about Owen's schools was not their
existence but his views on their functions, on learning and
teaching processes, and on discipline. He thought that education should be an instrument of social change, but that social
change was to be accompanied by the elimination of class
antagonisms.[21] Human beings began as 'passive and wonder-
fully contrived compounds' with a 'plastic quality' which
could be moulded at will. When he urged that there should
be a national system of education, he regarded this as an
essential prelude to social co-operation. 'Train any population
rationally and they will be rational' was to him self-evident,
and the main consequence of this proposition was the solution
of law and order problems which increasingly excited the
attention of Lord Liverpool's government. Wide provision of
nursery schools of the type established at New Lanark would
make it possible for more women to take paid work; at his
own mills this tendency was quite marked. Family incomes
could thus be increased without raising wage-rates.

New Lanark parents indicated that they regarded educational provision for their children as a special reward for their loyalty and good service to the master of New Lanark when they presented him with an address on 11 January 1817. Nor should we forget that the mills and village required a variety of skills and services so that Owen's insistence on training in 'useful arts' had a local practical utility. He thought that the best teaching should aim at the child's full comprehension without rote learning; he believed that it was important to educate the senses and to stimulate enquiry by a process of 'natural learning' where the child's powers of observation and judgement were trained in natural situations. Corporal punishment was forbidden, for Owen believed it right to keep learning a spontaneous and happy activity and the ultimate punishment ought to be communal pity for the delinquent rather than personal violence. As Mrs Browning has strongly argued, Owen was particularly fortunate in his teachers who devised interesting curricula backed by the imaginative use of visual aids.[22]

Nonetheless, there were clear connections between Owen's principles of education and those of scientific management. It was 'habits of order, regularity, temperance and industry' which, on his own admission, Owen was trying to inculcate. As outside interest in his schools developed, Owen gained indirect advantages from what was essentially a tourist phenomenon. The people naturally acquired a special pride in their village and in themselves. This did no harm to their general motivation for work; indeed, in such an environment, output and productivity gains were likely. What he had done was to kill class hatred with kindness and to replace communal divisions with social unity, pride and purpose.

Owen's views on education were also central to his utopian vision and his millenarian forecasts. He had become increasingly alarmed about the effects of the industrial system on humanity, and this is most obvious in his *Observations on the*

Effect of the Manufacturing System (1815), written before the results of peacetime depression had made themselves manifest. Those made rich by the new system lusted for more wealth and material possessions: [23]

> The acquisition of wealth, and the desire which it naturally creates for a continued increase, have introduced a fondness for essentially injurious luxuries ... and they have also generated a disposition which strongly impels its possessors to sacrifice the best feelings of human nature to this love of accumulation.

As for the poor, 'from whose labour this wealth is now drawn', they were 'infinitely more degraded and miserable than they were before the introduction of these manufactories, upon the success of which their bare subsistence now depends'.[24] What was necessary was an educational system which would train people to live peacefully and happily with their neighbours. Employers needed to be taught that to grind the faces of their workers in a competitive labour market might superficially appear to be good economics but it was political and social nonsense. Workers had to be educated rationally in a planned environment.

In 1817 Owen institutionalised his claims for the communal relationships which he had established at New Lanark. His *Report to the Committee of the Association for the Relief of the Manufacturing and Labouring Poor* (March 1817) contained his plans for the settlement of 500 to 1,500 paupers in 'villages of co-operation'. Work mainly in agriculture was to be provided for these communities, and once they became self-supporting, they could begin to repay the capital costs of their establishment, either as a rent or as an interest charge. The initial capital for such establishments might be raised, Owen believed, by nationalising the funds of certain public charities, by borrowing on the security of the poor rates and by offering the private capital market the stimulus of preference-type interest rates. The abundance of capital in Britain so impressed Owen that his attention to fund-raising was less marked that his regard for the benefits accruing to the community from such settlements. Although the individuals living in co-operation would certainly gain, Owen had little doubt that the community would derive the greatest benefits. The burden of poor relief would be diminished; communal purpose and unity would be encouraged. As he had previously claimed in *A New View of Society*, the elimination of crime, punishment, depravity, idleness and poverty would follow. Simultaneously, Owen was enjoining radicals not to mislead the poor and to abandon political agitation; faith in the British Constitution and in the moral regeneration of their rulers was all that they required.

Increasingly, Owen turned towards political economy for solutions to the problems besetting British society, and as he did so, he became more and more convinced of the necessity for accurate statistical information.[25] Hence his admiration of Patrick Colquhoun whose national income statistics he found so fascinating. Owen by 1820 was advancing the view that trends in wages and numbers of able-bodied unemployed should be charted, county by county, on a quarterly basis.[26] This was necessary preliminary work before any state action could be taken with proper prior knowledge. It was this sense that legislation had to be based upon proper information that makes Owen often appear remarkably scientific and quantitative both in his language and in his analogies.

Unemployment for him meant so much waste of human resources and a wilful diminution in the gross national product. Even more, as a man of imaginative conscience, he viewed it as an act of cruelty perpetrated by an inefficient society on its weakest members. Low per capita incomes, low productivity, idleness, crime and ignorance were all functions of a backward social, economic and moral system.

Both his contemporaries, Malthus and Ricardo, were essentially pessimistic about the economic potentiality of industrial society. Malthus was obsessed with the growth of population which he thought would outstrip subsistence and income. Ricardo, although refusing to accept that a total failure of demand could occur and preferring to believe instead that one person's costs must be another's income, enunciated his views of the law of diminishing returns on land and the inevitability of declining profits.[27]

Owen was prepared to accept—with Malthus—that a total collapse of markets was possible, but he rejected outright the pessimism of Malthus.[28] Similarly, although he accepted the Ricardian view of the labour theory of value—which Marx was also later to assimilate into his synthesis—he could not accept Ricardo's dreary views on money or wages.[29] Instead, Owen moved towards a theory of state-intervention and under-consumption. State-induced inflation was Owen's solution for the economic problems facing British society, and he remained constant to it throughout his life. So that all the able-bodied, who wanted work, could be employed, it was necessary for the government to intervene at downturns in the economy. A Speenhamland policy of subsidies to the poor had nothing to commend it; in fact, it was a positive hindrance to their betterment:

> Benevolence says, that the destitute must not starve; and to this declaration political wisdom readily assents. Yet can that system be right, which compels the industrious, temperate and compara-tively virtuous to support the ignorant, the idle and comparatively vicious?[30]

Many followers of Ricardo argued after 1815 that the main problem of the age was overproduction; upon these Owen poured scorn:

> Is it possible that there can be too many productions desirable and useful to society? [sic] and is it not to the interests of all that they should be produced with the least expense and labour, and with the smallest degree of misery and moral degradation to the working classes, and, of course, in the greatest abundance to the higher classes, in return for their wealth?[31]

While Malthus and his followers regarded the Corn Law of

1815 as essential, Owen followed Ricardo in favouring its abolition not only because of its restrictive effects on international trade but also because he reasoned that it affected the living standard of the poor adversely.[32] Equally, Owen opposed the unrestricted application of machinery if it lowered wages and lessened total employment. Better wages and shorter hours for most people ought to be included in the objectives of capitalists, along with cheaper production and better profits.[33] A more equitable distribution of national income was ignored by both Malthus and Ricardo; for Owen it was a necessary precondition for greater levels of national economic achievement.[34]

As Owen moved towards a theory of under-consumption, he joined a notable group of heretic economists, for there was wider interest in this possible explanation of the slump after the Napoleonic wars than is generally realised.[35] Thomas Attwood of Birmingham, in *The Remedy or Thoughts on the Present Distresses* (1816), blamed cessation of government spending, a thought which Owen greatly expanded in his *Report to the County of Lanark* (1820). Instead of giving credit to landowners and abolishing income tax which so aided the commercial interest, Owen advocated a national minimum wage and an inflationist currency of labour notes. Both Owen and Attwood recognised that there existed a discrepancy between increasing industrial output and the supply of specie. Thus, an increase in the money supply through labour notes was one means of increasing effective demand and thereby inflating a deflated economy. As practical businessmen, Owen and Attwood rejected orthodox classical economics because they did not expect 'the dismal science' to work. However, the government followed the advice of David Ricardo and the Bullionists and in 1819 embarked on a return to gold payments which made the depression worse. In mitigation, for Ricardo, it should be allowed that he, unlike Owen and Attwood, saw no possibility of achieving full employment and, therefore, did not concern himself with what he clearly regarded as utopian fantasies.

The need to consider the relationship of the money supply to the growth of the Gross National Product and the importance of increasing purchasing power during slumps in order to increase consumption, remained heresy for more than a hundred years after the *Report to the County of Lanark*. Yet Owen certainly considered himself to be a political economist with practical experience that ought to carry more weight than mere book-learning. It seems possible that Owen's management experience helped to form his economic thought for during depressions he had had to turn away men seeking work.[36] Like Attwood, he must also have relied heavily on empiricism. He saw the government's policies in action and found them wanting; he believed that such measures encouraged civil strife and disorder and prevented social harmony. Earlier, mercantilist thinkers like John Bellers whom Owen came so much to admire, had emphasised the importance of providing work for the honest poor. Contemporaries, like the handloom weavers of Scotland and the miners of Lanarkshire, had agitated for minimum wages enforced on employers by justices of the peace. As a JP for Lanarkshire, Owen was surely aware of this local controversy. In addition, the concept of a national minimum wage was also a forlorn political issue among a few Tory back-benchers.

It has often been emphasised that Owen had many weaknesses, but lack of originality was not one of them. His career shows a brilliant deviant quality. To give up a successful business career for the roles of social reformer and community builder—on the American frontier or in Hampshire—cannot be simply regarded as signs of a guilty conscience. No doubt, Owen was affected by the inhumanity and wastefulness of capitalism—'the paradox of poverty in the midst of plenty'—but his response was not that of the sentimentalist. He lacked neither the capacity nor the ruthlessness 'to buy cheap and to sell dear'. It was because of the social divisions produced by the capitalist variety of industrialisation that he produced gradually a socialist-type synthesis, which is better described as millennialist. The constant underlying principle for his actions was his belief in his own ability to save Britain from social and political disaster. His exposition of the coming millennium may have reduced his political effectiveness, since his apocalyptic language and incapacity for compromise did not endear him to most politicians. But it was exactly this statement of the better world-to-come than won Owen his most fervent working-class supporters.[37]

Owenism developed a mass following in the 1820s and early 1830s, and although it went through a number of phases, it remained concerned with the prophecy of a new society. Owen himself, after his return from New Harmony in 1828, temporarily led this mass movement. But whether he really became more radical in this period is at least doubtful. His involvement in the Grand National Consolidated Trades Union, perhaps the most significant popular movement of the early 1830s, did not mean that any basic changes in his thought had occurred. Even when he supported the idea of a general strike, he thought that it could be conducted without class hatred or violence. He expected 'superior minds among all classes of society, male and female' to rally to the call in order that the new society could overtake the old suddenly like 'a thief in the night'. Owen's sectarian position prevented him from becoming the permanent leader of the working classes but throughout his life and afterwards he remained a respected 'father figure'—philanthropist, reformer, inspirer of social advances.[38]

To examine the careers of a few leading Owenites and ex-Owenites is rather like taking a roll-call of the most significant social, political and economic agitations of the Victorian age. John Finch (1784-1857), one of the founders of Liverpool Co-operative Society, secretary of the city's branch of the

Association of All Classes of All Nations and president of the Liverpool Rational School Society, believed that Owenism marked a return to fundamental and practical Christianity. An active temperance advocate, his belief in Owen and the millennium was unshakeable.[39] William Pare (1803-73) of Birmingham, the organiser of the first Co-operative Congress in 1869 and first secretary of the Central Co-operative Board, remembered Owen's maxim that statistics should be accurately compiled to support any meaningful argument. Indeed his socialist opinions were considerably reinforced by his quantitative abilities.[40]

Men like James Hole (1820-95) of Leeds campaigned for scientific education, mechanics' institutes, improved housing for the working classes and urged upon their followers the merits of 'association' (ie Owenite co-operation) for achieving specific social improvements. In the 1890s he was advocating public ownership of the railways.[41] George Jacob Holyoake (1817-1906), the great exponent of secularism, was, of course, one of Owen's early biographers and a significant contributor to the mythology surrounding Owen. Holyoake extracted from Owenism an element which he described as 'free thought' and he handed down to Charles Bradlaugh a number of active ex-Owenite secularist societies, the core of modern humanism. In Owenism Holyoake also discovered the true source of 'rational', as opposed to 'enthusiastic', co-operation; in the process, he turned Owen into an epic figure in the history of British co-operation.[42]

But the influence of Owen on reform and protest movements was often negative—but curiously important. Despite Owen's strictures against political agitations, many Radicals were prepared to accept Owen's other ideas. Among the London Chartists there were ex-Owenites, notably William Lovett (1800-77) and James Bronterre O'Brien (1801-61).[43] Henry Hetherington, the leader of the radical agitation against the press laws, inveighed, earlier, in the *Poor Man's Guardian*, against Owen's refusal to become involved in the Reform Bill agitation of 1831-2 but in his *Last Will and Testament* declared himself an Owenite socialist at heart.[44] Owen's paternalism alienated many, and his refusal to define exactly how the millennium was to be produced without revolution drove away others.[45] But the origins of British democratic socialism are to be found in the activities of men like Lovett and Hetherington, and the language and ideas of Owenism survived piecemeal in British co-operation and in the minds of men like Robert Blatchford whose influential *Merrie England* (1894) contains several 'echoes of Owen'.[46]

The concept of a 'co-operative commonwealth' which the Christian Socialists preached in the 1850s had roots in Owenism—and not merely because the Christian Socialists also recruited ex-Owenites.[47] Essentially, Owen challenged the fundamental structure of a society, which increasingly confused the maximum profit with the greatest good, with a moral and ethical synthesis that emphasised the basic dignity of every man and woman. This moral attitude towards the irresponsible use of economic power was not confined to Owen or Owenites, or indeed to the Christian Socialists. For this reason it could not wither away and die, as Owenism did. But Robert Owen's contribution was an essential preliminary to the social, economic and political advancement of the working classes, because working men were given a sense of their dignity as individuals and a concept of 'association' which enabled them to seek greater power and influence in the Victorian community. As he lived on into the Victorian Age, Owen represented for the more affluent—whose partial assessments often survive best—outworn but initially fashionable ideas originating in the Age of Reason. Harriet Martineau expressed this best:

> His certainty that we might make life a Heaven and his hallucination that we are going to do so immediately under his guidance, have caused his wisdom to be overlooked in his absurdity ... I

own I became weary of him, while ashamed, every time I witnessed his fine temper and manners, of having felt so.[48]

At least, she felt ashamed!

Notes to this chapter are on pages 218-20

O'CONNOR, O'CONNELL AND THE ATTITUDES OF IRISH IMMIGRANTS TOWARDS CHARTISM IN THE NORTH OF ENGLAND 1838-48

J. H. Treble

IN RECENT years several writers have argued that Irish immigrants 'made their most important contribution to the growth of political radicalism among the working-classes in nineteenth-century Britain' through their participation in the Chartist movement.[1] And at first glance this seems to be a valid enough contention, for Irish names abound in the ranks of the Chartist leadership. Feargus O'Connor was born in County Cork and gained his first political experience as an Irish Repeal MP in the 1830s.[2] Bronterre O'Brien was another prominent Chartist who was of Irish stock, as was J. Deegan of Stalybridge, one of the few Catholic speakers at the 1839 National Convention.[3] At a more parochial level Christopher Doyle and Patrick Brophy, two of the most powerful figures in Lancastrian Chartism, had links with Ireland,[4] while across the Pennines, Leeds Chartists owed something in 1838-9 to the fire and zeal of two Irish textile workers, Charles Connor and George White.[5] A similar service to 'the good cause' was rendered by Peter Hoey at Barnsley; James Duffy in Sheffield; and John West in Hull.[6] A further degree of plausibility is given to the thesis of Irish commitment to the Chartist movement when one turns to examine the occupational structure and the socio-economic background of these immigrant com-

C

munities. For in virtually every one of the areas of rapid economic growth in the North of England—Liverpool, Leeds, Manchester, Bradford—the Irish were placed firmly at the foot of the economic ladder and subjected to the twin evils of underemployment and low wages. If, therefore, Chartism derived—as many historians have maintained—much of its support from those threatened by technological and seasonal unemployment and below-subsistence earnings, it should logically have attracted to its standard many of the immigrant handloom weavers and unskilled labourers in the northern towns.

In the last analysis, however, both these lines of approach are of strictly limited utility in elucidating the historical problem under review. In the first place an array of Irish names among the leadership does not in itself shed any light on the extent to which the bulk of the immigrant population gave its adherence to, or withheld its support from, the Chartist cause. Secondly, an untested hypothesis, no matter how plausible, does not begin to serve as a substitute for the rigorous process of historical investigation. It is in fact the purpose of this paper to suggest that the view described above presents an essentially misleading picture of immigrant alignments, and that despite the firm grip which individual Irishmen exercised over Chartism's destinies, the vast majority of their fellow-countrymen domiciled in Yorkshire, Cheshire and Lancashire had little contact with the movement until 1848, the 'Year of Revolutions'.

I

Always a key determinant in shaping Irish attitudes towards any political issue in the 1830s and 1840s was the teaching voice of Daniel O'Connell, not inaccurately described by one of his contemporaries as 'the lay pontiff of Catholicity'.[7] As the director of the successful campaign for Catholic Emancipation in the late 1820s, 'the Liberator', as he was styled, exercised a sway over his compatriots unequalled, and for the most part unchallenged, by any other politician. Feargus O'Connor, who by the end of 1838 had emerged as the most influential figure in North of England Chartism, was well aware of this dominance. Unfortunately, however, for the progress of his projected Anglo-Irish alliance, he had by that time already irrevocably alienated O'Connell. Since the nature of this quarrel clearly had a crucial bearing on the immigrants' political outlook, it is necessary to begin this study by looking at the *casus belli* between these two Irish radicals.

It should be stressed at the outset that their antagonism was not simply a product of the political situation of the late 1830s. Its antecedents can be traced back to 1833 when Feargus O'Connor had made a bid to seize the initiative from 'the Liberator' on the question of the advisability or otherwise of pressing for an early debate on the Repeal of the Act of Union in the House of Commons. Although on that occasion he had ultimately bowed to the wishes of the majority of Irish Repeal MPs, he did succeed in the short-term in sowing the seeds of dissension among the Repeal press, the *Freeman's Journal* supporting his stand while the *Pilot* endorsed the more cautious approach of 'the Liberator'.[8] For the next two years little more was heard of the quarrel, although as events were to prove, the breach had been papered over rather than closed. Certainly at the end of 1835 and the early months of 1836, when O'Connor was addressing Radical Societies in Yorkshire, there were few outward signs of disharmony between them. And for this state of affairs some of the credit must go to O'Connor, who was trying at this early stage to establish an understanding between the English and Irish nations, based on a joint programme of universal male suffrage and redress of the wrongs which successive governments had inflicted on Ireland. The particular form in which these protests were made not merely did nothing to antagonise

O'Connell; it succeeded in eliciting a measure of approval from him, since nearly all these radical bodies made positive gestures of support for Ireland's cause. At Barnsley, for example, the local Radical Society resolved to organise a subscription for the relatives of those who had fallen victim 'to the savage brutality of the unfeeling tithe-collectors and parsons of Rathcormac and other places'.[9] Elsewhere in the county funds were raised for the 'Grand National Tribute' which was to be used to help O'Connell to defray his expenses in defending his return as MP for Dublin. Forty pounds were contributed for this purpose from Bradford alone, while reformers in other Yorkshire towns tried to express their solidarity with 'the Liberator' by inviting him to officiate at specially arranged dinners.[10]

Amidst all this activity, O'Connor was careful to stress the political virtues of O'Connell. 'The Irishman,' he wrote, 'who forgets his [O'Connell's] unstained triumphs over the almost inconceivable and terrific political array opposed to him, the man who forgets his sacrifices when remuneration was either hopeless, or so remote in the distant horizon as to make the longest life, but a mere rung in the political ladder, such a man, I say, will merit the reproaches of the good and the virtuous.'[11] Viewed against this background it is scarcely surprising to discover that O'Connell in April 1836 presided over a Hull gathering at which radical toasts were drunk to 'The People' and 'Feargus O'Connor esq.'[12] Yet before the end of the same year the two men had come to the final parting of the ways.

The renewal of hostilities can be directly attributed to the widely divergent positions which they had assumed towards the Whig administration of Melbourne. To O'Connell it was a matter of the utmost importance that nothing should be done to jeopardise the Whigs' continuing hold on high office since they were attempting to honour the spirit of the Lichfield House Compact by remedying or promising to remedy some of the most deeply-felt grievances of Catholic Ireland. As he had proclaimed in January 1836 to an audience in Liverpool, the Whigs 'have not coalesced with me, but I am ready to coalesce with them, because they are doing justice to Ireland'.[13] O'Connor on the other hand was increasingly scathing in his attacks on both the partial nature of the 1832 Reform Act and the harsh Benthamite logic which informed the Whigs' New Poor Law. When during the course of 1837-8 he identified himself with the Tory-Radical campaign in the North of England against 'the bastille system' and when later he merged the Anti-Poor Law agitation into the wider demand for 'the Six Points', he merely confirmed O'Connell's fears that he was among 'the most active opponents of practical reform' and a zealous supporter of the Tory opposition.[14] Given these diametrically opposed philosophies, there was an air of inevitability about the ensuing verbal exchanges.

On this occasion O'Connell made the opening move. In late 1836 and early 1837 he condemned in unequivocal terms his rival's association with the English Radicals and gave him notice to quit Irish politics: 'He may be a Radical Reformer ...if he be, let him stick to the Radicals of England'.[15] O'Connor, however, was the last person to receive such an admonition without retaliation. During the course of 1837 he published in reply a series of letters which were designed to destroy 'the Liberator's' hold over the Irish masses. O'Connell, he asserted, had effectively betrayed Ireland's interests by abandoning his political convictions for Whig patronage. 'Unhappy Ireland' had as a result been 'divided into two parties; the one a set of needy place-hunters, bending beneath your nod, while the people...are starving'. O'Connell was accused: 'You have balanced lucre against greatness, and instead of laying up a store of honour for ages yet to come, you have prostituted your country, and offered her, "a bleeding sacrifice", at the altar of your idol; but riches will perish while your true picture will be drawn in history's pages'.[16]

It must be admitted that the initial use of such emotive language was more calculated to pander to prejudice and to confirm entrenched positions than to promote a rational discussion of the basic issues separating the protagonists. None the less by the time one enters the Chartist period proper it does become possible to disentangle from the heated insults certain fundamental points of disagreement.

At the end of 1838 and the beginning of 1839 O'Connell was attacking his opponent on three main grounds. Firstly he argued that 'the torch and dagger' oratory of O'Connor, Oastler and Rayner Stephens threatened the whole fabric of civil society and 'comes literally within the law of high treason'.[17] Secondly he tried to show that the violence of the language employed by Chartists retarded rather than accelerated the pace of parliamentary reform. As he was to write in April 1840, 'the misconduct of these men [the imprisoned Chartist leaders] has interfered with the progress of rational reform; they have frightened the timid; they have terrified the wealthy; they have disgusted and alienated the wise and the good; and they have nearly ruined the cause which they professed to advocate'.[18] Concessions, he concluded, should be wrung from unwilling governments by moral force methods alone since 'no human revolution is worth the effusion of one single drop of blood'.[19] Significantly enough, both the Catholic Association in the 1820s and the Precursor Society—founded by O'Connell in August 1838 to press for Irish corporation reform, the abolition of tithes and an increase in the number of MPs returned for Irish constituencies—conformed to this central tenet of 'the Liberator's' creed. Thirdly O'Connell tended to treat Tory-Radicalism and Chartism as synonymous movements, deeply hostile to the Whigs and thus indifferent to Ireland's future fate. This line of attack, although a gross distortion of the truth—the principal spokesmen of Tory-Radicalism displayed little interest in universal suffrage[20]—was possibly motivated by more personal considerations; for Oastler was a bitter critic of Roman Catholicism in all its forms while O'Connell and Rayner Stephens had clashed bitterly on the issue of factory reform in 1837.[21]

The counter-offensive of North of England Chartism to this comprehensive indictment of its recent proceedings took its tone from O'Connor although it was not exclusively his own work. O'Connell, it was alleged, was hostile towards the aspirations of the British working classes on every social question of major importance. He had prevaricated on the Ten Hours' issue, abandoned his pledge to support universal suffrage, and actively campaigned against trade unionism. Furthermore his attack on physical force oratory and his assertion that talk of revolution was commonplace in the northern counties misinterpreted the basic purpose behind the call to arms. In J. Deegan's words, pikes were being manufactured in Manchester 'to protect the constitution of the country and the labour of the poor'.[22] Such weapons were only needed as a guarantee against an attack on the liberties of the people by their rulers. But perhaps more damaging than these accusations to O'Connell's reputation was the firmly held belief among Chartists in the North of England that he was playing the rôle of unofficial 'Public Prosecutor' on behalf of the Whigs against the legitimate protests of an oppressed people. Thus Rayner Stephens' arrest in December 1838 was directly attributed to the 'Dictator to the Whig Cabinet, the base, bloody and brutal traitor, Daniel O'Connell'.[23] This judgement, delivered by Peter Bussey in January 1839, was, however, mild compared with the general reaction among Yorkshire Chartists. In Halifax O'Connell was liked to 'Satan amongst the Angels of Heaven', while at Hull it was resolved that the portrait of that 'arch traitor of the people, shall be publicly burnt at the room of the Working Men's Association'. 'We pray,' concluded this Hull remonstrance, 'that such may be the fate of all such apostates.'[24]

Paradoxically enough it was while this orgy of mutual

denigration was taking place that O'Connor made his first serious bid to realise his dream of a link-up between the English and Irish working classes. Speaking at a 'monster meeting', held on Kersal Moor in September 1838, he emphasised that 'we want yet with us those brave Irishmen whose ancestors with our own were obliged to wade up to the knees in blood for the defence of their religion, for God, and for their country. We must have them; we must take them out of the lions' den, and allow Daniel [O'Connell] to remain in the lions' den alone'.[25] Once this note had been sounded it was quickly taken up by the delegates attending the first National Charter Convention in February 1839. On O'Connor's suggestion and perhaps consciously emulating earlier moves in the same direction by Lovett and the London Working Men's Association,[26] the assembled delegates appointed a committee which was entrusted with the dual task of considering the best way of enrolling in their ranks the Irish nation and of drawing up a document on the Irish question.[27] The end-product of these deliberations was an *Address to the People of Ireland*. The authors of this manifesto believed that Ireland's economic and social ills stemmed from the same source as those of the British working classes—from the lack of a self-defence mechanism, 'to be plain, from a want of the Suffrage which, we contend, of right belongs to, and in justice ought to be exercised by, every sane man of twenty-one years of age, and untainted with crime'. If, however, Ireland wished to attain this goal, it could not do so under O'Connell's leadership; for 'upon each and every' issue which had recently affected the British working-man, 'your leader [was] arrayed against the principles of justice which he professed to support'. It followed, therefore, that the Irish people should join forces with the Chartists under the banner of 'Universal Suffrage and No Surrender'.[28]

During the course of the next few months these overtures met with an enthusiastic response in only a few, narrowly circumscribed areas of immigrant settlement. Pre-eminent among such localities and until 1848 in every respect the outstanding exception to the general pattern of Irish immigrant alignments, was Barnsley where the closely-knit Irish community had a long tradition of militancy behind them in the linen industry. Many of the town's Irish flax weavers, for example, had played a prominent part in 1829 in a bitterly contested strike of some five months' duration against the local linen manufacturers. This clash of capital and labour was marked by at least one authenticated act of arson and a series of coercive measures against strike-breaking domestic workers.[29] Viewed against this backcloth it is perhaps not surprising to find that Barnsley's magistrates could report in August 1839 the existence of 'dirks of a formidable character and in considerable numbers, beside fire-arms... in the possession of a deluded portion of the working-classes, who consist ... of individuals who have come from Ireland, Scotland, and Lancashire, and are by occupation linen-weavers'. When in the wake of these discoveries 'illegal' meetings were temporarily prohibited, it was 'some newly imported Irishmen... [who] declared vehemently' against the 'cowardice' of the local Chartist leadership in complying with this edict.[30] Sheffield appears to be the only other place in the West Riding where immigrants reacted in a similar manner to the vitriolic oratory of O'Connor, although there only a small number of Irishmen was involved. In the end a mere 'half a dozen' Irishmen under the leadership of James Duffy, an immigrant book-seller, participated in the tragi-comic proceedings which surrounded an almost completely abortive uprising in the town in January 1840.[31] There was very little divergence from this pattern in the neighbouring county of Lancashire, where Irish rank-and-file commitment to the Chartist cause was principally confined to Manchester itself. Even there the scattered and sparse nature of the evidence flatly challenges the assertion of R. J. Richardson, one of Manchester's elected

delegates to the National Convention, that he was the representative of the 30,000 Irishmen and Irishwomen living in
the cotton capital of Britain.[32]

Yet the scant impact of Chartism in its formative phase on
immigrant society did not reflect the presence of widespread
apathy among the Irish to either an extension of the franchise
or the host of socio-economic problems which confronted the
unskilled worker. Rather it denoted the extent to which
O'Connell's advice to shun 'the insane or dishonest Radicals
of England, who instead of appealing to common sense, declare their reliance on arms',[33] was obeyed with undeviating
fidelity by the vast majority of his compatriots in the northern
counties.

The validity of this conclusion can be underlined in three
ways. Firstly local organisers of the Precursor Society faith-
fully echoed 'the Liberator's' condemnation of physical-force
methods. George Smyth, for instance, writing on behalf of
Liverpool's 3,000 Precursors, labelled certain of the Chartist
leaders as 'ignorant revolutionists' who 'call upon the people
to arm for the purpose of exciting a civil commotion, which
would, undoubtedly, end in the destruction of their misguided
adherents'.[34] A similar verbal onslaught on 'the torch-and-
dagger Tory-Radicals of this country—the base hirelings and
partizans of the Tory faction' was made at Huddersfield,
Stalybridge and Ashton-under-Lyne,[35] while James Byrne,
organising secretary of the Precursors working on the Chester
to Birkenhead railroad, assured O'Connell that he 'need not
care for the abuse of Feargus O'Connor, supporter of the corn
laws, the maledictions of the torch-light preacher, or the whip
of Oastler'. Such calumnies merely demonstrated, in immigrant eyes, the extent to which the English Chartists were
prepared to subordinate Ireland's true interests to their own
selfish ends. In Byrne's words, 'Who is he that's hated most
in Ireland and over the world? The renegade that exchanges
the shamrock for the rose, and panders to the vices of the

Tory-Radicals, for a petty pittance, to calumniate O'Connell, the Liberator of his country, the champion of civil and religious liberty, the unpurchaseable foe of tyranny of every shade and clime'.[36] In the second place although the Precursor Society never produced anything like the mass following commanded by O'Connell in his earlier Catholic Emancipation campaign, it could none the less legitimately claim to be the only important outlet for the immigrants' political energies during its thirteen months' life-span. By the end of 1838 flourishing Precursor committees had emerged at Liverpool and Manchester, pledged to co-operate with 'the Liberator' to obtain 'from the British legislature a full and equal participation in all rights and privileges of the British constitution; or, in the denial of those, to demand from your country... a *Local Legislature*'.[37] Outside these two towns the new movement spread slowly but surely through the North of England. By the time it was dissolved by O'Connell in September 1839, it had also taken root in Stalybridge, Chester, Ashton-under-Lyne, Huddersfield, Bradford, Leeds and Wakefield, although it must be admitted that in none of these districts did it command the active support of more than a minority of the resident Irish.[38] Thirdly, as Chartist speakers themselves acknowledged, all their assiduous wooing of the Irish people achieved nothing because O'Connell's compatriots continued to follow his lead 'right or wrong'.[39] 'The Liberator' therefore was completely justified when in January 1839 he maintained that

> the attempts of the Tory Radicals to produce confusion and civil strife have always failed among the Irish resident in England... With few exceptions, the Irishmen who live in England have totally avoided any communication with that body; and they have acted in a similar way in Scotland. They show that they are convinced that the only sure path to justice and prosperity is that of peace and good order.[40]

II

There was no indication that this picture would undergo fundamental change in the near future. Partly this was because of the effect of the Newport Rising of November 1839 on O'Connell's outlook. That event confirmed him in his opinion that the logical sequel to intemperate language was armed revolt against the authority of the Crown, and that to have associated his countrymen in any way with the Chartist cause would have been tantamount to undermining the delicate social health of the Irish nation.[41] But apart from O'Connell's reaction, this resort to physical force had adverse consequences for the Chartist movement itself. In the short term it produced not merely widespread disillusionment among some of its working-class adherents; it also triggered off a series of legal prosecutions against those leaders who had so readily employed 'torch and dagger' oratory in the euphoric atmosphere of 1838-9. By the early months of 1840 most of the major figures in North of England Chartism, including O'Connor himself, were serving prison sentences for their invocation of the language of physical force. Chartism, then, for most of 1840 was more concerned with recovering its own sense of purpose and analysing its own errors of judgement than with mounting a fresh initiative to capture the backing of the Irish people.

Yet if the Chartists were thus compelled to settle for a policy of comparative inactivity, it was far otherwise with O'Connell. From the spring of 1840 he was busy laying the foundations of the last major agitation of his long political career—the campaign for the repeal of the Act of Union. In one sense of course there was nothing new in his demand for the restoration of a domestic parliament on Dublin Green. He had largely fought the 1832 General Election on that very issue and had emerged triumphantly from the hustings with a following of 39 Repeal MPs.[42] Whereas, however, he had

then made little attempt to take the Repeal message to the
Irish peasantry, in the 1840s his prime concern was to rally
the masses behind the Loyal National Repeal Association. As
with Catholic Emancipation, the Repeal issue, according to
O'Connell, should permeate every corner of Ireland so that
the House of Commons would recognise, and then yield to
the peacefully expressed corporate will of the Irish people on
a question of the utmost significance for their future well-
being.[43]

Among the earliest supporters of this new agitation were
the Irish inhabitants of Manchester and Liverpool. In September 1840 Luke Healy could assure O'Connell that 'he had
no doubt, from the intense feeling which was entertained for
Repeal, that before Christmas there would be 5,000 Repealers
in Manchester and the surrounding districts alone'.[44] Tangible proof that this claim was scarcely exaggerated was provided both by the size of Manchester's contribution to the
Repeal coffers—£208 12s [£208.60] in the nine months from
April 1840 to January 1841—and by the fact that 1,000
females alone had been enrolled as Associates before the end
of December 1840.[45] If less spectacular progress was recorded
in the same period among the Irish population of Liverpool,
the achievements there were still impressive. By April 1841
ten Repeal Wardens were organising their fellow-countrymen
in the town and some £38 had been collected for the Repeal
Rent in the previous quarter.[46] There were similar displays
of enthusiasm for their native-land among immigrants in
Preston, Ashton-under-Lyne and Warrington,[47] while in
Cheshire local Repeal Associations were set up at Stalybridge,
Stockport and Macclesfield.[48] An identical pattern was discernible during 1840-41 in most of the large Yorkshire towns:
Huddersfield, Leeds, Bradford, Middlesbrough, Dewsbury,
Sheffield and Hull all possessed Repeal organisations long
before O'Connell launched his 'monster meeting' campaign
in 1843.[49]

After this impressive start the new movement continued to prosper. By the autumn of 1843 the Leeds Association had opened five Repeal Reading Rooms and contributed £80 in the previous nine months to the Repeal Rent.[50] Repealers in Manchester and Liverpool, similarly moved by the seeming effectiveness of the 'monster meeting' rallies had also increased considerably their donations to the Dublin-based headquarters of the Association.[51] But apart from this record of progress in these now firmly established centres, new Repeal bodies were to spring up during 1842-3 in such places as Barnsley and Bolton.[52] These signs of rapid growth indicated in unmistakable terms that the immigrant communities in the North of England were overwhelmingly committed in the early 1840s to the Loyal National Repeal Association's attempt to restore some measure of political autonomy to the Irish nation.[53]

The logical corollary of these developments was to reduce still further O'Connor's already slender hopes of bridging the gap in understanding between English Chartists and Irish immigrants. Indeed it can be argued that the manner in which the Repeal question was handled in the northern towns increased rather than reduced the size of that gap. To some extent this was because Repeal in an English context became inextricably linked with the idea of securing an improvement in the immigrant's lot. Repeal, it was asserted, would bestow economic benefits on the working-classes of both nations; for it would 'give permanent employment and happiness' to those who were now living in the deepest poverty 'in the damp cellars' of Manchester.[54] In other words the Irish economy, under the benign guidance of a domestic legislature, would undergo such spectacular expansion and diversification that Irish exiles, 'temporary sojourners in another land', would receive adequate 'remuneration of their skill and toil' in their homeland.[55] But the voluntary repatriation of Irishmen on this scale could only have major repercussions on the living standards of the English working classes, since it would at one stroke reduce the severe pressures which the immigrant community exerted on the English labour market and thus lead to a sharp upward movement in the real wages of the indigenous labour-force.[56] It was therefore in the interests of English working-men to hasten this happy day by 'giving us [the immigrant population] your assistance to achieve our long-lost rights'.[57]

Assessed strictly from the economist's standpoint, such rhetoric contained many unsatisfactory features. There was no real discussion of the mechanics of economic growth: Repeal itself, acting very much after the manner of the philosopher's stone, was to be the route to instant wealth. Again, a crude reiteration of the wage-fund theory was thought to be a sufficient explanation of the infinitely complex subject of the impact of Irish immigration on wage-levels in the North of England. These intellectual weaknesses were to be overlooked by almost all sections of immigrant society. What they did grasp—and here the very vagueness of the message facilitated its spread—was that Repeal held out the prospect of a better life and that it seemed to offer a speedier realisation of a material improvement in their lot than the socio-economic programme of the Chartists. Such a line of argument could by very definition only add to the list of formidable obstacles which O'Connor had to surmount before he could begin to make inroads into O'Connell's 'grass roots' support.

The formulation however of a rival creed was by no means the sole fresh barrier which 'the Liberator' erected in the early 1840s to insulate his fellow-countrymen from the 'seductive' oratory of Chartist leaders. As in Ireland, O'Connell realised the supreme importance of actively involving in the Repeal campaign the Roman Catholic clergy staffing the northern missions. For the Catholic priesthood was not only the local and visible embodiment of the *magisterium Sanctae Romanae Ecclesiae*; it possessed an influence over its flock which no other element in society could hope to emulate. The extent of that influence had already been displayed in widely disparate fields during the course of the 1830s. In 1832 Catholic priests had intervened in drastic and decisive fashion to terminate immigrant participation in the cholera riots which had convulsed Manchester and Liverpool.[58] Again in the mid and late 1830s the same ecclesiastical authority was equally successful in persuading most Irishmen domiciled in the North of England to steer clear of trade unionism.[59] Last but by no means least the clergy fulfilled a vital social function when they acted as agents for remitting the funds of their parishioners to needy relatives in Ireland.[60] Given this background there was much commonsense in O'Connell's advice to Repealers to co-operate with their pastors. Even more fortunate for his general strategy there was abundant proof at the very inception of the Repeal agitation that the vast majority of priests in England were wholeheartedly committed to his new political programme. Nowhere was this more apparent than in Lancashire and Yorkshire where with few exceptions the clergy, whether of Irish or English extraction, played a prominent part in organising Repeal Associations at the local level.[61]

In two inter-related ways these developments were to aggravate O'Connor's difficulties in making effective contact with the immigrant community. On the positive side clerical endorsement of the Loyal National Repeal Association automatically predisposed the Irish Catholic populations in Manchester, Liverpool, Leeds and other towns to follow their priests' lead and enrol themselves and their families in the ranks of O'Connell's Repeal Associates. On the negative side the Catholic clergy tended to assume the same hostile stance towards Chartism as 'the Liberator' had done in the closing months of 1838. In a few areas such clerical condemnation of the Chartist movement had predated the foundation of the Repeal Association. Thus as early as June 1839 the Rev J.

Collins advised the Liverpool Precursors 'not to join the Chartists, as the latter were an illegal body, and no Catholic who belonged to them could receive the sacraments of their church', while the Rev G. Gibson of St Patrick's cautioned his flock from the pulpit 'against attending their [Chartist] meetings even from a motive of curiosity'.[62] After 1840 this type of attack seems to have increased. In Birkenhead, for instance, the Rev Henderson, 'Catholic pastor of the place', on hearing that itinerant Chartists had converted 'a few Irish labourers to their principles, . . . delivered an admirable and patriotic address to his congregation, in which he dwelt with great force upon the services of O'Connell in the cause of his country, and earnestly admonished them of the dangers of co-operating with the torch and dagger men'.[63] An identical policy was followed in Manchester by the Rev Daniel Hearne where virtually every Chartist attempt at fraternisation with the local Repealers was frustrated by the vigilance of this Irish-born priest.[64]

The vigorous nature of this campaign, however, was not simply the product of clerical loyalty to the political views of O'Connell. It derived some of its impetus from the attitudes of individual Chartists towards organised religion. Chartist disruption of Anglican services; the thinly-veiled deistical writings which occasionally appeared in the columns of the *Northern Star*; and the presence of known unbelievers in the ranks of the Chartist leadership convinced the Catholic clergy that Chartism was more than a movement which aimed at the violent overthrow of existing institutions. It was also hostile to the revealed truths of Christianity itself. It was basically for this reason that individual priests went in certain cases so far as to invoke spiritual sanctions against Chartists who were members of the Roman Catholic Church.[65] Although such a policy never seems to have been given official espiscopal approval,[66] it was yet another factor in deterring most Irish Catholics—even if the inclination had been there—from

D

joining forces with English Chartism.

One significant consequence, therefore, of the spectacular expansion of the Repeal Association in the North of England was a further deterioration in the relationship between the supporters of O'Connor and the Irish followers of O'Connell. What was perhaps more unexpected was the precise form in which these disagreements were expressed; for during the course of 1841-2 Repealers and Chartists passed from exchanging insults about the virtues and vices of their respective champions to employing physical force means to break up one another's meetings.

The first occasion when the use of such tactics was threatened on any scale was at a rally of the Leeds Parliamentary Reform Association in January 1841 to which O'Connell had been invited to deliver an address on the household suffrage question. As soon as these arrangements were made public, the *Northern Star* had entered the arena. This meeting, it assured its largely working-class readership, was merely a middle-class move to 'sell you to O'CONNELL, who would sell you to the Devil'. Chartists should thus organise themselves to frustrate the intentions of the household suffrage party. Above all it was essential that they should demonstrate to 'the Liberator' the undying hatred in which he was held by the English working classes. To achieve this goal it was necessary for 'the people, *en masse*, from every town, village, and hamlet within thirty-six miles' to 'be in Leeds on that day to do *honour* to O'CONNELL—to show him the estimation in which he is beholden by the people of England'.[67] Feargus O'Connor underlined this inflammatory appeal by writing from his prison cell to Yorkshire Chartists. All he required of them in return for his many services to the movement was 'but *one*, one, ONE, *only* ONE *day*, devoted to your cause and my defence'.[68] In other words, it was proposed to disrupt the proceedings of the Leeds gathering by relying on the vocal and physical strength of the mob.

Although the meeting itself passed off without any major disruption, this was less because Chartists had failed to answer their leader's call—individual groups in fact had made their way to Leeds from places as far afield as Glasgow, Sunderland and Birmingham[69]—than because O'Connell, seriously delayed on the crossing from Ireland, never put in an appearance.[70] But even if he had avoided a direct confrontation with militant Chartism, he had none the less been seriously shaken by these developments. Writing to a friend five days after the rally he declared that 'I am afraid Feargus intended me personal mischief; but if he did, he had been signally disappointed'.[71] Three months later he returned to the same theme, asserting that the *Northern Star* and O'Connor had written in deliberately provocative terms for a very specific purpose: 'I declare to heaven—and I sincerely tell you I do not exaggerate when I say so—it was done for the purpose of putting me to death'.[72]

There could be little doubt that such frenzied hyperbole reinforced the determination of the O'Connellite Irish who had settled in Lancashire to employ similar methods against the Chartist movement in their adopted county. Yet although they were to obtain control as early as May 1841 of one Chartist gathering in Manchester when they effectively defeated a vote of censure on 'the Liberator',[73] the majority of their initial clashes with the Chartists occurred not at rallies summoned to support the 'Six Points', but on the neutral platform of the Anti-Corn Law League.

III

Almost from its inception the League had received the blessing of O'Connell. The repeal of the Corn Laws, he had announced at Manchester in January 1840, 'will be equally beneficial to both parts of the empire and pre-eminently so to Ireland'.[74] Irishmen were thus under an obligation to agitate for the removal of those duties which threatened to perpetuate 'injustice to the poor'.[75] In 1843 he was still following the same line of attack. The government, he asserted, as long as it clung to protection, was committing a criminal offence against the people of the United Kingdom. 'That criminality has a double aspect—the criminality in preventing the purchase of food elsewhere and the criminality in making food dear at home.'[76] Once O'Connell had given this lead, the more socially conscious elements among the Catholic clergy joined in the campaign for the total abolition of the 'provision laws'. The Rev McDonald, for example, journeyed from Birmingham to a Manchester gathering in order to address the audience along with 'the Liberator'.[77] At a less elevated level the Rev P. Kaye was active on the League's behalf in Bradford, while in 'the cotton capital' itself the Rev D. Hearne worked tirelessly for the cause over a period of years.[78]

Most Chartists on the other hand remained extremely suspicious of the League's intentions.[79] For although there were few dedicated protectionists in the Chartist ranks, many believed that the Corn Law issue was another middle-class ruse to divert the working-man away from the paths of constructive social reform. According to this thesis, abolition of the 'provision laws' would only bestow lasting benefits on the whole of society if it were preceded by the granting of universal male suffrage. Otherwise 'the [money] saving effected by the repeal of these laws'[80] would merely find its way into the pockets of 'the millocracy'. In essence Chartists were arguing that industrialists alone would benefit from lower grain prices under the existing franchise. Falling wheat prices would mean correspondingly lower money wages for the working-classes and correspondingly higher profits for their employers. Accepting explicitly the validity of this analysis, many Chartist societies availed themselves of every opportunity to disrupt the League's meetings in the North of England.

At first these tactics met with little resistance from the

League's organisers who were genuinely taken by surprise at these displays of open hostility. Belatedly, however, in 1840 the Anti-Corn League's hierarchy, confronted by such determined opposition, accepted the fact that the intellectual force of their arguments was not by itself sufficient to carry the day. Among other things they required a working-class base to ensure that their message would be received by the multitudes, if not enthusiastically, then at least free from Chartist interruption. Hence their decision to set up Operative Anti-Corn Law Associations in Lancashire. But in the short-term a much more significant move was the approach which the League made to the leaders of Manchester's immigrant population for their support. The sequel to these talks was an agreement, concluded in the early months of 1840, between the League and the Manchester Irish 'to join their forces to break the Chartist control of public meetings'.[81]

One of the first fruits of this *rapprochement* was the speedy promotion of the principal working-class spokesmen of O'Connell's Repeal of the Union agitation to prominent positions within the Anti-Corn Law movement. J. J. Finnegan, for instance, an immigrant weaver and scathing critic of O'Connor, was immediately employed as a full-time lecturer in the League's pay. Before the end of 1840 he had already toured Ireland on behalf of 'the good cause' and had more than held his own in public debate with James Leach, a rising figure at that time in Lancastrian Chartism.[82] At a more parochial level John Kelly, an Irish-born printer and a local organiser of 'the Liberator's' Repeal campaign, had emerged in the early 1840s as a pillar of the Manchester Operative Anti-Corn Law Association,[83] where he received the enthusiastic backing of T. Falvey, an immigrant domestic worker and a Macclesfield-based Repeal Warden.[84] Even when the League resorted to physical-force methods, it tended to rely on the strength of such 'Irish lambs' as Michael M'Donough who was in his own right both a Repeal Warden and Volunteer, and William Duffy[85] to secure victory over Chartist opposition. The Corn Laws thus became another social question which divided Irish Catholics from English Chartists, although in this case differences between the two sides were not confined to sterile mutual recrimination. Increasingly during 1841-2 verbal clashes were to be followed by the use of violence.

The first major test of this newly-forged alliance was in June 1841 at an outdoor League meeting in Stevenson's Square, Manchester. Almost as soon as this rally had begun, 'the Chartists showed their preparations for a row by drawing forth short staves, with which they began to lay about them'. The response of the League's Irish supporters to these acts of provocation was instantaneous: 'our Irish friends, made desperate at seeing this, and particularly by the brutal conduct of a fellow who nearly killed a poor man with a blow from an iron bar, rushed at the [Chartist] flags, tore them down, and laid about them to such good effect as to drive the Chartists out of the square'.[86] Again in October 1841 and January 1842 Irish immigrants were to obtain similar triumphs in the Manchester area at the expense of the Chartists.[87]

Yet if these humiliations severely damaged the standing of the National Charter Association in Lancashire, the final blow had still to descend. Hitherto the Irish had restricted their physical-force activities to League meetings. But in March 1842 the fateful decision was taken to carry the fight into the Chartist camp itself. Mindful of the reception which had been prepared for O'Connell in Leeds, they awaited a suitable opportunity of exacting their revenge. That opportunity came when O'Connor appeared at Manchester's Hall of Science to deliver a lecture on the Repeal of the Act of Union. Amidst scenes of indescribable chaos Irish Repealers succeeded in bringing the evening's proceedings to a premature close with scarcely a word of the scheduled address having been uttered.[88] It was now the turn of O'Connor to assume the role of outraged innocence. The gathering, he alleged, had been wrecked largely as a result of the machinations of the Anti-Corn Law League. Watkin, he went on, having begun the day by circulating anti-Chartist propaganda among the town's Irish population, had then hired 'a large portion of bludgeon men', acting under such immigrant leaders as Finnegan and Duffy, to stifle all rational discussion of the Repeal issue.[89]

These accusations tended to be dismissed by the bulk of contemporary opinion as mere fabrication. Yet in reality they were less wide of the mark than even O'Connor realised. For if on this particular occasion 'the moral force cowards', as O'Connor described the League's hierarchy, had not supplied money to defray all the expenses 'of physical force aggression and printing',[90] there is evidence to show that certain Irishmen were receiving payments from the Manchester branch of the Anti-Corn Law League.[91] Whether or not such 'Irish lambs' were normally bought as cheaply as the *Northern Star* suggested—it only cost, it asserted, 'a good swig of whisky and a few shillings' to secure the services of Irish brawn[92]—the League's spokesmen were less than honest when they denied the existence of an arrangement from which each party benefited.

IV

It is against this unpromising background that the fresh overtures which English Chartists made to the Irish people in the years 1841-3 have to be set. In its earliest phase this new initiative seemed to lack any form of central direction. Every move depended on the vigour and enthusiasm of local leaders. As a result progress was bound to be erratic and gains were few. In Preston and Manchester, for example, attempts by the local Chartist Societies to attract Irish audiences by staging a reconstruction of the trial of Robert Emmet ended in total failure.[93] In other areas of heavy immigrant settlement in the North of England similar modest gestures of support for O'Connor's projected Anglo-Irish *entente* met with scarcely any better fate. Indeed, from a Chartist point of view the only glimmer of light during the bleak year of 1841 came from Birmingham where George White, formerly a pillar of Bradford and Leeds Chartism and now a reporter with the *Northern Star*, succeeded in producing 'great wavering' among the town's Repealers.[94]

It was principally to counteract this threat that O'Connell was asked in September 1841 'to adopt some speedy means' of containing Chartism. Failure to act on this advice, he was warned, would be attended with the direst consequences for the solidarity and unity of the Midlands Repeal movement; for 'these [Chartist] vagabonds, when they find a portion of the [Irish] people inclined their way, will call a public meeting in the name of Repeal, and pass a vote of censure on Mr. O'Connell, and will give cheers for Feargus and Repeal'.[95] Within a week this plea had been answered in decisive fashion from Dublin. T. M. Ray, Secretary of the Loyal National Repeal Association, was instructed to write to all Repeal bodies in England 'cautioning them against any species of connexion with the Chartists, and begging them to exclude all known Chartists from their meetings, and stating that otherwise they must be excluded from being members of' the Repeal organisation. This edict was accompanied by a detailed exposition of the necessity for such a policy. The Chartists, it was asserted, were 'the worst enemies of Ireland' since they had aided the Tories at the 1841 General Election, tried to coerce 'rational Reformers' into silence and calumniated 'the Liberator' for the sole purpose of weakening the Repeal cause.[96]

The impact of these instructions on Repeal opinion was immediate. Before the end of September the Birmingham Irish were able to claim that 'the replies of the association . . .

have had the desired effect in exterminating the Chartists
from our meetings',[97] while from Stockport came an assurance
that 'there is very little danger...of the Repealers being
seduced by the wiles of the Chartists'.[98] Matters were carried
still further in Manchester where a Repeal rally was held for
the specific purpose of enabling local immigrants to express
'their want of confidence in Feargus O'Connor as a leader'.
After a prolonged debate resolutions were carried warning

> the people against being led away by specious promises to support
> and assist Feargus O'Connor, who has shown by his foul abuse
> and denunciation of O'Connell (the great leader of the people of
> Ireland), that he merely espouses the repeal for the purpose of
> undermining the influence and paralyzing the efforts of a much
> wiser, much more patriotic, and much more honest man.[99]

It is thus reasonable to conclude that by the autumn of 1841
the sporadic and largely parochial attempts of the northern
Chartists to reach at least a *modus vivendi* with the Irish
Repealers living in their midst had ended in almost total
failure.

In some respects the most unexpected sequel to these re-
buffs was that Chartist disillusionment with the seeming
inflexibility of immigrant opinion was of short duration; for
by January 1842 they were again trying to persuade the Irish
people that tangible benefits would accrue to Ireland from a
Repeal-Chartist alliance. Their message, simply put, was that
Repeal accompanied by the 'Six Points' would in the long-
term be more advantageous to Ireland than a straightforward
dissolution of the existing Union. Once sounded this message
which had received the personal endorsement of O'Connor,
was to be heard from Chartist platforms in virtually every
major town in the North of England. Bronterre O'Brien, for
example, went to great lengths, when speaking at Newcastle-
upon-Tyne, to point out to his compatriots that 'a new feature'
had been added to the Second National Petition. This was
nothing less than a demand that the existing Legislative
Union between Great Britain and Ireland should be re-

pealed.[100] Other Chartists followed the same line of attack both at Sheffield, where James Duffy, 'an old veteran' in the struggle for the Charter, was honoured by the presence of 'a great number of our Irish brethren', and at Manchester.[101] In a very limited sense this line of approach did achieve a modicum of success. Using Irish orators to hold forth on Irish subjects for the first time produced substantial immigrant attendances at meetings held under the auspices of the Chartist movement.[102] This was something which the manoeuvres of 1838-9 and 1841 had never come within striking distance of accomplishing. But to be placed against this credit side of the balance sheet was the fact that few immigrants showed any signs of transferring their loyalties from O'Connell to O'Connor. After Parliament's summary rejection of the Second Chartist Petition, the gap which remained between O'Connor's Irish policy and current political realities still remained wide.[103]

It was perhaps for this reason that O'Connor in the spring of 1843 decreed yet another change of strategy. Since the 'Imperial Chartists' had been unable to obtain a formal agreement between the National Charter Association and the Loyal National Repeal Association, they should now try to spread Chartist principles by infiltrating local Repeal societies. By acting in this fashion it might ultimately be possible to wrest control of the English-based part of the Repeal organisation from O'Connell's hands. For a brief period in May-June 1843 this switch of direction seemed likely to produce a rich harvest in certain parts of the northern counties. At Bradford, for instance, where several Chartists had made contributions to the Repeal Rent as early as January 1843,[104] there were positive signs towards the end of May of increasing fraternisation between Repealers and the supporters of the 'Six Points'.[105] An identical pattern emerged at Sheffield where George Julian Harney became 'the first Englishman and Chartist' to join the local Repeal body[106] and at Hull where, despite the advice of

Rev Coppinger that Repealers should beware of 'listening to the "big mouthers",' John West and other Chartists were enrolled as Repeal Associates.[107] Other towns where there was some indication that the old animosities were being softened by this new approach included Barnsley, Leeds and Manchester,[108] although in these last two places there was no evidence of Chartists being admitted to the ranks of the local Repealers.

Unfortunately, however, for the future of this plan Repeal leaders in Dublin were quick to spot the danger of allowing Chartists uninterrupted access to meetings at which policy decisions were taken. On the last day of May 1843 a fresh edict was issued by T. M. Ray to Repeal Wardens in Britain ordering them to return all subscriptions they had received from persons connected with the O'Connorite agitation. Furthermore local officials were left in no doubt as to the reasoning behind such a move: some of the Chartist leaders, it was noted, 'are now in the pay of the Tories, and are now come to create confusion, when the attainment of Repeal is obvious, and can be marred only by contact with those who have been reckless of law and order'.[109] This move was by itself sufficient to bring the romance between the two sides to an abrupt but predictable conclusion.[110] By the end of June Chartists in the northern towns had reverted to their 1842 tactics of trying to secure immigrant support for Chartist-run Repeal meetings, albeit with much less satisfactory results than on the earlier occasion.[111]

After 1843, in fact, O'Connor appeared to believe that the prospect of an Anglo-Irish alliance depended more on O'Connell's committing serious errors of judgement in his conduct of the Repeal campaign than on any policy decision which the Chartists might take to promote that goal. Thus in October-November 1844, he sought to make the most of O'Connell's temporary flirtation with federalist notions by undertaking a lecture of the North of England to expose 'the Federal humbug'.[112] 'FEDERALISM,' he was to argue, 'MEANS PATRONAGE, NOT REPEAL: – MEANS WHIGGERY, AND NOT IRELAND FOR THE IRISH.'[113] None the less the advantages to be wrung from this *faux pas* were essentially limited, and most of these were subsequently lost through Chartist denunciation of the Tory government's decision to treble the Maynooth Grant.[114]

At the beginning of 1846 therefore the problem of bridging the gap separating Irish Repealers from English Chartists appeared to be as intractable as ever: the bulk of the immigrant population, still deeply immersed in its own campaign for an Irish legislature, continued to display open hostility towards English Chartism. What was perhaps more surprising was that as the events of the year unfolded, this now familiar pattern was not to be disturbed in the slightest degree by either the traumatic experience of 'the Famine' or the secession of the 'Young Ireland' group in July from the Repeal Association. For while the secession produced serious disaffection among many Repeal societies in the northern towns at the 'tyrannical proceedings' of Conciliation Hall, there was no indication in the autumn of 1846 that immigrant supporters of the 'Young Irelanders' showed any desire to reach an understanding with local Chartist organisations. In virtually every case they were to reaffirm their commitment to Repeal but to go on to assert that that goal could not be attained unless the existing leadership of the Loyal National Repeal Association showed a greater degree of flexibility and tolerance than hitherto and unless it was prepared to subordinate personal animosities to the greater good of a unified nationalist movement. During the closing months of 1846, therefore, and for most of 1847 the Repeal movement in the North of England suffered from internal divisions which could trace their origins back to a specifically Irish context. Although Conciliation Hall continued to receive the backing of the overwhelming majority of immigrants both before and after

Daniel O'Connell's death in May 1847, a sizeable minority was attracted to the Irish Confederation, the rival nationalist organisation founded in January 1847 by the 'Young Irelanders' to press in a vigorous but peaceful agitation for Repeal. Before the end of 1847 that minority had displayed its strength by establishing Confederate Clubs at Leeds, Manchester, Liverpool, Stalybridge, Rochdale and Sheffield.[115]

In the short run this fresh development offered few crumbs to North of England Chartism since all these bodies accepted without question the anti-Chartist stance of the principal spokesmen of the Confederation. That stance had been defined as early as March 1847 when Richard O'Gorman wrote to William Smith O'Brien, the Confederation's outstanding figure, about a proposal which had originated among Dublin radicals, to bring O'Connor over to Ireland for a mass rally. O'Connor, he asserted,

> is quite sharp enough to take advantage of the vacancy [caused by lack of Confederate activity] and turn it to account - What do you think of Chartist meetings by torch light with that mountebank at the Peoples [sic] head? I fear it much - If we don't take care that [sic] we have broken one idol [Daniel O'Connell], but to find another and more degrading worship start up in its place.[116]

Two months later the deliberations of the Confederate Council again made it abundantly clear that Chartism was still regarded as a force which was inimical to Ireland's true interests. Captain Bryan, a Confederate who had been asked to preside at a Dublin gathering in 'support of Chartist principles', was informed, when he sought guidance on the point, that his presence at such a meeting would be prejudicial to the Confederation's political standing, 'but that the Council did not assume to itself the power of controuling [sic] or in any way interfering with the acts of its members'. In the absence of any precise directive Captain Bryan offered his resignation, but was persuaded to abstain from such action until after the Council had taken a further look at the topic. A week later its decision was announced: Bryan could, without fear of losing his membership, take the chair of any rally which was 'not inconsistent with the fundamental principles of the Confederation'.[117] The delightful ambiguity of this ruling indicated only too well the dilemma in which the Confederate leaders had found themselves: while they abhorred Chartism they wanted to avoid at all costs giving the impression that they made a more searching probe of their members' outside interests than had been the practice at Conciliation Hall under John O'Connell. In the last analysis, therefore, they were relying on the individual's conscience to guide his political conduct, although they were at the same time hinting that support for the Charter was an act of bad faith. Last but not least John Mitchel was using the columns of *The Nation* in August 1847 to repudiate the whole idea of a Confederation-Chartist alliance.

> We desire no fraternisation between the Irish people and the Chartists, not on account of the bugbear of physical force, but simply because some of their five points are to us an abomination and the whole tone and spirit of their proceedings, though well enough for England, are so essentially English that their adoption in Ireland would neither be ... desirable. Between us and them there is a gulf fixed, and we desire not to bridge it over, but to make it wider and deeper.[118]

'The Liberator' himself could not have surpassed the seeming finality of this last pronouncement.

English Chartists for their part were equally outspoken during 1846-7 in their comments about the 'Young Irelanders'. At the 1846 National Chartist Convention which met just after the secession had occurred, delegates had subjected O'Connor's dream of a link-up between the English and Irish working-classes to some searching criticism. Richard Marsden of Preston, for example, thought 'it folly to obtrude their assistance upon the Irish people'; in his opinion the Chartists 'had ... already degraded themselves by servilely courting the sympathies [of Ireland]'. George Julian Harney concurred with these sentiments, although he felt that 'an address which set forth the real principles of Chartism, in reply to Mr. O'Connell's calumnies, would be well timed and advisable'. None the less, even if this were done, delegates should still not place too much trust in the Secessionists.

> Smith O'Brien and his friends were no advocates of democratic principles, all they wanted was an Irish middle-class supremacy dignified by a national flag; as regarded the mass of the Irish people, the Young Irelanders no more desired to invest them with democratic franchise than did O'Connell and his partisans.[119]

The extent to which this advice was followed by Irish Chartists living in London was amply demonstrated when in August-September 1847 they set up the Irish Democratic Confederation to press for Repeal and—as if bidding defiance to Mitchel's calumnies—for an Irish Parliament 'based on the full, free, and fair representation of the whole people of Ireland'.[120]

The initial anti-seceders' bias of the ordinary members of this new organisation was confirmed when the Executive Committee, perhaps yielding to the blandishments of its President, Feargus O'Connor, issued an address which referred in friendly terms to 'Old and Young Irelanders'.[121] Rank-and-file reaction to this document indicated in unmistakable terms that the time for such honeyed phrases and peaceful overtures was long since past. For instance, Michael Seagrave of the Barnsley branch of the IDC—Barnsley was the only place in the North of England where Irish Chartists were sufficiently numerous or interested enough to affiliate themselves to the parent body—felt that it was quite mistaken to anticipate positive gestures 'from the Young Irelanders as a body. Their office organ, the NATION, was silent when Ireland's patriots [O'Connor and the leaders of the Irish Universal Suffrage Association] were denounced. Its editor now occasionally trumpets forth their names to acquire popularity, but studiously keeps back their principles as "abominations".' Yet having rapped the Executive of the IDC over the knuckles for its ill-advised manifesto, he concluded by stressing, as Irish Chartists had done before him, that O'Connor alone could 'win Ireland for the Irish... I unhesitatingly assert, without fear of contradiction, that there is no other man in existence in whom Irishmen can or ought to place an equal degree of confidence as in Mr. O'Connor.'[122] It was true that by mid-November 1847 there were some signs in Barnsley itself that this 'hard line' attitude was undergoing minor modifications,[123] but to be offset against this switch in tactics was the fact that no Irish Confederation Club in the northern counties showed any inclination to abandon their well-worn stance of calculated aloofness from English Chartism.[124] Within four months, however, this outwardly unpromising situation was to alter beyond all recognition: by March 1848 O'Connor's cherished dream of an Anglo-Irish *entente* had become an accomplished fact.

Two factors contributed powerfully to this unexpected turn of events. In chronological order they were the impact of the social radicalism of James Fintan Lalor's thought on an influential section of the Confederate Council and the galvanising effect which the French Revolution of February 1848 exercised on Repealers of all shades of opinion. By the end of November 1847 both John Mitchel and Devin Reilly had been persuaded by Lalor to press for the extension of the system of the Ulster tenant right to the whole of Ireland. Given the continuation of 'the potato blight' and the disturbing social consequences which would inevitably follow in the wake of widespread and arbitrary evictions, they believed it was essential that the Confederation should give precedence to Lalor's campaign for the reform of land tenure. Although Mitchel and Reilly made no immediate impact on the Council's thinking and although they were to remain in a permanent minority within the Confederation, their argument that socio-economic issues should in the short term be the prime concern of the 'Young Ireland' movement led to a fundamen-

tal appraisal of the Confederation's position on a whole host
of interrelated issues. Among them was the question of its
relationship with Chartism. It was to be in this field—and
perhaps partly as the result of Mitchel's prodding—that a
striking change of emphasis had taken place by January 1848.
For at the first anniversary celebrations of the Irish Confederation James Leach, a prominent Manchester Chartist, was
invited to Dublin by the Council as a guest-speaker.[125] Of
equal significance Mitchel at the same gathering tried to
establish a limited form of understanding with the Chartists.
If he did not at this stage withdraw the savage attack on the
'five points' which he had made a few months earlier, he still
emphasised the need for a policy of co-operation based on the
self-interest of both parties. Mitchel argued,

> Thus far, . . . we can carry out our bargain. Let us, then, each by
> the best mode we can, pull down the common enemy [the Whig
> government]—down with him at all events. (Great cheering). And
> when that is done we will not quarrel with the people of England
> for establishing the Charter in their own country—they have a
> right to the Charter if they want it—they have a right to establish
> that or any other institution they please.[126]

Once this breakthrough had been achieved, strenuous
attempts were made during the course of the next few weeks
to replace the formerly strained relations between the two
sides by a more friendly climate of opinion. On the Confederation's side Mitchel completed his conversion to the idea
of a Chartist-Irish Confederation alliance by admitting the
error of his ways. Writing in the *United Irishman* he described
how 'our moral-force agitation' had led him and others to
entertain 'a strong aversion and suspicion against English
Chartists, their principles and objects'. These views were no
longer, and indeed never had been, tenable since every Chartist supported Repeal. 'They are our brothers and allies: we
are bound to help them to their ends, as they offer to help us
to ours. Their enemy and ours is one—the gold-broking,
blood-bartering, government of England; and the main task

E

for us both is one—to pull down that Moloch, and trample it under our feet.' Now, therefore, was the time to cement an alliance with the English Chartists—an alliance which should be concluded at a joint rally, arranged for St Patrick's Day in Manchester, which should define 'our common purpose, and pointing out where our roads diverge, and at what point the British and the Irish are to wend their separate roads'.[127]

In the North of England, where the Confederation's cause continued to flourish, Mitchel's advice was in fact by this time merely endorsing existing practice. For almost as soon as the Confederation's birthday celebrations were concluded, Chartists and Confederates had begun to hold meetings in order to discuss among other things the desirability of co-ordinating their future activities. James Leach, for example, addressed a gathering of Stalybridge Confederates shortly after his return from Dublin and was gratified on that occasion to hear an attack on himself by John O'Connell forcibly answered by B. S. Treanor, President of the local Confederation Club.[128] Similar examples of fraternisation were to be found at Rochdale—where the Owen Roe O'Neil Club made use of the rooms of 'our kind friends', the Chartists; at Manchester; at Liverpool where Dr Reynolds, an Irish Chartist, was the honoured guest of the local Confederates; and at Leeds where the peripatetic George White was one of the principal speakers at the Flood Confederate Club.[129]

Yet notwithstanding these fundamental departures from traditional immigrant attitudes towards Chartism, several of the senior elements in the Confederation's ranks were as late as February 1848 still uneasy about current trends in political thinking. Much of their opposition, it is true, was directed against the social radicalism and militant republicanism which were increasingly dominating the writings of John Mitchel. But there also remained a residual hostility to any idea of an Anglo-Irish *entente* along the lines which O'Connor had been outlining for most of the preceding

decade. The most articulate and influential representative
of this strand of opinion was William Smith O'Brien who,
when invited to attend a Chartist-Confederate meeting in
Manchester on St Patrick's Day, made it clear 'that I could
not take any part in your proceedings if it be intended to
[connect?] Chartism with Repeal'. Although he admitted
that 'I do not entertain the objections which I once feel
[sic] to Chartists', he concluded by emphasising that 'I cannot conceive any proceeding more calculated to retard the
success of Repeal cause than the attempt to identify the
Repeal with Chartism'.[130] At the time these sentiments were
committed to paper—28 February—there was nothing to
suggest that either Smith O'Brien or those others who sub-
scribed to this anti-Chartist thesis would in the short-term
abandon their rigidly defined position. Within little more
than a week, however, the Confederate Council had both
accepted the Manchester invitation and appointed a powerful deputation to represent them. Subsequent events in Dublin compelled the Council to make some alterations in the
personnel of its delegation,[131] but at the end of the day it
was still able to send one of its most prominent members,
Thomas Meagher, and to offer the hand of friendship to the
English Chartists.[132] After this Manchester gathering it was
for the first time possible to speak of a *rapprochement* between Chartism and the Confederation at the national level
and to point to renewed attempts at the local level to translate this informal alliance into a practical programme of
co-operation.

Such a transformation owed much to the overthrow in the
last days of February 1848 of the 'July Monarchy' of Louis
Philippe; for that event had a catalystic effect on the views of
such cautious figures as Gavan Duffy and Smith O'Brien.
Significantly enough, if neither of these two spokesmen of the
conservative wing of the Council was willing at this stage to
advocate an immediate uprising, they were no longer pre-

pared to rule out the use of physical force as a last resort. Indeed, Smith O'Brien saw some virtue in persuading the Irish people to form themselves into a national guard. The sedition trials of the two Confederate leaders—Meagher and Smith O'Brien himself in May 1848—and the sentence of fourteen years' transportation imposed upon John Mitchel in the same month merely helped to reinforce their growing faith in the efficacy of a military uprising as the best, or perhaps the only, way of obtaining a domestic legislature from Westminster.[133]

Once this type of strategy was given serious consideration, English Chartism assumed a position of special importance. For in combination with the Confederate Clubs in the northern counties it could mount, in the event of an Irish rebellion, a diversionary operation in English which could limit the reinforcements available for service in Ireland at the very time when the final struggle for independence was being waged.[134] It was partly for this reason that from late March 1848 Confederates and Chartists in the North of England were integrating their activities ever more closely. At Oldham, for example, Doheny, after describing himself as an 'Irish Chartist', tried to persuade his audience that

> the present time, when thrones were crumbling and despots were being flung away, was the time for Irish freedom and English Chartism. (Applause). He was accredited to say, on behalf of the Irish people, 'The charter, the whole charter and nothing but the charter'; and he asked them in return for 'Ireland, all Ireland, and nothing but Ireland for the Irish'.[135]

A similar story was recounted in Leeds where the local Confederate Club gave its 'adhesion to the Chartists, and appointed a deputation, to attend their meetings'; while the alliance was carried even further in Manchester where a joint committee of Confederates, Conciliation Hall Repealers and Chartists was established to 'watch passing events and act as might be required'.[136] The extent to which this type of activity met with the Confederate Council's approval was strikingly demonstrated when Mitchel in one of his last public appearances and Doheny were sent over to Liverpool at the end of April to promote good relations between English Chartists and Irish Repealers.[137]

Fraternisation on this scale was accompanied both by 'physical force' speeches from Confederate leaders of the immigrant communities in Leeds, Liverpool and Manchester and, after Mitchel's savage sentence, by joint drillings between Chartists and Confederates.[138] Yet few of the local magistrates in either Lancashire or Yorkshire were intimidated by these manoeuvres; for as they knew from past experience, 'physical force' oratory, if it were to command respect, had to be matched by organisation and military strength. All the Chartists and Confederates had to offer in these vital areas were a few firearms and an ill assorted collection of pikes. When, therefore, *Habeas Corpus* was finally suspended in Ireland and Smith O'Brien launched a totally ineffective rising in Tipperary, the Chartist-Irish Confederation alliance in Yorkshire and Lancashire created scarcely any problems for the forces of law and order. Instead of engaging in a concerted and well-planned diversionary operation, Chartists and Confederates found themselves—as at Liverpool—confronted by a determined magistracy, backed up by troops and a formidable number of special constables prepared to take appropriate action against all potential leaders of an insurrection.[139] With the ensuing arrests of local Chartist and Confederate spokesmen,[140] the short-lived Chartist-Confederation understanding came to an abrupt conclusion. By the autumn of 1848 both Repeal and the campaign for the 'Six Points' hardly evoked any ripple of enthusiasm among the working classes in the northern towns.

For the immigrant population in particular it was a bitter blow to realise that after almost a decade of agitation there was no hope in the short-term of obtaining an Irish Parliament on Dublin Green. Yet it was a blow with which they had to come to terms; for as they looked at the fearsome devastation which 'the Famine' had wreaked in their native-land and as they tended to the needs of those relatives and friends who had come to Britain to escape the worst consequences of 'the potato blight', they realised in their hearts that *Cathleen ni Hoolihan* had a long and arduous journey ahead of her before she was to be transformed into a beautiful 'young woman' who 'walked like a queen'.[141]

Notes to this chapter are on pages 220-29.

DICKENS AND THE SELF-HELP IDEA
Robin Gilmour

I

'OF ALL the great Victorian writers, he was probably the most antagonistic to the Victorian Age itself.'[1] At first sight nothing could seem more remote from the alienated Dickens of Edmund Wilson's influential thesis than the idea I propose to discuss here. Self-help is one of the mainstream Victorian notions that has travelled least well into the twentieth century, and it is still associated in the popular mind with the more unpleasant aspects of Victorian life—with *laisser-faire* economics, with the cult of success and the worship of respectability, with hypocritical attempts on the part of middle-class propagandists to inculcate their own values and goals in the working population. There is of course some truth in the popular view, but I believe self-help deserves more sympathetic consideration than it sometimes gets, especially from those interested—as the student of the Victorian novel inevitably is —in the crucial and highly complex question of class in the Victorian Age.

The period (as everyone knows) saw the rise of the middle classes into political and social influence, and self-help was an essential part of their creed: it championed the values of achievement over those of birth and station, and as such was a weapon in their quarrel with the established order. Dickens' relationship to this process of social evolution was fundamental to his criticism of Victorian society, and I would suggest that the self-help idea, properly considered, can help us to understand that criticism. In particular, his 'antagonism' to the Victorian Age can be charted in his progressive alienation from the idea of the self-made man, and the corresponding emphasis in his later fiction on the idea of the gentleman, conceived in moral rather than class terms. To consider this topic, however, it is first necessary to look at the self-help idea and at the extent of Dickens' own allegiance to it.

Self-help is usually associated with Samuel Smiles. He was not the earliest nor the only writer in the field, but he is certainly the most representative. His *Self-Help* (1859) was as popular and influential as it was, not because it said anything essentially new, but because it gave succinct and memorable expression to ideas already widely current in the mid-Victorian period. It has to be said at once that Smiles is a repetitive and not very subtle thinker, and his works will never merit more than a footnote in the official histories of ideas; yet there is a sense in which he and others like him are valuable to us for that very reason. We catch in their more ephemeral writings a note which is sometimes missing from the enduring masterpieces—an echo from that evanescent context of social and moral assumptions which Lionel Trilling has called, in an apt phrase, 'a culture's hum and buzz of implication'.[2] In Smiles' case the hum comes from the engine-room of the Victorian period. His purpose in writing *Self-Help*, so he wrote in his *Autobiography*, was 'principally to illustrate and enforce the power of George Stephenson's great word— PERSEVERANCE'.[3] Significantly, Smiles aligned himself with the great railway pioneer whose biography he had published in 1857, and it was the character of these 'parvenus' that he sought to celebrate:

> There is no doubt about the parvenus. They are the men who do the great work of the world. . . For the parvenus are of the people, belong to them, and spring from them. In recognising the great parvenu spirit of this age we merely recognise what, in other

words, is designated as the dignity of labour, the rights of industry, the power of intellect. For real honour is due to the man who
honestly carves out for himself by his own native energy a name
and a fortune, diligently exercising the powers and faculties
which belong to him as a man.[4]

Smiles' heroes were the pioneering engineers, inventors, and
industrialists of the early Victorian Age, whose efforts had
largely been responsible for making England the workshop of
the world. In this sense the creed of self-help was complementary to Smiles' industrial biographies: he was interpreting
the achievement and values of men who were doing, and
knew they were doing, 'the great work of the world'.

It is a mistake, however, to see *Self-Help* as the mere glori-
fication of worldly success, for although Smiles believed that
'every man's first duty is, to improve, to educate, and elevate
himself',[5] it was not the success but the character of the self-
made man that he valued. In the Preface to the 1866 edition
of *Self-Help* he defended himself against the charge that he
had paid insufficient attention to the fact of failure by observing that, in the case of the successful man 'it is not the result
... that is to be regarded so much as the aim and the effort,
the patience, the courage, and the endeavour with which
desirable and worthy objects are pursued'. There is a central
emphasis on character in Smiles which is mostly absent from
later success literature. He celebrates individualism not so
much as a means to worldly success but as the path to independence and self-fulfilment, and if one can detect a pattern
in the hundreds of examples scattered throughout his writings
it would be his admiration for those who have risen from
humble origins to the dignity and independence of a productive life. In stressing the individual's capacity to elevate
himself morally and intellectually he offered a career of 'self-
culture' (as he called it) as something to be pursued for its
own sake, irrespective of its market value.

Dickens was an exact contemporary of Smiles, and for much
of his life he shared many of the ideas and beliefs which find

a classic expression in *Self-Help*. Firstly, and most obviously, he was to a large extent a self-made man: the story of his early life, in Forster's biography, was not available to Smiles at the time of writing *Self-Help*, but it might well have found a place in his history of individuals who had successfully raised themselves in the face of adverse circumstances. The son of a Navy pay clerk who was imprisoned for debt, Dickens experienced the misery of working as a wage-slave in a blacking-factory; yet he struggled out of the debt-ridden shabbiness of his background to establish himself as the most successful English novelist of the nineteenth century. In his own profession he was as great a pioneer as George Stephenson, and he would have endorsed Smiles' conviction that 'real honour is due to the man who honestly carves out for himself by his own native energy a name and a fortune, diligently exercising the powers and faculties which belong to him as a man'. Close to the spirit of Smiles' words are these lines from a play by Bulwer Lytton, which Dickens knew by heart and liked to quote:

> Then did I seek to rise
> Out of the prison of my mean estate;
> And, with such jewels as the exploring mind
> Brings from the caves of knowledge, buy my ransom
> From those twin jailers of the daring heart—
> Low birth and iron fortune.[6]

Dickens also shared Smiles' belief that the road to success lay chiefly 'through the energetic use of simple means and ordinary qualities, with which nearly all human individuals have been more or less endowed'.[7] In *David Copperfield*, which is partly autobiographical, the emphasis falls not on the hero's gifts as a writer but on his application to the self-help virtues: hard work, perseverance, 'patient and continuous energy', earnestness. 'I have never believed it possible,' David Copperfield observes towards the end of the novel, 'that any natural or improved ability can claim immunity from the companionship of the steady, plain, hard-working qualities, and hope to gain its end' (ch 42). Twenty years after writing this Dickens expressed the same idea in a speech to the Birmingham and Midland Institute:

> The one serviceable, safe, certain, remunerative, attainable quality in every study and in every pursuit is the quality of attention. My own invention or imagination, such as it is, I can most truthfully assure you, would never have served me as it has, but for the habit of commonplace, humble, patient, daily, toiling, drudging attention. [*Applause.*][8]

It is in Dickens' speeches, indeed, that we get the clearest evidence of his allegiance to the self-help idea. He was a frequent speaker at Mechanics' Institutes and Athenaeums (themselves the institutions of self-help) and his speeches frequently stress the moral which forms the opening sentence of Smiles' work: 'Heaven helps those who help themselves'. Like Smiles, but more emphatically, he stressed self-help as an end in itself: members of the Birmingham and Midland Institute were urged to 'Persevere ... not because self-improvement is at all certain to lead to worldly success, but because it is good and right of itself...'[9] The same spirit was evident a quarter of a century earlier, when in 1843 he spoke to the Manchester Athenaeum of the 'consolations' of self-help:

> The man who lives from day to day by the daily exercise in his sphere of hand or head, and seeks to improve himself in such a place as the Athenaeum, acquires for himself that property of soul which has in all times upheld struggling men in every degree, but self-made men especially and always. [*Applause.*] He secures to himself that faithful companion which, while it has ever lent the light of its countenance to men of rank and eminence who have deserved it, has ever shed its brightest consolations on men of low estate and almost hopeless means. [*Applause.*] It took its patient seat beside Sir Walter Raleigh in his dungeon-study in the Tower; and it laid its head upon the block with More. But it did not disdain to watch the stars with Ferguson, the shepherd's boy; it walked the streets in mean attire with Crabbe; it was a poor barber here in Lancashire with Arkwright...[10]

And so on: Dickens' attitude is less buoyant than Smiles', but with its earnest and hortatory tone and roll-call of famous names, this passage would not be out of context in *Self-Help*. It represents, of course, a statement for public consumption: his imaginative attitude, as we shall see later, is a good deal more complex.

II

So far I have tried to place the self-help idea in a sympathetic light, stressing Smiles' concern with character and suggesting certain similarities with Dickens' conscious moral outlook. But one cannot read very far in the literature of self-help without encountering a basic ambivalence in the attitude to 'getting on'. Despite Smiles' emphasis on the moral value of a self-help career, and despite his attacks on snobbery and social climbing, there is a class resonance about the idea of 'raising' or 'elevating' oneself which his disclaimers do not quite dispel. This ambivalence manifests itself in a tension between moral and social value, and it is most acute at the point where the self-help idea merges into the idea of the gentleman—as it does for both Smiles and Dickens. The final chapter of *Self-Help* is entitled, significantly, 'Character: The True Gentleman'. If, for Smiles, 'the crown and glory of life is Character', then the crown and glory of character is the ideal of the gentleman. The true self-helper can become the 'true gentleman':

> There never yet existed a gentleman but was lord of a great heart. And this may exhibit itself under the hodden grey of the peasant as well as under the laced coat of the noble... Riches and rank have no necessary connexion with genuine gentlemanly qualities. The poor man may be a true gentleman,—in spirit and in daily life. He may be honest, truthful, upright, polite, temperate, courageous, self-respecting, and self-supporting,—that is, be a true gentleman. The poor man with a rich spirit is in all ways superior to the rich man with a poor spirit.[11]

The classlessness of the gentlemanly ideal was much canvassed in the Victorian period, and Smiles' statement represents what was, so to speak, the official view of the matter. Yet the student of the period must be careful, as Geoffrey Best points out, 'not to confuse the moral ideal with the social reality'.[12] In practice the two were often far apart. The theorists of self-help might extol the innate moral worth of the self-made man, but in the real world his status as a gentleman was not self-evident and was often measured by more traditional standards. Moreover—and this was something Smiles never really faced squarely—the impulse to self-improvement often came from a desire to 'get on' in a narrowly social and material sense.

This ambiguity runs throughout self-help literature and it emerges very clearly in a book which, although published three years before *Self-Help*, is very close to it in tone and attitude. *John Halifax, Gentleman* can be seen as the classic self-help novel. It was written by Dinah Mulock, who later married George Lillie Craik, author of *The Pursuit of Knowledge under Difficulties* (1831), a seminal work in the self-improvement genre which profoundly influenced Smiles.[13] *John Halifax, Gentleman* is an uncritical fictional celebration of a poor boy's rise in the world and, being fiction, it reveals many of the unconscious assumptions involved in such a rise. It was published in 1856, and although the action is set at the end of the eighteenth and beginning of the nineteenth century, it is a characteristically mid-Victorian work. This story of the orphan boy who rises from tanner's lad to prosperous mill-owner could only have been written, one feels, in the years after the Great Exhibition, the high noon of Victorian prosperity. The aggressive ring of the title, with its emphasis on the word 'Gentleman', suggests the self-assertive insecurity of the new Victorian middle class, conscious of their emergence into commercial prominence but uncertain of their precise place in the traditional hierarchy. Mrs Craik's treatment of this emergent type is entirely uncritical: there is no suggestion of irony in the quasi-religious solemnity with which she celebrates the moral and domestic pieties of the

new middle class. In *John Halifax, Gentleman* we are un-
ashamedly offered the hero as Victorian businessman and
paterfamilias:

> ... my eyes naturally sought the father as he stood among his
> boys, taller than any of them, and possessing far more than they
> that quality for which John Halifax had always been remarkable
> —dignity. True, Nature had favoured him beyond most men,
> giving him the stately, handsome presence, befitting middle age,
> throwing a kind of apostolic grace over the high, half-bald crown,
> and touching with a softened gray the still curly locks behind.
> But these were mere accidents; the true dignity lay in himself and
> his own personal character, independent of any exterior. [ch 30][14]

If John Halifax ends up as a commercial patriarch, he starts
out as the archetypal self-help hero. Although he believes his
father to have been 'a scholar and a gentleman' (ch 1), this
hint of genteel birth is never proved and we learn that 'his
pedigree began and ended with his own honest name' (ch 2).
He is an orphan, alone in the world and uneducated—he is in
his teens before he learns to write his own name. But he is the
possessor of a 'firm, indomitable will' (ch 8), and he is quite
prepared to pursue knowledge under difficulties. He educates
himself and, like Smiles' great hero George Stephenson,
spends his leisure time constructing models of the machines
he is later to employ in his factory. He prospers in the tanner's
yard, marries a 'lady'—Ursula March—and using her capital
sets himself up as a mill-owner. When his landlord, Lord
Luxmore, diverts the stream which powers the mill, John
proves his independence and resourcefulness by installing
steam machinery in his factory, and his prosperity steadily
increases—even in the lean years, for John Halifax is too
prudent to invest his capital in risky foreign speculations. In
short, we are in the world of *Self-Help*, where character is destiny and God helps those who help themselves. 'I am what God
made me,' John Halifax declares at the outset of his career,
'and what, with His blessing, I will make myself' (ch 14).
There are some interesting parallels between Mrs Craik's

novel and *Great Expectations*, and I shall argue later that Pip's efforts to become a gentleman should be seen in the light of the Smilesian concept of 'self-culture' which is common to both novels. Like Pip, John Halifax feels ashamed of his 'ugly hands' and of his employment in manual labour, and his ambitions are similarly confused with a sexual motive: he wants to marry Ursula, although he knows that she is a 'gentlewoman' and he only a 'tradesman' (ch 15). His friends advise him to respect his station—as Joe and Biddy advise Pip—but he perseveres, marries Ursula, and becomes in time a landed proprietor; unlike Pip, he becomes a 'prosperous man' who 'drove daily to and from his mills, in as tasteful an equipage as any of the country gentry...' (ch 29). The difference between the two novels lies in the attitude to success: whereas *John Halifax, Gentleman* is a laudatory celebration of a successful self-help career, Dickens sets out to explore the inner assumptions and contradictions which such a career of 'great expectations' involves, and there is a whole dimension of irony in his novel which is quite absent from Mrs Craik's.

Yet it is precisely this lack of irony in *John Halifax, Gentleman* which makes it interesting. Mrs Craik's very closeness to her subject, her uncritical relationship to the self-help idea, makes her novel a revealing document. When, towards the end, John Halifax starts to rehearse the story of his rise from humble origins, his son interrupts him with the comment, 'We are gentlefolks now' (ch 29); the hero's reply, 'We always were, my son', is quoted by Taine in his essay on 'Landed Proprietors and English Gentlemen', and it illustrates perfectly the ambiguity surrounding the idea of the gentleman in self-help literature.[15] For although Mrs Craik is here saying, with Smiles, that the poor man can become a gentleman, that what matters is independence and integrity and dignity, at the same time John Halifax is only secure in social status when he has *justified* himself by acquiring the symbols of hereditary class—the large estate, the county acquaintance, an aristocratic son-in-law, a carriage that is as 'tasteful . . . as any of the country gentry'. Moreover, these achievements figure in the novel as themselves the *reward* of a lifetime's self-help: success is measured in terms of a breakthrough into a rigid social hierarchy. The whole drift of the novel bears out the truth of Asa Briggs' observation that 'in the battle between the self-made man and the gentleman, the self-made man won in England only if he became a gentleman himself, or tried to turn his son into one'.[16]

This battle was not only fought out on the Victorian social front; it also took place in the minds and hearts of the Victorians themselves. The ambivalence in the self-help idea which I have examined in *John Halifax, Gentleman* was shared by Dickens for much of his creative life, and was only finally resolved in *Great Expectations*. The depth of perception and honesty of feeling in that late novel are the product of Dickens' imaginative mastery of the ambiguities involved in becoming a 'gentleman', and represent the culmination of a long process of debate in his art between the idea of the gentleman and the values of self-help and the self-made man. To trace that debate, as I want to do now, is to chart the outlines of his quarrel with the Victorian Age itself and to measure the extent of his alienation from some of its most cherished beliefs.

III

I have so far discussed that part of Dickens which identified with the self-help values, the self-made man who took pride in having overcome Bulwer Lytton's 'twin jailers of the daring heart—low birth and iron fortune'; but this is not the whole story. There was another part of Dickens, equally important, which insisted on his gentlemanly status, not as something earned (after the manner of John Halifax) but something inherited, a birthright. It is this part which is uppermost in his account of the blacking-factory episode: in the shame he felt at having been set to work with 'common men and boys' and in the corresponding insistence on the fact that 'though perfectly familiar with them, my conduct and manners were different enough from theirs to place a space between us. They, and the men, always spoke of me as "the young gentleman".'[17] In his early novels these two attitudes co-exist without awareness of contradiction: for a young hero like Nicholas Nickleby to 'get on' is not so much to achieve status as to recover it, to reclaim and to re-assert a lost inheritance. Thus we learn at the end of *Nicholas Nickleby* (1838-9) that 'the first act of Nicholas, when he became a rich and prosperous merchant, was to buy his father's old house' (ch 65). We are never allowed to forget that Nicholas is a gentleman's son. (There is a similar suggestion, not developed, in John Halifax's belief that his father was a 'scholar and a gentleman'.)

Of the early novels *Oliver Twist* (1837-8) is closest to the memory of the blacking-factory experience, and is Dickens' first fictional attempt to come to terms with the feelings of moral outrage and social disinheritance which we can see in his autobiographical account. The novel presents a situation which is to recur, with modifications, in *David Copperfield* and *Great Expectations*: a small, innately genteel child is forced to suffer social humiliation, he escapes to the comfort and security of a middle-class home, and is then threatened with a return to his former degraded condition. This nightmare of disinheritance, as it may be called, is perhaps the most characteristic of all Dickensian nightmares, and it is given terrifying expression in such scenes as the invasion of Oliver's country retreat by Fagan and Monks, or his recapture by Nancy, when the child cries out in agony—'I don't belong to them. I don't know them. Help! Help!' (ch 15). In the end, of course, Oliver is restored to his inheritance: the workhouse child is discovered to be of gentle birth, thus justifying (symbolically if not realistically) the improbable gentility of

F

speech and manner he displays throughout. The moral that 'birth will out' can be seen as Dickens' fictional vindication of his childhood insistence on being 'the young gentleman', a status which his father's imprisonment for debt and his own menial employment in the blacking-factory had threatened to destroy.

There is a similar tension between status and situation in Dickens' next novel, *Nicholas Nickleby*, although here the pressures on the hero's gentility are economic. Where Oliver had been a child and an entirely passive hero, Nicholas is a young man faced with the necessity of 'getting on in the world' (ch 15) as a result of his father's financial ruin and death. His situation would seem to require the practice of self-help, but in the event Nicholas makes a rather pathetic showing. We are told that he applies himself with 'steadiness and persever-ance' (ch 37) in the Cheerybles' office, but this is in the context of what has already become, for Nicholas, a family affair: the Cheeryble brothers are simply Mr Brownlow writ large. Out-side their office he shows considerable reluctance to 'get on' in any way that will threaten his respectability: the employ-ment agency fills him with acute embarrassment, and when he does get a job with the Crummles troupe, he works under a pseudonym. When asked by Mr Gregsbury to name the duties of an MP's secretary, Nicholas can think of few 'beyond the general one of making himself as agreeable and useful as he can, consistently with his own respectability...' (ch 16). Respectability, one tends to feel, is Nicholas' chief concern—a concern shared by his creator. Work can only be conceived as a possibility for the young hero when it poses no threat at all to his 'respectability': hence the cosy, familial unreality of the Cheerybles' business. Nicholas must always be able to assert his genteel status in the face of taunts like Sir Mulberry Hawk's that he is 'an errand boy':

> 'You are an errand-boy for aught I know,' said Sir Mulberry Hawk.

'I am the son of a country gentleman,' returned Nicholas, 'your equal in birth and education, and your superior I trust in everything besides...' [ch 32].

In Nicholas' reply one hears that mixture of self-assertion and social defensiveness characteristic of the new Victorian middle class which was coming into being at this time. Dickens cannot see his hero's predicament objectively because he is still too close to the expectations of this class to examine its values critically. The result is a novel which raises the problem of 'getting on' in this society only to resolve it, through the benevolence of the Cheerybles, in the form of the restored inheritance.

The pre-occupation with inherited status in *Oliver Twist* and *Nicholas Nickleby* is related, in ways I have suggested, to Dickens' interpretation of his experience and background— an interpretation which at this stage suggests an eagerness to be identified with the established rather than aspiring sections of the Victorian middle class. The essential development of his social thought, however, is towards an increasingly critical understanding of this class and of his own relationship to it. Words like 'genteel' and 'respectable' acquire altogether more complex associations in the later novels, as Dickens becomes more aware of the negative aspects of Victorian respectability. When Kate Nickleby is described as possessing 'true gentility of manner' (ch 28), there is no irony in the phrase; when, a decade later in *Dombey and Son* (1846-8), Mr Dombey describes the grotesquely affected Mrs Skewton as being 'perfectly genteel' (ch 21), the word has acquired a prim, negative connotation, reinforcing our sense of the life-destroying nature of Dombey's habitual propriety.

At the same time as Dickens becomes more openly critical of middle-class life, and of the deadening power of tradition and social convention, there is a new emphasis in his work on the self-help values and a new willingness to recognise and affirm the element of the self-made man in his own character and history. When we reach *David Copperfield* (1849-50), there has been a significant shift away from the fact of inheritance towards the celebration of the self-help values of hard work, earnestness, and perseverance; and David's story offers a much more convincing exploration than anything in the previous novels of what life might be like for an orphaned child with his way to make in the world. Before discussing *David Copperfield*, however, I want to look briefly at the previous novel, *Dombey and Son*, where we can see evidence of a division in Dickens' response to the Victorian scene.

Dombey and Son is a novel about business; it is also a novel which records, with impressive accuracy and open-mindedness, the first impact of the railways on Britain. Dickens' presentation of Mr Dombey as a representative contemporary man who embodies the hardening features of an increasingly influential commercial class, goes hand-in-hand with the recognition that the society which Dombey and his like are starting to dominate is undergoing a process of social upheaval brought about by the railways. Dickens is careful to distinguish between these two areas of contemporary life, and the distinction is made explicit in chapter 20, when Dombey responds with sullen introspection to the railroad which takes him to Birmingham after the death of his son Paul, 'tinging the scene of transition before him with the morbid colours of his own mind, and making it a ruin and a picture of decay, instead of hopeful change, and promise of better things...' (ch 20). It is the 'hopeful change', the 'promise of better things', that Dickens celebrates in the new railroad. He records with awed fascination the 'hundred thousand shapes and substances of incompleteness' as the railway invades Stagg's Gardens in chapter 6, yet the final tendency of this unheaval is beneficent: '...the new streets that had stopped disheartened in the mud and waggon-ruts formed towns within themselves, originating wholesome comforts and conveniences... Bridges that had led to nothing, led to villas, gardens, churches, healthy public walks...' (ch 15). Dickens' affirmation of this 'hopeful change' provides the touchstone for his criticism of Dombeyism. For Mr Dombey is shown throughout the novel as the enemy of change, hostile to the transforming power of love and fellow-feeling; he is 'the beadle of private life; the beadle of our business and our bosoms' (ch 5). With his quasi-aristocratic conception of business and his deadening respectability—mirrored in the 'tall, dark, dreadfully genteel street' (ch 3) where he lives—Dombey is representative of a social class which, on coming to power and influence, is showing itself increasingly hostile to the life of instinct and natural feeling, and therefore to the life of the imagination. In this thematic opposition we can see, as Steven Marcus points out, a deep division in Dickens' attitude: 'On the one hand he is affirming the changing world symbolized by the railroad, and on the other condemning the society which produced it'.[18] This is to put it too neatly, perhaps, but certainly in the years immediately after *Dombey* the values of the changing world —in which self-help plays an important part—provide the terms of Dickens' criticism of society.

IV

Although a much more inward and introspective work than *Dombey*, *David Copperfield* continues Dickens' enquiry into Victorian middle-class life—a fact Matthew Arnold recognised when he praised the novel as an 'all-containing treasure-house' of 'English middle-class civilisation'.[19] The continuity is evident in the character of Mr Murdstone, David's step-father, which Arnold singled out for particular praise. With his austerity and cult of 'firmness', his sadism sanctioned by his cruel religion, Murdstone represents an extension of Dickens' criticism of the hard and sterile elements in contemporary life. It is, I think, significant that Murdstone has a controlling interest in the wine warehouse where David is set to work, and which is the fictional re-creation of the blacking-factory where Dickens had suffered so much as a child. *David Copper-field* also shows a renewed—and considerably more critical—interest in the idea of the gentleman. It is true that like Oliver and Nicholas, David is the son of a gentleman, and like them is rescued from the worst consequences of poverty by the generosity of his Aunt Betsey: the inheritance theme is still there. But David has to work harder for his inheritance than any of the previous young protagonists, and Aunt Betsey is very far from being the convenient device that Mr Brownlow and the Cheerybles are. She is a fully realised woman, whose championing of 'earnestness' carries the authority of her experience of life: 'Earnestness is what that Somebody must look for, to sustain him and improve him, Trot. Deep, downright faithful earnestness' (ch 35). The idea of the gentleman, too, has been modified by the prevailing emphasis on earnestness and self-improvement. Respectability, such a key word in the early novels, here acquires a new and sinister connotation in the character of Littimer, Steerforth's manservant, 'who was in appearance a pattern of respectability' (ch 21), but in reality proves to be corrupt and treacherous. Steerforth himself embodies the negative aspects of the gentlemanly code which Dickens now rejects: the pride in status that leads to disregard for the feelings of others, lack of purpose and commitment, contempt for the values of duty and hard work. He is allowed personal charm, which he never loses (at least in David's eyes), and the redeeming touch of a momentary insight into his own predicament: 'I wish with all my soul I could guide myself better' (ch 22).

The waste and aimlessness of Steerforth's career provides a necessary foil to the slow process of maturation, of self-improvement and self-advancement, that is David's story. In this respect the novel is broadly affirmative of the self-help values, although Dickens' attitude to success is rather more complex. Although we see David at the end 'advanced in fame and fortune' (ch 63), we are not allowed to forget those characters who have suffered defeat at the hands of life: David's mother, Little Em'ly, Ham, Mr Peggotty. Although David's career seems to testify to the value of prudence, there is Micawber to remind us of the fact of imprudence and in doing so to bear witness, as Mrs Leavis acutely remarks, 'to a pre-Victorian enjoyment of living that Dickens indignantly saw being destroyed by the Murdstones and Littimers'.[20] Although Aunt Betsey urges David to become 'a fine firm fellow, with a will of your own' (ch 19), and to be 'firm and self-reliant' (ch 34), we remember also Mr Murdstone and the destructive potential of his firmness of will. Most of all, perhaps, there is the character of Uriah Heep to demonstrate the twisted, hypocritical form that self-help can take in this society for someone who shares neither David's advantages nor his basic decency:

> Father and me was both brought up at a foundation school for boys... They taught us all a deal of umbleness—not much else that I know of, from morning to night. We was to be umble to this person, and umble to that; and to pull off our caps here, and to make bows there; and always to know our place, and abase ourselves before our betters. And we had such a lot of betters! Father got the monitor-medal by being umble. So did I. Father got made a sexton by being umble. He had the character, among the gentlefolks, of being such a well-behaved man, that they were determined to bring him in. "Be umble, Uriah," says father to me, "and you'll get on". It was what was always being dinned into you and me at school; it's what goes down best. "Be umble," says father, "and you'll do!" And really it ain't done bad! [ch 39]

'Be umble ... and you'll get on': Uriah's competitive humility is a weed that is seen to have grown in the shade of what Arnold called 'the Murdstonian drive in business and the Murdstonian religion'.[21]

If *David Copperfield* is a story of success, it is a success tempered by compassion and a full recognition of the element of failure and defeat in life. It is this central humanity which renders acceptable the self-help values enforced in David's story: hard work, earnestness, prudence, self-reliance, perseverance. The total communication of the novel is of course considerably more complex than these values suggest (the point is often made that David Copperfield could never have written *David Copperfield*) but Dickens' affirmation of them at this stage of his career is important. They provide him with a system of values which enables him to articulate his criticism of the repressive, life-denying forces in contemporary life (the Dombey/Murdstone forces) while at the same time proclaiming his allegiance to the new forces of the changing world embodied in the railroad in *Dombey*. The ethic of self-help, that is to say, is congenial to a Dickens who is still open-minded about contemporary society, still genuinely affirmative of some manifestations of Victorian progress. Thus in the opening address to *Household Words*, written while still at work on *David Copperfield*, Dickens can speak of his faith in 'the progress of mankind' and of 'the privilege of living in this summer-dawn of time':

> The mightier inventions of this age are not, to our thinking, all material, but have a kind of souls in their stupendous bodies which may find expression in Household Words. The traveller whom we accompany on his railroad or his steamboat journey, may gain, we hope, some compensation for incidents which these later generations have outlived, in new associations with the Power that bears him onward . . . even with the towering chimneys he may see, spirting out fire and smoke upon the prospect. The swart giants, Slaves of the Lamp of Knowledge, have their thousand and one tales, no less than the Genii of the East. . .[22]

It is in something of this spirit that Mr Rouncewell the ironmaster is conceived in *Bleak House* (1852-3), and that Dickens launches his attack on the world of fashion and the Court of Chancery, 'things of precedent and usage; over-sleeping Rip Van Winkles, who have played at strange games through a deal of thundery weather. . .' (ch 2).

Bleak House opposes past and present more emphatically than any of Dickens' previous works, and the ironmaster has an essential part to play in this opposition. He is a secondary character in the action, but his meeting with Sir Leicester Dedlock in chapter 28 is thematically central, a confrontation which reveals Dickens' delicate balancing of social forces in this novel. Sir Leicester is first presented to us as 'an honourable, obstinate, truthful, high-spirited, intensely prejudiced, perfectly unreasonable man' (ch 2)—conflicting attributes which suggest an ambivalence in Dickens' attitude to the character. In his social role as a powerful baronet he is criticised (as the family name of Dedlock implies) for his rigidity and opposition to change: like Dombey to this extent, Sir Leicester and his class are shown to be incapable of receiving 'any impress from the moving age' (ch 12). As an individual, however, he is shown to be a good man, honourable and scrupulous in fulfilling his responsibilities—a positive quality in a novel where irresponsibility is thoroughly anatomised— and an 'excellent master . . . holding it a part of his state to be so' (ch 7). He is chivalrous to his wife, conscientious in his attitude to his dependent relatives, and invariably courteous to his social inferiors. Dickens' ability to portray these qualities in a man whose social role he is criticising is evidence of the complexity of his mature art, for he does not make a straightforward division between the man and his position. Sir Leicester's qualities are directly related to his conception of his social role, and Dickens can do justice to this fact even while making a considered rejection of the role itself.

Rouncewell, on the other hand, is a man whose social role Dickens respects: the ironmaster is 'always on the flight' (ch 28), an embodiment of the will, energy, and purposefulness of the moving age. He has a 'strong Saxon face . . . a picture of resolution and perseverance', and Dickens describes him in terms that recall Mrs Craik's John Halifax:

> He is a little over fifty perhaps, of a good figure, like his mother; and has a clear voice, a broad forehead from which his dark hair has retired, and a shrewd, though open face. He is a responsible-looking gentleman dressed in black, portly enough, but strong and active. Has a perfectly natural and easy air, and is not in the

least embarrassed by the great presence into which he comes.
[ch 28]

It is not difficult to see where Rouncewell stands in the
scheme of values in *Bleak House*. A man who has made his
way in the world and expects his son to make his; hard-
working, persevering, and earnest ('I think it is rather our
way to be in earnest,' he tells Lady Dedlock in chapter 48),
yet 'responsible-looking' and 'natural and easy'; he embodies
the best aspects of a self-help career as Dickens sees it at this
time. Unlike the lawyers in the Court of Chancery, the ironmaster combines hard work with humanity, perseverance
with responsibility; he is thus a focal figure in the thematic
structure of the novel, providing a contemporary image of
purposeful activity which offsets both the laziness and irresponsibility of characters like Turveydrop and Skimpole, and
the equally irresponsible but joyless and destructive industry
of lawyers like Mr Vholes.[23]

When the aristocrat and the ironmaster meet in chapter 28
to discuss the future of Lady Dedlock's maid Rosa, it is a
representative confrontation of the old order and the new in
which the best features of both are on display.[24] The two men
are poles apart in political and social attitudes, yet they meet
on the common ground of the personal qualities they share:
courtesy, a sense of responsibility, respect for another's right
to hold opinions different from one's own. Rouncewell, the
son of the housekeeper, enters the drawing-room of Chesney
Wold with a becoming mixture of dignity and tact, and Sir
Leicester for his part shows instinctive courtesy when, 'with
all the nature of a gentleman shining in him', he offers his
visitor the hospitality of Chesney Wold. Dickens shows that
the future belongs to the energetic ironmaster, whereas Sir
Leicester is childless and fixed in the past, yet it would be
wrong to conclude from this, as Ruskin did in 1870, that
Dickens was 'a pure modernist—a leader of the steam-whistle
party *par excellence*—and he had no understanding of any

power of antiquity. . . . His hero is essentially the ironmaster.'[25] The total perspective of *Bleak House* is more complex than Ruskin allows, and a response to the 'power of antiquity' is part of it. Dickens' admiration for the energetic contemporary man is tempered by his deeply felt response to the dignity and established order that Chesney Wold represents:

> Sir Leicester is content enough that the ironmaster should feel that there is no hurry there; there, in that ancient house, rooted in that quiet park, where the ivy and the moss have had time to mature, and the gnarled and warted elms, and the umbrageous oaks, stand deep in the fern and leaves of a hundred years; and where the sun-dial on the terrace has dumbly recorded for centuries that time, which was as much the property of every Dedlock —while he lasted—as the house and the lands. Sir Leicester sits down in an easy chair, opposing his repose and that of Chesney Wold to the restless flights of ironmasters. [ch 28]

It is not only Sir Leicester who opposes the ancestral repose of Chesney Wold to 'the restless flights of ironmasters'. There are many such passages of lyrical evocation in *Bleak House,* and they contribute a contrary rhythm to the novel's affirmation of the moving age, culminating in Trooper George's visit to the 'iron country farther north' in chapter 63. George has refused a post in his brother's factory to become the right-hand man of the ageing and infirm Sir Leicester, and it is the values of the old order he brings with him on the journey north. The 'fresh green woods' of Chesney Wold are in our minds as we witness the landscape of the moving age: '. . . coalpits and ashes, high chimneys and red bricks, blighted verdure, scorching fires, and a heavy never-lightening cloud of smoke, become the features of the scenery'. When George enters his brother's yard, we see 'a great perplexity of iron lying about', some of it 'twisted and wrenched into eccentric and perverse forms', and 'mountains of it broken-up, and rusty in its age'. The whole scene is an assault on the senses, 'a place to make a man's head ache', as George observes. The criticism is there, though not on the level of statement, and it contributes to the complexity of the total picture: the moving age has the purpose and energy which the old order lacks, yet it is creating a landscape which is dirty, incoherent, and potentially inhuman; the old order is dying because it is out of touch with the needs of contemporary society, yet even in its decay, Chesney Wold offers an image of a desirable natural harmony which the moving age is destroying.

V

I have discussed the opposition between the aristocrat and the ironmaster at some length because it seems to me to show the complexity and essential open-mindedness of Dickens' response to the changing world in *Bleak House*. It is, of course, a classic confrontation of the gentleman and the self-made man, and the fact that neither is allowed the final word suggests that Dickens has not yet resolved the debate within himself. But if the debate is still open in *Bleak House*, there is in his next novel, *Hard Times* (1854), what one can only describe as a violent revulsion from the self-made man and from the idea of self-help conceived in terms of social ambition. Dickens has moved north to discover that Mr Rouncewell has been replaced by Mr Bounderby, and his qualified admiration for the ironmaster who has risen from the ranks gives way to contempt for that 'Bully of humility', Bounderby, 'a man who could never sufficiently vaunt himself a self-made man' (Bk I, ch 4), and who proves in the end to be a 'self-made Humbug' (Bk III, ch 5). This is an important development in Dickens' social thinking and it amounts to a rejection of the self-made man as a potentially regenerative contemporary figure. The idea that a new class of energetic and ambitious self-made men will help to transform English society is now abandoned: the social evils of *Hard Times* are not, as in *Bleak House*, the legacy of the past, but the creation of the new men of mid-Victorian England—bankers, industrialists, trade unionists, utilitarians. The moving age is seen to have created the bleak philosophy of Gradgrind and the soul-destroying monotony of Coketown, symbolised in the piston of the steam-engine which 'worked monotonously up and down like the head of an elephant in a state of melancholy madness' (Bk I, ch 5).

It is in keeping with this change in Dickens' attitude that the hero of his next novel, *Little Dorrit* (1855-7), should be a middle-aged failure, alienated equally from his background and from the contemporary world. Nothing could be further from the mature David Copperfield or Mr Rouncewell than Arthur Clennam, who confesses on his first appearance: 'I am such a waif and stray everywhere, that I am liable to be drifted where any current may set... I have no will' (Bk I, ch 2). In the scheme of values of *Bleak House* such an attitude would have consigned him to the category of drones like Skimpole, who also says 'I have no Will...' (ch 31), but it is a measure of Dickens' alienation from these values that he can show Clennam's aimlessness to be not only honest but an honourable and essentially justifiable response to the contemporary world as portrayed in *Little Dorrit*. Ambition in the sense of 'getting on' is now seen to be incompatible with humanity and responsibility in a society dominated by the corrupt financier Mr Merdle, 'whom it was heresy to regard as anything less than all the British Merchants since the days of Whittington rolled into one' (Bk II, ch 12). Dickens' moral and social positives are now located in the Christian passivity and lack of will of the heroine, Little Dorrit, and in the humble, self-effacing professionalism of the inventor, Daniel Doyce:

> He never said, I discovered this adaptation or invented that combination; but showed the whole thing as if the Divine artificer had made it, and he had happened to find; so modest he was about it, such a pleasant touch of respect was mingled with his quiet admiration of it, and so calmly convinced he was that it was established on irrefragable laws. [Bk II, ch 8]

Dickens actually uses the word 'self-help' when Clennam

describes Doyce as 'the honest, self-helpful, indefatigable old man who has worked his way all through his life' (Bk II, ch 26), and the inventor clearly embodies the self-help qualities which his creator still respects: perseverance, earnestness, professionalism. But Doyce has no ambition in the worldly sense, and it is significant that there is no role for him in contemporary society, such as Rouncewell and Bounderby enjoy: the Circumlocution Office repeatedly rejects his invention, and he pursues his research with the lonely independence and humility of the true artist. Dickens' characterisation of Doyce shows the self-help idea purged of its attributes of pride, will, and social ambition. The emphasis is now almost exclusively moral, and in celebrating the inventor's humble self-forgetfulness Dickens aligns him with the Christian virtues embodied in Little Dorrit herself.

Whether or not Lionel Trilling is correct in his suggestion that Dickens was passing through 'a crisis of the will' at the time of writing *Little Dorrit*,[26] it is clear that the rejection of self-help as a social creed in that novel and *Hard Times* is not simply to be explained in terms of a change in his attitude to contemporary society; it reflects also, and perhaps more fundamentally, a change in his attitude to himself. We have seen in previous novels like *Nicholas Nickleby* and *David Copperfield* how intimately Dickens' response to the contemporary world is related to his interpretation of his own experience, and there may well be something of Dickens' own bewilderment and confusion in the sad, troubled figure of Clennam.[27] Certainly these two interests, social and autobiographical, converge in the character of Pip in *Great Expectations*: this fable of a poor boy's rise into uneasy gentility catches up the ambiguities in Dickens' most intimate experience, and the result is a novel which is in many ways his most profound commentary on Victorian civilisation and its values. Pip's career of great expectations brings together self-help, inheritance, and the idea of the gentleman—lifelong preoccupations of Dickens which he subjects here to a new and searching scrutiny.

VI

Great Expectations (1860-1) is the climax of the debate between the self-made man and the gentleman in Dickens, and he resolves it by showing that the self-made man in fact aspires to the status of the gentleman. The novel thus brings into the open an ambiguity which, as we have seen, is latent in the self-help idea and in works like *John Halifax, Gentleman*. To 'get on' for Pip is, quite simply, to become a gentleman: the nakedness of that ambition is unclouded by even the nominal 'career' which an earlier character like Nicholas Nickleby is given. Pip's career is becoming a gentleman, and it is characteristic of the painful honesty of Dickens' mature art that he shows Pip embarking on it without the genteel ancestry vouchsafed to his previous heroes. While Oliver, Nicholas, and David are gentlemen by birth and have only to knock on the right door, so to speak, to reclaim their inheritance, Pip is never anything but the blacksmith's boy: the gentility for which he hankers has to be painfully acquired, it is for much of the book precariously held, and although he does succeed in the end in attaining to it, this state is very different from the one he had imagined in his childhood fantasies—it is finally a moral, and not a social category. But it is a mistake to read this novel as a 'snob's progress';[28] Pip's great expectations are too complex to be reduced to the crude category of snobbery. I have already noted the parallels between *Great Expectations* and *John Halifax, Gentleman,* and with Mrs Craik's novel in mind we can see that Pip's early struggles are essentially those of the self-help hero. Initially, his career falls into a classic nineteenth-century pattern: like Newcomen and Faraday, two of Smiles' heroes, Pip is a blacksmith's boy, and like them he has a 'hunger for information' (ch 15) which his narrow provincial world fails to satisfy. 'The Pursuit of Knowledge under Difficulties' is the running title Dickens added in 1868 to the scene in chapter 2 where Pip arouses his sister's anger by persistent questions about the convict-hulks, and the ironic reference to Craik's work serves to underline Pip's predicament. He has indeed to pursue knowledge under difficulties, and when set against his sister's tyranny and the total inadequacy of the village dame-school, his early struggles to teach himself to read and write have a representative pathos which justifies the use of one of Smiles' favourite terms: self-culture.

Pip's predicament in this environment is defined with wonderful skill and economy in the first two chapters. Magwitch turns Pip upside down, calls him a 'young dog', and threatens him with unspecified tortures; yet this intimidation is only an extreme version of the treatment he already receives at the hands of other adults. He returns home in chapter 2 to a household where he has to endure the rigours of his sister's 'hard and heavy hand', arbitrary thrashings from Tickler, violent dosings of tarwater which make him conscious of 'going about, smelling like a new fence'. His sister's system of bringing up by hand is sanctioned by a primitive rural society, and it is harsh, unjust, brutalising, and morally diminishing. Pip has had to sustain from infancy 'a perpetual conflict with injustice' and this has made him 'morally timid and very sensitive' (ch 8). His effort at self-culture is an attempt to struggle out of brutality and ignorance into the light of decency and self-respect, and this essentially moral struggle only becomes confused with social ambition when he visits Satis House and meets Miss Havisham and Estella. It is Estella, in calling him coarse and common, who gives a social category to the sense of humiliation that is already strong within him. With a sense of inevitability which Dickens conveys beautifully and surely means us to share, Pip's unfocussed aspirations acquire a social direction and a sexual motive: he will become a gentleman and marry the lady.

It is at this stage that Dickens introduces the inheritance theme, but with a sting in its tail. Pip is taken up by an unknown patron whose declared plans for his future chime exactly with his own secret ambitions: he is to become a gentleman. In the earlier novels the fairy godparents—Mr Brownlow, the Cheerybles, Aunt Betsey—had rescued the young heroes from their social disinheritance, which in *Oliver Twist* and *David Copperfield* had taken the nightmare form of exile in the social underworld. In *Oliver Twist* especially, Dickens had seemed to insist on the complete separation, the utter incompatibility, of the genteel world of Mr Brownlow and the underworld of Fagin's den. Now, in *Great Expectations*, the two worlds are brought into significant relationship: Fagin and Mr Brownlow meet in the figure of Magwitch, the social outcast who turns out to be Pip's anonymous benefactor. In this startling reversal of the inheritance pattern, Pip is given the economic basis of the genteel life only to discover in the end that he owes it all to a man whose whole history and way of life seems a denial of the gentility to which he has aspired. His great expectations derive not, as he thinks, from the decaying gentility of Satis House and Miss Havisham, but from a transported convict and 'hunted dunghill dog' (ch 39), who for much of the novel is invested with the horror of Pip's childhood vision of him as a 'desperately violent man', whom he had seen 'down in the ditch, tearing and fighting like a wild beast' (ch 39). The fact that Magwitch is a man of essentially good impulses who has been victimised by society does not obscure Dickens' recognition of his violent and uncivilised nature, which reasserts itself at the end when he drowns Compeyson. It is to this man, who eats and drinks like an animal and dies a convicted felon in the prison infirmary, that Pip owes his status. The boldness of Dickens' conception confronts us with an irony of deep social implication: Pip's gentility has been made possible by what seems to be its antithesis.

G

This irony at the heart of *Great Expectations* is central to his definition (or rather re-definition) of the idea of the gentleman. In previous novels inheritance had confirmed the genteel status of the young hero; in Pip's case it seems to destroy it. For the blacksmith's boy who has pursued a lonely career of self-culture, who has associated the genteel life with the melancholy refinement of Satis House, who has for years believed that his innate or potential fitness to participate in that life was being recognised and rewarded by Miss Havisham, the discovery that Magwitch is his patron comes as a shattering revelation that transforms him, at a stroke, back into the blacksmith's boy: 'Miss Havisham's intentions towards me, all a mere dream; Estella not designed for me; I only suffered at Satis House as a convenience...' (ch 39). Those who read the novel as a 'snob's progress' see this revelation as the moment at which (to quote from a recent critic) 'Dickens exactly nails the absurdity that fed the Victorian idea of being or becoming a gentleman'.[29] But this is surely to miss completely the point Dickens is making about the idea of the gentleman in this novel. Magwitch's return does indeed destroy Pip's fantasy about the origins of his great expectations, but it has the paradoxical effect of revealing him as a true gentleman. The scaffolding crumbles but the building stands: in his subsequent behaviour to Magwitch, to Joe, to Miss Havisham, and to Herbert, Pip shows himself to be a gentleman—not the 'brought-up London gentleman' (ch 39) that Magwitch thinks he has created and that Pip inevitably associates with his attempt at self-culture, but a gentleman in a classless, moral sense. It is in this latter sense that Pip in his illness, recognising Joe and the breach in their friendship, blesses his old friend as a 'gentle Christian man' (ch 57); and Pip, too, reveals himself a 'gentle Christian man' when he conquers his revulsion to Magwitch and comes to love him, forgives Miss Havisham, and makes atonement to Joe and Biddy. The Pip we see at the end, working modestly for the firm in which his unselfishness has established Herbert as a partner, is indeed a gentleman in a moral sense of the term that ought to be as comprehensible to a modern reader as it would certainly have been to a Victorian.

Pip's story summarises Dickens' lifelong involvement with the idea of the gentleman; indeed, the novel can be seen as a symbolic account of his own most intimate experience. Like Pip, he had been inspired by great expectations, by those 'early hopes of growing up to be a learned and distinguished man', and like Pip he had felt those hopes 'crushed in [his] breast' by the insecurity and degradation of his early years in London.[30] He too had aspired to the status of a gentleman, and what was made possible for Pip by Magwitch's gift, Dickens had to achieve through the practice of his art. But although he was to a large extent a self-made man himself, the essential development of Dickens' social thinking lies through a rejection of the self-made man, towards an affirmation of a gentlemanly ideal which has been purged of its associations with class and social ambition. This development coincides, as we have seen, with Dickens' increasing alienation from the values of his society, and the quotation from Edmund Wilson's essay with which I began—that of all the great Victorian writers, he 'was probably the most antagonistic to the Victorian Age itself'—is certainly an accurate statement of the position he has reached by the time of his last completed novel.

Great Expectations is a novel of memory, set in the past; *Our Mutual Friend* (1864-5) returns us to the England of the 1860s, to a world in the throes of share speculation, where *nouveaux riches* like the Veneerings thrive and an aggressive, Philistine respectability dominates society in the shape of the pompous Mr Podsnap. It is a society which Dickens hates and distrusts, and the measure of his antagonism is revealed in his treatment of the two characters whose contrasted relationship lies at the heart of the action: Bradley Headstone and Eugene

Wrayburn. Once again, the self-made man and the gentleman are brought into confrontation, but now Dickens' sympathies all lie with the gentleman. Headstone is a schoolmaster who has achieved a precarious respectability by exercising the self-help values which Dickens had long shared and now repudiates: will, ambition, the struggle (in the words of Charley Hexam, the odious meritocrat who is Headstone's protégé) to 'become respectable in the scale of society' (Bk IV, ch 7). Even the earnestness which had been a characteristic moral imperative in previous novels—one thinks of Betsey Trotwood's recommendation of 'deep, downright, faithful earnestness'—now turns up, twisted and obsessive, in Headstone's tormented feelings for Lizzie Hexam. 'I only add that if it is any claim on you to be in earnest' he tells her, tearing the mortar from the graveyard wall, 'I am in thorough earnest, dreadful earnest' (Bk II, ch 15). On the other hand, the traditional gentleman is now a sympathetic figure, an ally in Dickens' campaign against the values of Veneering and Podsnap. Eugene Wrayburn, the public-school-educated gentleman, is allowed to confess to lack of purpose, to joke about earnestness, to question the value of energy—'If there is a word in the dictionary under any letter from A to Z that I abominate, it is energy' (Bk I, ch 3)—even his moments of insolence are forgiven to a man who shows himself capable, as Wrayburn does at the end, of stepping outside 'the scale of society'. As Angus Wilson points out, Steerforth is redeemed in Eugene Wrayburn: 'Loneliness, failure, pride, bitter rejection of all that made up Victorian progress and Victorian morality, a considered rejection of duty and hard work as moral ends, Dickens comes through to acceptance of these in the person of Eugene Wrayburn'.[31]

In *Our Mutual Friend* the conflict between the gentleman and the self-made man is brought in the end to mortal issue, as Headstone makes his brutal attack on his rival. But while the self-made man is destroyed by the inner violence which he cannot control, the gentleman is rescued from the river by Lizzie Hexam and nursed back to health. Wrayburn's ordeal, like Pip's, burns away his adventitious class trappings to reveal him as a gentleman in the moral sense, and his marriage with Lizzie is therefore not merely a symbolic union across the barriers of class, but a union which challenges these barriers, which denies 'the scale of society' that Lizzie's brother Charley is so assiduously climbing. It is fitting, then, that the last word of the novel should be given not to the 'Voice of Society', the voice of Podsnap and the assembled nonentities at the Veneerings' dinner-table, but to Twemlow, the impoverished relation of the mighty Lord Snigsworth. In standing up for the 'feelings of a gentleman' against the snobbery of Podsnap, Twemlow gives utterance to what we can safely assume is Dickens' final view of the matter:

> 'I say,' resumes Twemlow, 'if such feelings on the part of this gentleman, induced this gentleman to marry this lady, I think he is the greater gentleman for the action, and makes her the greater lady. I beg to say, that when I use the word, gentleman, I use it in the sense in which the degree may be attained by any man...'
> [Bk IV, ch 17]

Notes to this chapter are on pages 229-30

THE UNSCHOOLED PHILOSOPHER: AN UNLIKELY IMPRESSION OF JOHN STUART MILL

D. R. Gordon

MATTHEW ARNOLD, in the course of a defence of Christianity against attacks on it by John Stuart Mill in his essay *On Liberty*, described Mill's teaching as a 'somewhat degenerated and inadequate form of Hellenism'. To it he gave the name 'Millism'.[1] The office occupied by this name does not for the present purpose matter; what does is that in no sense whatsoever are there today any Millists, nor was there ever anything that might properly have been called Millism. Although among philosophers, Mill has had great detractors such as Bradley and Frege, he has attracted fairly low-grade devotees. Many outstanding thinkers have indeed admired the essay *On Liberty* but, as in the case of Mill's godson Bertrand Russell, more for its sentiments than its arguments.[2] If it is the fate of great thinkers to generate Schools of Thought, Mill is not a great thinker.

Edward Alexander says of Mill and Arnold that we should consider them as 'representative figures rather than as seminal minds' and adds: 'For the number and variety of minds penetrated by Arnold and Mill, great as they are, are less impressive than the number and variety of minds who find themselves represented in the writings of Arnold and Mill'.[3] In the case of Mill it is easy to read too much into this judgement and into the partly supporting judgement of Professor

Anschutz that 'somewhere or other in his writings you can discern traces of every wind that blew in the early nineteenth century'.[4] Someone who wrote over such wide theoretical and practical territories as Mill, who wrote so many book reviews, who conducted such a massive and thorough correspondence, could hardly help bearing the traces of many intellectual winds. Moreover, it does not follow from the fact that Mill is not a seminal thinker that he should be cast for the modest role of 'representative' figure. Mill may be less than the one, but he is surely more than the other.

Mill was a great philosophical intellectual yet it was true to say twenty years ago that he had not at that point figured as one of the rehabilitated Victorians. This can no longer be said and the new-found thirst for his writings has called forth the great new edition from the University of Toronto Press and, very significantly, the much-to-be-encouraged *Mill Newsletter* from the same source. Despite the rehabilitation, despite the fact that, with one or two exceptions, there is an enormously more sympathetic and reconstructive response to his work, the general judgement of Mill as conspicuously less than a great philosopher, has not been questioned. The rehabilitation of Hume in this century has ensured for him the first place among British philosophers. But Mill lacked too many of the qualities of the very greatest thinkers, the penetrating lucidity of Hume, the reconstructive imagination of Newton or Kant, and the logical power of a Keynes or a Wittgenstein to articulate the elements in a new conceptual scheme. Further, he lacked that thorough awareness of what he is about and of what difference is being made by what he is doing that the greatest theorists possess. But his thoughts have been fecund in this way, that some good philosophers, having had thoughts and theories of their own, have come to recognise that what perplexes them, for example about the relation of Fact to Value, or the nature of meaning, or the possibility of rational and liberal political policies in a world inhabited largely by ignorant men, is a crux at one place or another in Mill's writings. Accordingly, although there has been more than a whiff of the demand for Fair Play in the recent interest in Mill, it is to Mill that philosophers have returned, not (it seems plausible to predict) to Dugald Stewart. Mill said of the Scottish philosopher Brown that he failed to effect a synthesis, and produced only an eclecticism. Many think that this is Mill's own failing and that which reduces him to a representative figure. The new interest in Mill cannot be accounted for in this way. It can in another. Although not a great philosopher he is, over a surprisingly wide range of intellectual enquiry, a great precursor. Surely, therefore, whatever his defects, he must be credited with depth, and this is one thesis concerning Mill to be defended here.

Perhaps special interests should be declared at this point. Mill is the most-read moral philosopher of all time yet it is a fact, a puzzling fact, that he never wrote a book on the subject. There are interpretations of Mill that would make the fact unpuzzling, that he was prematurely aged from the middle 1850s, that he had the presage of an early death from consumption, and accordingly from that time conducted a tidying-up operation, and so forth. Perhaps a thesis such as this must find a place in a complete account of Mill's failure but it is by no means a sufficient explanation.

The examination of Mill's role as a precursor, it is claimed, requires consideration to be given to the fact that his ethical writings were oddly fragmentary; revealing the causes of this fragmentariness entails revealing the precursive nature of the demands he made of a rational ethic. There is, first of all, the problem of Mill's susceptibility to the influences of other writers. Although most critics point to this and also (probably rightly), to the consequent partial blight on his originality,[5] the nature of this susceptibility and its place in Mill's theorising, is less commonly examined. Mill was, of course, dominated by his father in his early life and there is much hair-raising testimony to this in the *Autobiography*. There is, for example, the manner in which he was taught Economics just after the publication of the great treatise of his father's close friend Ricardo:

> My father ... commenced instructing me in the science by a sort of lectures, which he delivered to me in our walks. He expounded each day a portion of the subject, and I gave him next day a written account of it, which he made me rewrite over and over again until it was clear, precise, and tolerably complete. In this manner I went through the whole extent of the science.[6]

As if this were not enough, he was then required to read Ricardo's *Principles*, 'giving a daily account of what I read, and discussing, in the best manner I could, the collateral points which offered themselves in our progress'.[7] History has dealt harshly with Mill's own *Political Economy* and he himself did not think much of it. One can see why. The word-for-word, painstaking, exhaustive indoctrination of a thirteen-year-old boy destroyed whatever chance he ever had to make more than an ephemeral 'representative' contribution to the subject. But it should be remembered that Economics was a matter on which James Mill was personally and professionally interested; indeed it was John Mill's notes based on his father's tuition that formed the basis of the elder Mill's *Elements*.[8] One might add that if the kind of mind-stifling training programme cited were entirely typical of Mill's education, he would henceforward have been *less* rather than more susceptible to literary and intellectual influence. It may have been so with the *Political Economy*. But Mill, who was perfectly and accurately aware of the nature of his father's dominance and its effects on him, put a *different* and more interesting twist into the matter. He laid emphasis not on his lack of originality but rather on his lack of self-propulsion. Writing of his father, in the original manuscript of the *Autobiography* he says:

> To have been, through childhood, under the constant rule of a strong will, certainly is not favourable to strength of will... The

things I ought *not* to do were mostly provided for by his precepts
...but the things I *ought* to do I hardly ever did of my own
motion, but waited till he told me to do them... I thus acquired
a habit of backwardness, of waiting to following the lead of
others, an absence of moral spontaneity, an inactivity of the
moral sense, and even to a large extent, of the intellect, unless
roused by the appeal of someone else,—for which a large abatement must be made from the benefits, either moral or intellectual,
which flowed from any other parts of my education.[9]

The importance of these expunged passages and the larger
passage from which they come, could hardly be overestimated
but, immediately, two things emerge: first, that Mill needed
catalysts for his thought, and secondly, that he believed that
there was 'a large abatement' to his defect of will. Taken
together, they suggest the thesis that the abatement did not
go so far as to remove Mill's defect, but also that the defect
did not make Mill a mere philosophical sponge, a mere
absorber and (failed) synthesiser of other people's thought.

Although it would be bizarre to suppose that anyone could
be found who would accord to Mill the lowly status given—
say—to G. H. Lewes, what has been said still needs saying,
since Mill's standing, particularly as a moral philosopher, still
suffers from the image of him as a muffed Wordsworthian
Benthamite. What is the truth of the matter? In what manner
was Mill open to influence and to the direction of his will?

There seems no reason to question the remark made by
Mill about the impact on him of Carlyle that 'the good his
writings did me, was not as philosophy to instruct, but as
poetry to animate'.[10] Although this reads more like the rejection than the recognition of Carlyle as a central intellectual
influence, animation, the activation of his mind, is, throughout Mill's life, a key both to what he did and to what he did
not do. That Mill is thoroughly aware of this is shown by the
care that he takes to locate the points of intellectual impact
on him and to stress what is owing to himself. He relates, for
example, how he was held back for five years in the writing
of his *System of Logic* by the lack of a 'comprehensive and at

the same time accurate view of the whole circle of physical science' on the basis of which to write his philosophy of Induction. He feared that he might have to do the work himself but:

> Happily for me, Dr. Whewell, early in this year (sc. 1837), published his History of the Inductive Sciences. I read it with eagerness, and found in it a considerable approximation to what I wanted. *Much, if not most of the philosophy of the work appeared open to objection; but the materials were there, for my own thoughts to work upon.* . .[11]

Even in the most central cases where there are candid expressions of indebtedness there are important qualifications, as, for example, in the case of Comte, to whom Mill owed much. Again on Philosophy of Science, and writing of the *Cours de Philosophie Positive* he says:

> My theory of Induction was substantially completed before I knew of Comte's book; and it is perhaps well that I came to it by a different road from his, since the consequence has been that my treatise contains, what his certainly does not, a reduction of the inductive process to strict rules and to a scientific test, such as the syllogism is for ratiocination. . . Nevertheless, I gained much from Comte, with which to enrich my chapters in the subsequent rewriting. . .[12]

The initial answer to the problem of animation is obvious enough: Mill was activated, was catalysed by materials to work upon and doctrines to oppose. Later it will be made clear that part of the answer to the question raised regarding his ethics is that in this field, he had neither sufficient materials to work on nor had he (or felt he had) worthwhile enough teachings to oppose. For the present, it may be suggested that he was less amenable to influence than is commonly suggested. He is the constant External Examiner (and he would have been a fearsome one!) working from a stable methodological position, helping, except in the case of Comte,[13] to make small reputations, destroying great ones such as Hamilton's. In a celebrated judgement of the *Autobiography*, Carlyle said:

It is wholly the life of a logic-chopping ꞏgine, little more of human in it than if it had been done by a thing of mechanized iron. Autobiography of a steam-engine. . .[14]

What good reason is there to doubt the justice of this? Carlyle's seems, at first sight, a grotesque opinion, especially if we bear in mind the delicate explorations by Mill in the *Autobiography* of his own upbringing and his mental crisis and his account, later on in the book, of the influence on him of his wife. As to the latter, Mill was notoriously weak-minded on the subject of Harriet Taylor, especially in the attribution to her of most of the good ideas in the essay *On Liberty*. All this is excusable in the light of the account he gives in the original manuscript, of his adolescent and unsatisfied need for love, as well as for intellectual stimulation, in the Mill home. At any rate, few scholars now accept Mill's own judgement of her intellectual impact on him, and are more ready to agree with Alexander Bain's view that she helped him by 'intelligently controverting' his ideas.[15]

The matter of Mill's mental crisis is more crucial, for there is a clear opposition between the accounts given of him as the constant External Examiner, the logic-chopping engine, the man with a stable methodology, and of him as the man who wrote confusedly on questions of value from the incompatible positions of the Benthamite and the Wordsworthian. This is important for it may well be the case that Mill never became a Wordsworthian except in a very narrow, easily explained sense, and that, accordingly, his ethical difficulties lie elsewhere. Writing of the crisis he says:

> For I now saw, *or thought I saw*, what I had always before received with incredulity—that the habit of analysis has a tendency to wear away the feelings. . .[16]

Again

> . . . all those to whom I looked up, were of opinion that the pleasure of sympathy with human beings, and the feelings which made the good of others . . . the object of existence, were the greatest and surest source of happiness. . . My education, *I*

thought, had failed to create these feelings in sufficient strength to resist the dissolving influence of analysis, while the whole course of my intellectual cultivation had made precocious and premature analysis the inveterate habit of mind...[17]

Again

Analytic habits may ... even strengthen the associations between causes and effects, means and ends, but tend altogether to weaken those which are ... a *mere* matter of feeling. They are therefore (*I thought*) favourable to prudence and clear sightedness, but a perpetual worm at the root both of the passions and of the virtues...[18]

As a result of these thoughts, Mill's opinions and character, so he related, underwent two kinds of change. They have often been remarked upon: he surrenders the Utilitarian principle as a direct end:

Those only are happy (*I thought*) who have their minds fixed on some other pursuit than their own business ... even on some art or pursuit, followed not as a means, but as itself an ideal end. Aiming thus at something else, they find happiness by the way.[19]

Secondly, he gives for the first time prime importance to the 'internal culture of the individual':

I ceased to attach almost exclusive importance to the ordering of outward circumstances, and the training of the human being for speculation and for action.

The cultivation of the feelings became one of the cardinal points in my ethical and philosophical creed.[20]

There is much of interest in these passages, and much that is equivocal, but some central features are clear enough: Mill is writing of a transitional stage, that is, a stage which he out-grew. It is not so much analysis he objects to but 'precocious and premature' analysis, analysis uninformed by the raw data of emotion and passion which his upbringing had hitherto denied him. His great mentor Bentham is criticised on pre-cisely the same score. In the 1838 essay on *Bentham* he claims that Bentham's philosophy is limited by his 'general concep-tion of human nature and life [which] furnished him with an unusually slender stock of premises'. Bentham's knowledge is bounded because:

> He had neither internal experience nor external; the quiet, even tenor of his life, and his healthiness of mind, conspired to exclude him from both. He never knew prosperity and adversity, passion nor satiety... He knew no dejection, no heaviness of heart. He never felt life a sore and a weary burthen. He was a boy to the last.[21]

But Mill, unlike Bentham, broke these bounds. He *had* a deep mental crisis, he *did* feel 'life a sore and a weary burthen'— *but he got over it*. Mill did not become a Romantic. The reiterations of 'I thought' or 'as I reflected' in many places in the chapter on his mental crisis indicate clearly Mill's neutralising of the story of the effect of habits of analysis on the feelings. Poetry has become both a window and a mirror; from it he can encounter a new world of phenomena which had eluded him; from it, too, he can learn more about himself and see in a new way the virtues of the kind of life he had grown to hate. With relief, it seems, he says of Wordsworth: 'I needed to be made to feel that there was real, permanent happiness in tranquil contemplation. Wordsworth taught me this...'[22]

Of course, there were a great many developments. His view of the nature of happiness, of the relation of means to ends, and his doctrine concerning the point of the Principle of Utility, all developed on fresh lines. But the problems to which they gave rise are not necessarily the problems of a confused mind; they are not necessarily the products of a Benthamite structure suffused with, then eroded by, Romanticism. They are with philosophers still and Mill raised them.

It may begin to seem plausible, then, to suggest that there are not two internally warring John Stuart Mills, a man of feeling and a man of intellect, and plausible to suggest that of the two accounts of him already mentioned, that of Carlyle is more nearly correct. Again on his mental crisis, and writing of his love of music, Mill says:

[It was] characteristic of ... the general tone of my mind at this period of my life, that I was seriously tormented by the thought of the exhaustibility of musical combinations. The octave consists only of five tones and two semi-tones, which can be put together in only a limited number of ways, of which but a small proportion are beautiful; most of these, it seemed to me, must have been already discovered, and there could not be room for a long succession of Mozarts and Webers, to strike out ... entirely new and surpassingly rich veins of musical beauty.[23]

Mill never got out of this habit of mind; *it merely ceased to worry him*, and this is the truth in what Carlyle said. Mill cannot for more than a very short period enjoy; he has to ask himself the nature of his enjoyment. He does not feel; he recommends the cultivation of feelings. He cannot quite rush into the street and tell people that and why they should read Wordsworth; a careful Associationist like him must say that the reason he enjoys Wordsworth is that he loves 'rural objects and natural scenery'[24] and Wordsworth places before him 'beautiful pictures of natural scenery'.[25] In justice it must be said that Mill qualifies this last comment severely, but he is, in fact, rather obscure on his other reasons for taking to Wordsworth, except in a general way that Wordsworth is 'the poet of unpoetical natures', precisely those which require poetic cultivation.[26] But the general point about Mill remains. Its proof is, for once, given by the exception. In the one case where he had a profound emotional relationship with a woman, that is with Harriet Taylor, he did not know how to talk about it and declined into a sentimentality and maudlin to be found nowhere else in his writings. Finally on this point, Mill's considered judgement, reminiscent of that of Holbach in the previous century, is this: 'The intensest feeling of the beauty of a cloud lighted by the setting sun, is no hindrance to my knowing that the cloud is vapour of water, subject to all the laws of vapours in a state of suspension'.[27]

There is really little doubt which of the two, the feeling or the knowledge, Mill was by his nature best fitted to have. From the body of his work there is no reason to suppose that,

after his crisis, he ever felt the slightest difficulty in keeping
aesthetic experiences well within his metaphysical grasp. On
matters of feeling he is, finally, a bore, and for some, a kind of
mangle. We need not confine ourselves to religious attitudes
and experiences when we appraise Arnold's question: 'How
short could Mill write Job?'[28]

Questions as to the proper interpretation of Mill's ethical and
political writings are, at the present time, hotly debated by
philosophers. After a great flurry around the essay on *Utilitarianism*, of which no one has ever succeeded in giving a
unified interpretation, scholars are now reaching out for *The
Spirit of the Age*, the 1833 and 1838 papers on Bentham, the
reviews, the *Logic*, in attempts to get the key to his moral
philosophy. If as has been considered, there is good warrant
for doubting that there are two unjoinable parts to Mill's
nature, if there is no longer the same excuse for claiming that
he is a feather for gusty intellectual winds and for claiming
that his ethical thought is a 'mishmash' of influences, how are
the incoherences, real and apparent, in his moral thought, to
be explained? Questions of personality and motivation, questions as to the causality of a man's opinions and theories arise
when we are trying to understand them, and centrally, when
we find them to be wrong or incoherent, in trying to account
for their wrongness or incoherence. Sometimes the job is not
hard; sometimes it is easy to find that the premises are false or
the argument invalid. Sometimes it is even easier than this:
we can attack the man and by a few simple exercises on his
personal history, show cause why his views just had to be silly.
In the light of Mill's *Autobiography*, it is not difficult to see
why those who rejected his views turned to his psyche as an
object for abuse. The materials for such abuse were ready to
hand. Carlyle and Arnold could say that Mill was a mere
artefact, or (if the anachronism be allowable) a kind of data-
processing machine. Benthamites could thunder that he had

gone soft in the head and all Romantic. It cannot any longer simply be argued that, in ethics and social philosophy, Mill's arguments are simply bad or confused. Indeed, part of the recent rehabilitation consists in the attempt to show that some of them are better than they were thought to be, even cogent. Mill saw further than his detractors, and their rejection of him was due to their School-bound failure to see how great is the range of phenomena and logical facts with which ethics has to cope. Mill's problems are very intractable and because we can see that better today than was possible in the late nineteenth century, we have a keener appreciation of his contribution. A professed feature of recent philosophy has been the dissolution of Schools of Philosophy; one is no longer required to be a Rationalist or an Empiricist in epistemology, a realist or an idealist in ontology, a deductivist or an inductivist in the philosophy of science, or a deontologist or teleologist in ethics. That there were no Millists is at least in part due to this, that there has been in the last hundred years, no slot in the possible range of -isms into which Mill could easily be put. Most of his best ideas cut across Schools of Thought. For a variety of reasons, it took another age to get rid of this pigeon-hole conception of philosophical doctrines, or rather, to be properly cautious and historical, to change the list of options.

We now see how difficult Mill's problems were. How is it possible to reconcile the demand for individual liberty with the attempt to secure the interests of everyone equally? How is it possible to reconcile the attempt to discover laws of progress, of social dynamics, with the putative fact of human agency, the power of human beings to change the world, to make things happen? How is it possible to use the consequences of actions as a guide to their worth without flouting the morality one is trying to give a general account of? How, if we are to be rational moralists, imbued with the canons of discovery and proof in physical science, can we do what we cannot do and yet must do, argue from factual premises to

H

evaluative conclusions? This last, the inference from Fact to Value, was until a few years ago, the cardinal sin in Ethics, and Mill was held to be first among the guilty. The question is, can we prove, from a range of facts mainly about human beings and their propensities and the situation in which they find themselves, that happiness, or self-realisation, or freedom is alone intrinsically desirable? The hypothesis would be worth trying out that this was Mill's master question in ethics and social philosophy, that he was beaten by it, and that it was partly for this reason that he never wrote a treatise on ethics and never followed up the suggestive but often elusive later chapters of the *System of Logic,* and particularly the last chapter of all, 'Of the Logic of Practice; including Morality and Policy'.

Why is it that this much-read and famous moralist never wrote a book on ethics? The simplest answer is a direct traverse, to say that he did write such a book, the *Utilitarianism* of 1861. But that was hardly a book, certainly not from the author of the *Logic,* the *Political Economy* or *An Examination of Sir William Hamilton's Philosophy.* It was, rather, a hasty compilation of semi-popular essays mostly written in the year of, or soon after, his wife's death. There is no evidence that Mill thought well of it. In the *Autobiography* he makes one reference to it as 'the little work...'[29] and there is a similar reference to it as 'the little volume' in later editions of the *Logic.*[30] If we cannot really count the *Utilitarianism,* what then is the answer? Is it an unsurprising fact that Mill never wrote a treatise on moral philosophy? It seems not. It will not do to say, at least *simpliciter,* that Mill's powers were declining, for in the period of 'decline' he wrote and published the *Hamilton,* the *Auguste Comte and Positivism, The Subjection of Women, Representative Government,* apart altogether from many shorter pieces and the publication of his great edition of *Dissertations and Discussions.* Nor will it do to say that he did not wish to underline his 'disloyalty' to Bentham any more than he had done, for he was perfectly clear in his own mind that his criticism of Bentham was fair. Indeed he says quite specifically in the *Autobiography*:

> The substance of this criticism I still think perfectly just; but I have sometimes doubted whether it was right to publish it at that time. I have felt that Bentham's philosophy, as an instrument to progress, has been to some extent discredited before it had done its work, and that to lend a hand towards lowering its reputation was doing more harm than service to improvement. Now, however, when a counter-reaction appears to be setting in towards what is good in Benthamism, I can look with more satisfaction on this criticism of its defects...[31]

True enough, this suggests some inhibition for about twelve years after the publication of the 1838 essay, but not much, especially when we remember that Mill, who did not consider Bentham a great philosopher but rather a 'great reformer in philosophy', thought even less of him as a moralist. A number of other reasons might also be given for Mill's failure to write ethics on a large scale: personal reasons such as the intellectual nuisance disvalue of Harriet Taylor during their seven-year married life; the grander reason of his earlier twelve-year dedication to the *Logic*, on the ground, among others, that the mental regeneration of Europe must precede its moral regeneration. Though some of these should, perhaps, find their way into a final account, none of them, singly or collectively, are sufficient.

The key question is this: did Mill consider the project of a treatise important? There is clear and unequivocal evidence covering a considerable portion of his life, that he did, and moreover, that he did not see himself doing it. As early as 1834 he says in a letter to John Pringle Nicol: 'Of all views I have yet seen taken of the Utilitarian scheme, I like Austin's best in his book on the Province of Jurisprudence; but even that falls very short of what is needed'.[32] Mill himself owed much to the great jurisprudent Austin, and to him he writes in 1847:

There are two books I have heard you speak of as projects: a continuation of "The Province of Jurisprudence"...the other which would be more important is a systematic treatise on morals. This last may wait long for anyone with the intellect and the courage to do it as it should be done. And until it is done we cannot expect much improvement in the common standard of moral judgments and sentiments.[33]

The influence of Austin on Mill is one of the most interesting and equivocal of influences, and it is perhaps fitting to treat this letter with some caution. He might be exaggerating the weakness of moral philosophy in order to encourage Austin, who, despite his great qualities of mind, suffered from a kind of stifling perfectionism that made it very difficult for him to write anything at all. At any rate he returns to the theme in a letter to William Stigant in 1854:

I very much wish it were in my power to refer you, or anyone, to a book, or set of books fitted to form a course of instruction in Moral Philosophy. None such, to my knowledge, exist. In my opinion, ethics, as a branch of philosophy, is still to be created. There are writings on the subject from which valuable thoughts may be gathered, or others (particularly Bentham) who have thrown some light but not sufficient on the mode of systematising it. But on the whole, everyone's ideas of morals must result from the action of his own intellect upon the materials supplied by life, and by the writers in all languages who have understood life best.[34]

Although there are differences between, and unclarities in, these letters, it is at least clear that Mill did not picture himself as the author of the required treatise on morals. Writing to Harriet Taylor in the same year as the Stigant letter he says:

...I hope we shall live to write together all we wish to leave written to most of which your living is quite as essential as mine, for even if the wreck I should be could work on with undiminished faculties, my faculties at the best are not adequate to the highest subjects and have already done almost the best they are adequate to...[35]

For want of an alternative reading, it is tempting to identify the 'highest subjects' with ethics. In the *Autobiography* he says: 'I had always a humble opinion of my own powers as an original thinker, except in abstract science (logic, metaphysics, and the theoretical principles of political economy). . .'[36]

The 'highest subjects' can hardly be these; nor can they be political subjects since, in Mill's considered (and accurate) view, *On Liberty* was 'likely to survive longer than anything with the possible exception of the "Logic"'.[37] It is tempting to take these sets of words written perhaps fifteen years apart and conclude that Mill did not consider himself up to the severe requirements he made of the moral philosopher cited in the Austin and Stigant letters. But it is not necessary to depend upon this attenuated evidence. For it is surely plain that he wanted this task done, knew that he could not do it, and accordingly did not contemplate doing it. Certain contributory factors have been mentioned above, but none of them will do unless and until we can give a clear reason for Mill's feeling, or half-feeling, that he was not up to the task. An hypothesis about this reason has already been suggested, namely that Mill found himself facing a range of problems clustering around the hallowed distinction between Fact and Value which he was never able satisfactorily to resolve. All his ethical writings are occasional pieces, and many of them come up against this problem hard. That Mill is both explicitly aware of this problem and that it is for others to deal with is clear from the cursory but ambitiously programmatic final chapter of the *Logic*. He says:

A proposition of which the predicate is expressed by the words *ought or should be*, is generally different from one which is expressed by *is*, or *will be*. It is true that, in the largest sense of the words, even these propositions assert something as a matter of fact . . . that the conduct recommended excites in the speaker's mind the feeling of approbation. This, however, does not go to the bottom of the matter; for the speaker's approbation is no sufficient reason why other people should approve; nor ought it to be a conclusive reason even with himself. For the purposes of practice, every one must be required to justify his approbation: and for this there is need of general premises, determining what are the proper objects of approbation. . .[38]

These 'general premises' together with their derived conclusions would constitute the Art of Life in all its departments, the Right, the Expedient, and the Noble, and this Art, Mill repeats, 'in the main, is unfortunately still to be created'.[39] After stating that what is needed is Principles of Practical Reason or a doctrine of Teleology, Mill cites the promotion of happiness as the ultimate principle of Teleology, and, apologising for his cursoriness, says rather grandly:

> I have indulged the hope that to some of those on whom the task will devolve of bringing those most important of all sciences into a more satisfactory state, these observations will be useful...[40]

But is the problem, the supposed problem of inferences from fact to value, unavoidable? Mill thought that it was, and the diagnosis of this is to be found in his lifetime hatred of the 'Intuitional' philosophy which, in the moral field, had 'recourse to the popular theory of a natural faculty, a sense or instinct, informing us of right and wrong'.[41] These opponents of his managed neatly to account for values by the simple expedient of treating them as special kinds of facts discernible by a special internal mechanism whose deliverances were incorrigible and final. Mill objected to this on pretty obvious theoretical grounds and in his *Auguste Comte and Positivism* he illustrates this, and also the manner of Comte's influence on him, the influence, that is, of an ally, who amply supports Mill's general 'Inductivist' position with a new battery of methodological weapons. Mill says:

> What is the whole doctrine of Intuitive Morality, which reigns supreme wherever the idolatry of Scripture texts has abated and the influence of Bentham's philosophy has not reached, but the metaphysical state of ethical science?... It has the universal diagnostic of the metaphysical mode of thought, in the Comtean sense of the word; that of erecting a mere creation of the mind into a test or *norma* of external truth, and presenting the abstract expression of the beliefs already entertained, as the reason and evidence which justifies them.[42]

Substantially the same point is made in the first chapter of *Utilitarianism* where Mill, contrasting the two schools of thought, argues that even where they both agree as to moral laws, they differ as to the source of their authority and the evidence for them:

> According to the one opinion, the principles of morals are evidence *a priori*, requiring nothing to command assent, except that the meaning of the terms be understood. According to the other doctrine, right and wrong, as well as truth and falsehood, are questions of observation and experience.[43]

Intuitionism then, is mistaken; it also destroys the possibility of moral progress. In the 1835 essay on *Sedgwick's Discourse*, he says:

> If it be true that man has a sense given to him to determine what is right and wrong, it follows that his moral judgements and feelings cannot be susceptible of any improvement... According to the theory of utility... the question, what is our duty, is as open to discussion as any other question... An appeal lies, as on all other subjects, from a received opinion, however generally entertained, to the decisions of cultivated reason.[44]

'The progress of intelligence,' 'more authentic and enlarged experience,' 'alterations in the condition of the human race,' will require 'altered rules of conduct'. In thus affirming the possibility of moral progress, in asserting the provisional nature of moral insights and rules of conduct, in rejecting the possibility of a brute standard of right and wrong, in claiming that the principles of morals are 'questions of observation and experience', Mill was claiming that there are no quasi-perceptual shortcuts to moral judgements and principles; if there are none, then we have to find an algorithm, 'principles of Practical Reason' perhaps, which will, from time to time, enable us to get there. If one does not *see* that an innocent man should not be allowed to suffer, how can it be *shown*? For Mill, of course, the central question is not as specific as that but rather the foundation question: how can one show that happiness is desirable and that we ought to pursue it? In this form there was no problem for Bentham. Men *can* only seek pleasure and the avoidance of pain. To Hume the problem had come in the form: how is it possible that a set of factual statements should entail a statement such as 'you ought not to let an innocent man suffer'? Hume put an absolute logical bar on such inferences but could quite cheerfully add that the fact remains that we do make such inferences, just as he could say that there was no justification for casual inferences but that we made them just the same. Mill's problem is an extraordinarily deep-going one; it is not simply the problem of finding a logically unexceptionable means of proving that happiness alone is desirable and thus outflanking or confuting Hume; the nagging question is, what *is* happiness? It is here that the authentic results of his mental crisis are made plain. Mill could not have assented to the Happiness Principle on 'intuitional' grounds; nor, for want of an adequate account of human experience, of human motivation, and of the laws of progress, could he accept Bentham's story as anything but dogmatic and static as to human motivation. He did not solve his problem but he approached it in a number of ways. In attempting to show that happiness is alone ultimately desirable, does it have to be shown that we ought to pursue it *directly*? Mill was unable to give a clear-cut answer. As early as 1834 in a letter to Carlyle he says:

> I have never, at least since I had convictions of my own, belonged to the benevolentiary, soup-kitchen school... I believe that [the good of the species] can in no other way be forwarded but by the means you speak of, namely, by each taking for his exclusive aim the development of what is best in himself.[45]

This theme of self-development occurs many times in his ethical and political writings, especially in the essay *On Liberty*. Compare with the 1834 remark, the words of 1859:

> [The free development of individuality is]... one of the principal ingredients of human happiness, and quite the chief ingredient of individual and social progress.[46]

It is clear that in the (perhaps conciliatory) letter to Carlyle, there is an exclusive concern with the self-development of the individual which the later essay does not possess. While it is not clear what the development by a person of what is best in himself has to do with happiness, the early remark is certainly consistent with another constant theme in Mill, that there are all sorts of objects in themselves worth pursuing; it is consistent, too, with the doleful, Stoical comment in Chapter Two of the *Utilitarianism* that 'in this condition of the world ... the conscious ability to do without happiness gives the best prospect of realising such happiness as is attainable'.[47] Mill is often said to have reconciled the Happiness Principle with the 'obvious' fact that people very often do not pursue it, by a blatant dodge, the dodge namely of claiming that there are some virtues and activities (such as love of the arts and the pursuit of them) which are themselves *part* of happiness, and accordingly, that in pursuing them, we *are* pursuing happiness directly. The criticism seems just although Mill's position seems unavoidable, given his puzzles about the nature of the ultimate end. The criticism is just, for we may ask *which* objects, which 'virtues' have this quality? Mill's distinction between quality and quantity of pleasure, his remark that 'it is better to be a human being dissatisfied than a pig satisfied; better to be a Socrates dissatisfied than a fool satisfied';[48] his judgement that those who are to have the last word on which of two pleasures is best worth having are 'those who are qualified by having knowledge of both'[49] and that 'they are the only competent judges'[50]—these, it is sometimes alleged, usher in the authoritarian message, the talk of the intellectual elite, the Coleridgean 'clerisy' which warp Mill's liberalism. Yet how, for him, could it have been otherwise? He had witnessed, in his own person, the kind of moral progress which follows the 'more authentic and enlarged experience' of which he was, not many years later, to write in *Sedgwick's Discourse*. Words worth had taught him that 'there was real, permanent happiness, in tranquil contemplation'. Arguing that Intuitionism is incompatible with progress, Mill says in *Sedgwick's Discourse*:

The question, what mankind in general ought to think and feel on the subject of their duty, must be determined by observing what, when no interest or passion can be seen to bias them, they think and feel already.

He adds in a variant:

Accordingly this is an admirable doctrine for those who have hitherto, by education and government, had the framing of the opinions and feelings of mankind mainly in their own hands. A general prejudice may, on this scheme, be at any time erected, by those who are disinterestedly attached to it, or by those whose convenience it suits, into a law of our universal nature.[51]

Should he have reconciled himself to moral toryism, to philosophies that were 'agreeable to human indolence, as well as to conservative interests generally'? Or was he right to strike out for moral reform in the knowledge that what lay ahead was a series of sensitive and profound explorations of the virtues and of moral feelings? Moral progress is not self-generating and while it is easy to see, after the manner of the letter to Carlyle, how, according to Mill, a man may develop 'what is best in himself', it is less easy to see how new knowledge, of social dynamics and of the 'Springs of Action' is to be made into an instrument of the moral development of a people without accusations of elitism being made. Mill did not invent this problem; but, if Dr Cowling is a reliable witness, he at least sharpened it.[52] Part of the trouble is that the Happiness Principle is invoked to satisfy two, often conflicting demands, the demands namely of the morality of individual ideals and of social morality. We feel that individuals should be free to develop what is best in themselves but only so long as what they do does not harm the interests of others. The individualist position Mill adopted in the Carlyle letter, the qualified position in the essay on *Liberty*. In the essay he did so by making his celebrated distinction between self-regarding and other-regarding actions, between actions, that is, which affect (the interests) only of the agent himself and those which affect (the interests) of others. The questions remain: who is to say what is in the interest of a person or persons, and by what authority? Who is to say that one pleasure is superior to another, and by what authority? Who is to say what happiness is, and by what authority? Part of Mill's answer was that we cannot, in a routine, mechanical, Benthamite way, apply the Greatest Happiness Principle to laws, principles, and policies, and then if they pass the test, put them into practice. Since, for Mill, the notions of happiness and interest were much more complex than Bentham pretended, and because his great mentor misunderstood the relationship between moral rules and the Happiness Principle, his view was false. Both these points will have to be elaborated.

Moral and legal rules meant nothing to Bentham, old moral and legal rules, that is. They all rested on a false metaphysics such as 'the law of nature', 'right reason', 'natural rights' or 'moral sense'; now that the truth was available, that 'Nature has placed mankind under the governance of two sovereign masters, *pain* and *pleasure*', the law and morality can be re-modelled.[53] Mill rejected this thesis. In his 1833 *Remarks on Bentham's Philosophy* (his first public exercise in ethics) he says that Bentham's opponents will simply reply that they see no good reason why Bentham's account of the Psychology of Morals is any better than theirs. When Bentham concentrates his attack on the moral toryism of his opponents, that is better, but (he is in effect saying) Bentham is just as much a tory if he thinks that the provisional character of moral rules is *merely* a matter of whether in fact they do or do not increase pleasure and minimise pain optimally. For the notions of pleasure and happiness are not perspicuous notions. Moreover, the moral bearings of an evil act, such as thieving or lying, are not exhausted by the evil consequences to society:

> All acts suppose certain dispositions, and habits of mind and heart, which may be in themselves states of enjoyment or of wretchedness, and which must be fruitful in *other* consequences, besides those particular acts.[54]

Accordingly, Bentham's moral philosophy is perfectly suit-

able for the field of legislation since 'the legislator enjoins or
prohibits an action, with very little regard to the general
moral excellence or turpitude which it implies . . . his object
is not to render people incapable of *desiring* a crime, but to
deter them from actually *committing* it'. But this excursion
into the Philosophy of Legislation is something of a diversion;
Mill is centrally interested in the moral progress of men and
societies. He is saying, in effect, that if the notion of happiness
were a clear and homogeneous one, then the 'benevolentiary,
soup-kitchen view' of human progress would do. But, notoriously it will not do. Mill himself was, by his access to poetry,
drawn imaginatively to the idea of happiness as richness of
life and experience, and, by the state of his mind at the onset
of his crisis, drawn away from the idea of happiness as satisfaction of desire. His troubled state had, after all, been brought
on by his realising that he was doing what he wanted to do
and yet was unhappy. The felicific calculus did not fit.

Mill's vicious assault on Bentham has three noteworthy
features; first of all, it is intensely autobiographical, the rejection of a past self. He is speaking as much of this past self
when he says:

> Man is conceived by Bentham as a being susceptible of pleasures
> and pains, and governed in all his conduct partly by the different
> modifications of self-interest . . . partly by sympathies, or occasion-
> ally antipathies, towards other beings. And here Bentham's con-
> ception of human nature stops.[55]

And again when he says:

> Knowing so little of human feelings, he knew still less of the
> influences by which these feelings are formed: all the more subtle
> workings both of the mind upon itself, and of external things
> upon the mind, escaped him. . .[56]

In the second place, Mill offers what amounts almost to a
job-specification for the future moral philosopher, and in
noting it, one can see at least one of the sources of his failure
to write a treatise on morals:

... to build either a philosophy or anything else, there must be materials. For the philosophy of matter, the materials are the properties of matter; for moral and political philosophy, the properties of man, and of man's position in the world. . . Human nature and human life are wide subjects, and whoever would embark in an enterprise requiring a thorough knowledge of them, has need both of large stores of his own, *and of all aids and appliances from elsewhere.* His qualifications for success will be proportional to two things: the degree in which his own nature and circumstances furnish him with a correct and complete picture of man's nature and circumstances; and his *capacity of deriving light from other minds.*[57]

It is plain that Mill started out on an ambitious course, a remarkably hard-headed and un-Wordsworthian course at that. He was asserting that, among other things, there was no moral phenomenonology, and that the prevailing moral psychology, that of Bentham, was wildly erroneous. The repeated remark that ethics, as a branch of philosophy, is still to be created, steadily acquires significance.

The third feature of Mill's attack on Bentham is the manner in which, with one major qualification, it points in the same direction as his attacks on Intuitionism. Both Bentham and the Intuitionists have rigid ideas as to what moves men to action, desire for pleasure or conscience. Both have fixed points in their systems of ideas: in the case of the Intuitionists, the moral compulsion to follow detectable and absolute moral rules; in the case of Bentham, the moral compulsion to work towards the detectable end of the Greatest Happiness of the Greatest Number. Both show a lack of response to the complexities of moral situations, the Intuitionist by simply denying that there are any; Bentham by thinking that the real problems for the moralist come primarily when he is required to tinker with the always-obsolescent rules of morality when they fail to serve the known end. In each of his papers on Bentham, Mill attacks him at precisely the same point, his Table of the Springs of Action is defective because Bentham must needs find a motive corresponding to each pleasure or pain, because in stating motives and interests he assumes that 'all our acts are determined by pains and pleasures *in prospect'*. He criticises Bentham's account of motives as neither accurate nor complete. The defect plainly is that of deciding on the end first, and then deciding what motives will suit that end. If they do not fit, then they are made to fit, or else excluded altogether. From his list of motives Bentham excludes

> conscience, or the feeling of duty: one would never imagine from reading him that any human being ever did an act merely because it is right, or abstained from it merely because it is wrong.[58]

Man is a seeker of ends, not only of means. Moreover he already has ends: Man must be recognised as:

> a being capable of pursuing spiritual perfection as an end; of desiring, for its own sake, the conformity of his own character to his standard of excellence...[59]

This, for Mill, is an obvious fact, and recognition of it should not be seen as a blow to the Happiness Principle but rather as deepening our understanding of it, by working out the relation to it of the moral rules and ends that men have thought it fit to have. The Intuitionists and Bentham are, accordingly, both wrong. Bentham distrusts moral rules to the point of ridicule, the Intuitionists will have nothing to do with ends which their opponents suppose rules to serve. But Bentham was superior for he had argued powerfully for an external standard for morality.

As will surely be plain, Mill's defence of external standards is complex: the Happiness Principle is a signal for us that moral rules may be changed in the light of new knowledge, and reflection; it is also important from a 'purely scientific point of view for the sake of the systematic unity and coherency of ethical philosophy'.[60] But happiness is:

> much too complex and indefinite an end to be sought, except through the medium of various secondary ends, concerning which there may be, and often is, agreement among persons who differ in their ultimate standard.[61]

It is not absolutely clear what Mill intended by according to the Happiness Principle a theoretical status, or what precisely he meant in the *Logic* when he said that the promotion of happiness is the 'justification and ought to be the controller of all ends, but is not itself the sole end'.[62] Not having the single vision either of Bentham or the Intuitionists, having been made sensitive by 'light from other minds' and an enriched view of the range of human feelings (we do not, he says, lie to add to happiness but because we dislike misleading people), he was alive on the one hand to the claims both of moral principles and the ends they serve, and on the other, to the point of the whole moral exercise, be it utility, the interests of men, or the Greatest Happiness. For Mill, in short, there is a kind of reciprocal relationship between them such that we cannot in any finalistic way determine the validity of secondary ends in terms of the *summum bonum*, for they constantly and continuously help us to learn more about the *summum bonum*. Because of the infinite variety of human responses, the infinite variety of the ends people hold dear to, this search for the ends of life is a task which can hardly be completed.

But the relationship between secondary and ultimate ends is *reciprocal*, entailing in turn the provisional character of (at least some) moral principles. Mill often tried to work analogies between theory and practice in morals, and 'elements' or 'general theory' or 'foundations' and particular truths in formal and natural science. His brief discussion of science in Chapter One of *Utilitarianism* peters out in ambivalence as to which should come first, axioms or theorems, general theory or particular truths. In this connection it is likely that students of Mill have paid insufficient attention to the self-conscious, if restrained Kantianism both of Chapter One of *Utilitarianism* and to the *Logic*. Mill does not object to Kant's formalism in producing a supreme principle of all categorical imperatives, for that (in a way) is what he is trying to do himself. He does not object to Kant's employment of a supreme principle which tells us what *morality* is, for that is what he (it seems) is doing himself. What he objects to is Kant's failure:

> to show that there would be any contradiction, any logical (not to say physical) impossibility, in the adoption by all rational beings of the most outrageously immoral rules of conduct.[63]

Kant had paid too little attention to 'particular truths'. In the light of what has already been suggested, it is not too conjectural to urge that, despite his great admiration for him, Mill objected to a doctrine whose teleology is so remote as to make it an unserious attempt to deal with the ends which, morally speaking, people set themselves and the (secular) point of it all. As to these secondary ends and secondary principles, we should not (as Bentham would like) consider them moral fossils, for they form part of the body of phenomena for which, throughout his mature life, Mill promoted the search.

It was said above that one of the reasons for the long-time depreciation of Mill was that he did not conveniently fit into the received doctrinal categories. (It ought to be better known, for example, that in the Philosophy of Science, he was a very errant Inductivist.) In recent years, much labour has gone into determining what kind of utilitarian Mill was. He was not a utilitarian at all, except in a sense which is perfectly consistent with an enlightened intuitionism; that is, with an intuitionism quite unlike that of Samuel Clarke.[64] The great Bradley, in a devastating attack on Mill in his *Ethical Studies* (published three years after Mill's death) said acutely that one of Mill's errors was to oppose the intuitional and utilitarian schools.[65] When Mill said that 'all action is for the sake of some end' he was uttering a truism. Bradley was prepared to say that if the end was happiness, he was glad to call himself a Utilitarian. His doctrine of self-realisation was totally different from Mill's doctrine of self-development, but, that apart, there is a quite extraordinary amount of common ground between him and the Mill presented here. Leaving Bradley, one might add that if all action is for the sake of some end, a

utilitarianism of some kind is logically inevitable. But which
kind? It is to the attempt to answer this question that Mill's
attentions were devoted. If it may now be taken for granted
that Mill's objection to Intuitionist ethics is essentially to the
presumption of a native, untutored, unprogressive, internal
standard of right or wrong, and leaving aside the likely
objection that the doctrine was not like that, it can be said
that the materials are available for the theses that, in ethics
(and not only in ethics) Mill was a great precursor, and that
the respect in which he anticipates recent central issues in
moral philosophy is also the respect in which his problems are
intractable. It is partly for this reason that it is misleading to
call him a Wordsworthian. *Of course*, he stresses the bearings
of action on the agent and his character rather than on what
he quaintly calls the 'specific' consequences.[66] With his 'engine' of a mind he had to go beyond mere Wordsworthianism.
Perhaps he was not a Wordsworthian because he knew that he
could not be, any more than he wanted to be, a Wordsworth.
Instead he invented Ethology, 'or the Science of the Formation of Character'. This is usually treated very seriously by
students of Mill, and in respect of his Philosophy of Science,
it should be so treated. But as a substitute for the Moral
Phenomenonology, which was not open to his unromantic
mind, and which is best represented at the present time in
some continental philosophy and fiction, Ethology was, even
programmatically, not a starter. Even in the modern guise of
Social Psychology, it would hardly have begun to satisfy Mill's
ethical demands.

What then, of the distinction between Fact and Value? Here
Mill once again is the precursor of contemporary debates. For
example, when he talked about progress in a celebrated chapter of the *Logic* he said that the word was not to be understood 'as synonymous with improvement and tendency to
improvement'. But he also said:

It is my belief ... that the general tendency is, and will con-

J

tinue to be ... one of improvement; a tendency towards a better and happier state. This however, is not a question of the method of the social science, but a theorem of the science itself.[67]

It is clear that in saying these things Mill has two hankerings: he is hankering for a Social Dynamics which will, in an 'astronomical' and not in a 'cyclical' way, explain the reciprocal relationship between:

> The circumstances in which mankind are placed ... [which] form the characters of the human beings ... [and the manner in which] human beings in their turn, mould and shape the circumstances, for themselves and for those who come after them.[68]

There is, so far, only the matter of discovering empirical laws of social change; there is no implication of improvement. But when he speaks of a tendency towards a better and a happier state being 'a theorem of the science itself', he exhibits another hankering and a philosophically troublesome one at that. It may be that what Mill means is that if there is 'progressive change' in the first sense, progress in the second sense is entailed by it. If, that is, change consists in the enlargement of our conception of wants, and responses, and wants again, an enlargement of our conception of happiness and secondary ends, then *pro tempore* we have shown what 'morality' means; the result is that we have discovered that *this* happiness and *these* secondary ends are desirable, and this is a truism, not a staggering truth. There are many logical creaks in all this. Who is Mill, who are *we*, to detect tendencies to improvement and through our agency to adjust the direction of change? It is here that the dangers of moral and political authoritarianism are said to lie. It is here, on the stage of societies and their political arrangements, that doubts grow about the wisdom of allotting power to those who have cultivated their minds, and are 'best able to judge'. It is worth noting that Bentham was accused by Mill of having a simplified view of interest as anything which a person likes. To what extent are attempts to persuade, to educate, to cultivate the feelings of plain men, authoritarian? Mill was hardly likely to have the enthusiasms he had about the ways of enriching the mind and let it go at that. Although all this entails a certain distrust of democracy, the primacy of Mill's liberalism remains. However, it can be and has been claimed that only a false objectivity masks the fact that a value judgement is made when it is said that the nature of happiness, and therefore of morality are given through the witnessings and the preferences of the wise. Once again we see Mill in the middle of a great and real dispute. It is the merit of Mill, of his 'naturalism', to have helped stimulate contemporary moral philosophers to unhallow the distinction between Fact and Value.[69]

In Mill's lifetime, the conditions of Philosophical Logic, Philosophy of Science, and Moral Philosophy, were very low. Through a self-confessed defect in his intellectual equipment, his need for animation, materials to work upon, and teachings to oppose, he had, over a wide range of problems, to do his own work. By the demands he made on all these and the Philosophy of History, Psychology, Sociology and Moral Phenomenology, his task was hopeless. Book Six of the *Logic* is witness to this. It is always interesting, almost always worthwhile but there is a distinctly hollow ring in the portentous science-inventing, in the calling for work to be done to complete the map of knowledge contained therein. The intransigence of Mill's ethical difficulties have been, perhaps, adequately illustrated. There are more. Briefly to give one example, contemporary writers have tried to distinguish two main varieties of Utilitarianism. The holder of one believes that it is evidence merely of rule-worship to follow moral rules except as rough guides, which may be overborne at any time by a direct appeal to the Happiness Principle. The holder of the second believes that it is not right but merely expedient, and ultimately self-serving, to act on the other view, and that it is rules of action, not specific actions, that are to be justified by appeal to the Happiness Principle.

Neither of these doctrines and their sundry variants, has been presented here, yet they, and the teaching that has been presented, are to be found in Mill. Significantly, too, Austin is considered the founding-father of one of them, so-called Rule Utilitarianism. Is Mill simply confused? Confused yes, but not simply. Confused perhaps by the early teaching of Austin. But it is interesting to observe how large a place the absorbing logic of acts and consequences has in present-day discussion. Here, too, Mill stands as a precursor and his writings serve as work-books.

A number of contentious and unworked things have been said here. The aim has simply been to present evidence, not ambitiously of a new Mill, but of a Mill different from the historical figure still often paraded. If, at least in ethics and social philosophy he is to be a representative figure, the age he correctly represents is something more like our own than his own. Because of the extraordinary range of activities that had to be undertaken, he could never have hoped to achieve the ethical result he wanted. That result, and for his reasons, is still not possible. He is a deeply important philosopher because he itemised and in some cases elaborated upon, the matters for enquiry that fall under the 'Art of Practice'. If, moreover, it is true to say of him that he refused to march under established intellectual banners, we have the real reason why his stock was, for such a long time, so low. Not having the highest genius he was not even a good disciple, therefore he was confused. But Mill was never a disciple; he was merely born one.

Notes to this chapter are on pages 230-33

DOSTOEVSKY'S ANTI-UTOPIANISM
Andrew A. J. Noble

FEW, IF ANY, writers equal Dostoevsky's capacity to combine the powers of the historical, social and religious thinker with the more personal and aesthetic creativity of the novelist. No one, not even the Henry James of *The Bostonians*, wherein we find themes very similar to those discussed in this chapter, approaches his ability to fuse together in the creative act both of these elements. Consequently, my intention is to discuss Dostoevsky's achievement as a diarist and essayist in the hope that this will be enlightening to those who, while aware of his great fictional powers are, perhaps, less conscious of the depth, penetration and originality of his non-fictional writing and of its relevance to his fiction. In particular, special attention will be paid to that unique and remarkable book, 'huge, crazy, vengeful, fulminating',[1] as Saul Bellow calls it, *The Diary of a Writer*.

As a way into the subject, and as an expression of Dostoevsky's power to fuse the political, social and philosophic with the substance of fiction, let us eavesdrop for a moment on a heated discussion in *Crime and Punishment*. The participants are Zossimov, a doctor in his mid-twenties and in spirit and belief a middle-aged liberal, Pyotr Petrovitch Luzhin, another middle-class liberal and capitalist, aspirant by virtue of financial status to the hand of Raskolnikov's sister Douania, Raskolnikov himself, the youthful revolutionary and murderer, and his good-hearted friend, Razumihin, who is also in love with Douania. Luzhin, a creature of reflexive pomposity and sycophancy, is holding forth on the future.

'You must admit', he went on, addressing Razumihin with a shade of triumph and superciliousness—he almost added 'young man'— 'that there is an advance, or, as they say now, progress in the name of science and economic truth. . .'
'A commonplace'. . .
'No, not a commonplace! Hitherto, for instance, if I were told "love thy neighbour", what came of it?' Pyotr Petrovitch went on, perhaps with excessive haste. 'It came to tearing my coat in half to share with my neighbour and we were both left half-naked. As a Russian proverb has it, "Catch several hares and you won't catch one". Science now tells us, love yourself before all men, for everything in the world rests on self-interest. You love yourself and manage your own affairs properly and your coat remains whole. Economic truth adds that the better private affairs are organised in society—the more whole coats, so to say—the firmer are its foundations and the better is the common welfare organised too. Therefore, in acquiring wealth solely and exclusively for myself, I am acquiring, so to speak, for all, and bringing to pass my neighbour's getting a little more than a torn coat; and that not from private, personal liberality, but as a consequence of the general advance. The idea is simple, but unhappily it has been a long time reaching us, being hindered by idealism and sentimentality'.[2]

From this paean to self-interest, empiricism and laisser-faire economics, Luzhin, borne on his customary tide of vanity and undertow of paranoia, proceeds to pronounce on the, to him, paradoxical increase of crime in Russia among all classes in spite of the diffusion of these new enlightened economic truths. As a self-confessed man of the highest rectitude he cannot understand it. He is especially concerned by the recent murder of the pawnbroker and her half-witted sister.

'But morality? And so to speak, principles. . .'
'But why do you worry about it?' Raskolnikov interposed suddenly. 'It's in accordance with your theory!'
'Why, carry out logically the theory you were advocating just now, and it follows that people may be killed. . .'
'Upon my word!' cried Luzhin.
'No, that's not so', put in Zossimov.
Raskolnikov lay with a white face and twitching upper lip, breathing painfully.

'There's a measure in all things', Luzhin went on superciliously. 'Economic ideas are not an incitement to murder, and one has but to suppose...'
'And is it true', Raskolnikov interposed once more suddenly, again in a voice quivering with fury and delight in insulting him, 'is it true that you told your *fiancée* ... within an hour of her acceptance, that what pleased you most ... was that she was a beggar ... because it was better to raise a wife from poverty, so that you may have complete control over her, and reproach her with being her benefactor?'[3]

In this brief conversation, so deep are its roots and so tentacular its consequences, everything I have to say in this chapter is concentrated. In Luzhin, and to a lesser extent Zossimov, we have represented a complacent, self-aggrandising liberalism that cannot connect the implications of their beliefs and actions with the very criminality which, as 'men of principle', they condemn. Manifest in them, too, is a kind of fashionable, one might even call it superstitious, realism about the hard and triumphant Western ideas of science and economics—ideas, one might add, which have little to do with a genuinely scientific philisophy but much to do with a politicised version of the theory of evolution. In Raskolnikov we come to a more lucid recognition of the drift of these ideas, but he himself has recognised not their terrible wrongness but rather their terrible logic, and his own action has become merely the more intimate, and consequently terrifying, acting-out of murder based on vainglory and economic theory. He, too, believes in the final reality of the distribution, or redistribution, of economic resources. Much as Raskolnikov hates Luzhin, at this stage in the novel they differ in their sense of values only in degree of consciousness of what they are doing. Both are advocates of power, especially of the importance of their own role within the power structure, and of the final reality of wealth.

Thus, the three main elements to which I wish to draw attention are present in this passage. First, Dostoevsky's analysis of the egotism he saw around him and his disclosure of the terrible discrepancy between our pride of role and our actual conduct. Luzhin, the respectable businessman, in his intimacies displays the most squalid emotions. Raskolnikov believes he is superhuman and ends by murdering two old women. Second, there is the fashion in which the two generations, the liberal, romantic generation of the 1840s, 'those bureaucrats who recited Schiller with tears in their eyes', and the nihilistic, socialistic, younger generation of the 1860s, as typified by Luzhin and Raskolnikov, come into conflict. Third, and perhaps most important, there is Dostoevsky's disbelief, expressed by Razmuhin, that the 'commonplace' prejudices of the nineteenth-century mind in favour of science and economics do provide a final solution to the human condition. It is, indeed, Dostoevsky's disbelief in such a solution to the problems of responsibility, individual freedom and communality that lies at the centre of all his major fiction. Christ's refusal, in 'The Grand Inquisitor' section of *The Brothers Karamazov*, to turn the stones into bread is his ultimate expression of this idea.

Throughout *The Diary of a Writer* there are consistent restatements of Dostoevsky's hostility towards the notion that there can possibly be any material, and finally utopian, solution to the problem of human existence. This is not to say that he underrates the possibilities and probable developments of natural science—one need not look for a state of mind symptomatic of a hybrid Luddite and *muzjik*. Indeed, as with all else, he is remarkably clear in his vision of what is technologically to come. For example, in his diary entry for January 1876 he anticipates a time when men 'would be walking or flying in the air; they would be flying over immense distances, ten times more quickly than they are now travelling; they would be extracting out of the earth fabulous harvests; maybe they would be chemically creating organisms'.[4] Unlike his contemporary and friend, Fyodorov, however, Dostoevsky did not foresee the coming of a period in which the ethical will and technological expertise would combine to humanise the blind forces of nature and bring history to a utopian conclusion. He was too aware of the undercurrents and dangers of the European and Russian situation in the nineteenth century. While it is not my present intention to discuss his vision of an inevitable European political and military catastrophe, we can touch upon it by reference to Dostoevsky's understanding of the implications of the quick-firing rifle and at the same time see to what ends he thought modern technology would be used. Thus in October 1877 he makes the following analysis of the Russian war with Turkey:

> I merely wish to express the formula that *with the modern rifle,* assisted by field fortifications, every army on the defensive, *in any European country,* has unexpectedly gained a terrible advantage over the attacking army. Now the force of defence exceeds the force of attack, and it is unquestionably more advantageous to him who defends himself to conduct a war than to him who is attacking.[5]

With his customary visionary logic, Dostoevsky proceeds to develop this fact into a thesis of the forthcoming war in France which he considers, given the 'synchronisation' of European political and national forces, inevitable.

> Now imagine that this whole million of defenders should resort to trench implements as energetically and broadly as nowadays the Turks do; imagine a talented general and excellent ideas,—in this event Germany would have to dispatch to France—not just half a million but a minimum of a million and a half! Undoubtedly someone in Germany is now thinking about this.[6]

Dostoevsky, therefore, has no doubt as to the practical and inevitable consequences of technology. It is the moral and spiritual consequences that he finds unacceptable. And so, in his diary for January 1876, he embarks on a fantasy concerning the human condition in the event of scientific discoveries becoming all bountiful and all benevolent.

> Of course, you understand that human science is still in its infancy —actually, it is only beginning to work... And, unexpectedly, a series of inventions would come showering down... All of a sud-

den all knowledge would descend on humankind, and—what is most important—altogether gratis, in the form of a gift! I ask you: what, in such an event, would happen to men? Oh, it goes without saying that, at first, they would all be seized with rapture. People would be ecstatically embracing each other; they would rush to study the discoveries (and this would take time); they would feel, so to speak, bestrewn with happiness, interred in material blessings... 'Well,' all our philanthropists would exclaim in unison, 'now that man is provided for, only now is he going to reveal himself! There are no more material privations, there is no more of that degrading "milieu" which used to be the cause of all vices, and now man is going to become beautiful and righteous... Only now has sublime life begun!'
But it is doubtful if these raptures would suffice even for one generation! People would suddenly realise that there is no freedom of spirit, no will, no personality; that someone has stolen something from them; that the human image has vanished and the bestial image of the slave, the cattle image has come into being, with that difference, however, that the cattle do not know that they are cattle whereas men would discover that they had become cattle. And mankind would begin rotting; people would be covered with sores and ulcers; they would start biting their tongues with pain, seeing that their lives had been taken away from them in exchange for bread, for "stones turned into bread". Men would grasp the fact that there is no happiness in inaction; that idling thought must die; that it is not possible to love one's neighbour by sacrificing to him one's labour; that it is a nasty thing to live gratuitously, and *that happiness is not in happiness but in its pursuit*. Tedium and anguish would ensue: everything has been accomplished—there is nothing more to accomplish; everything is known—there is nothing more to know. There would be crowds of suicides, and not as at present—merely in miserable tenement houses; people would be gathering in multitudes, seizing each other by the hand, and spontaneously annihilating themselves by the thousands by the means of some new device revealed to them along with other inventions.[7]

It is characteristic of Dostoevsky that this disbelief in the final value of scientific materialism is consistent with his disbelief in the creation of *self-appointed* values in human life. Inevitably, Dostoevsky thought that for man to become arbiter and judge of his own place in the universe meant that he took upon himself a role of destructive pride. Throughout the diary he remarked that it is not for man to speak the final word as to his own destiny, and this abhorrence of historical determinism is part of his fear that any kind of determinism would entrap the human spirit in hermetic and authoritarian structures. This is why he was, like Kierkegaard, so anti-Hegelian. Dostoevsky considered it inconceivable that the ideal should make itself manifest through logic and the state. For him the ideal is God who can be *approached* by the individual through Christian practice and belief and such an approach is the substance of our freedom. Compared with Hegel's plateau of lucid rationalism Dostoevsky postulates a world that is mysterious and unfathomable, a darkness lit by the spiritual virtue of few individuals and the given moment of mystical illumination. This, I would add, seems to me the reason why Russian thought and philosophy with its emphasis on the fundamental value of the immediate, lived consequences of ideas is superior to the tortuous dangers of the Germanic imposition of abstraction on reality. It is also the reason why Dostoevsky, not Hegel, is the prophet of so much of our own present experience.

Dostoevsky, therefore, had no expectation and every fear of the theories of political, social and historical determinism which he considered to be a direct consequence of the French Revolution. Whether these theories were bourgeois or socialist, he considered them morally and spiritually disastrous because they imposed a restricting materialistic form on human consciousness and freedom. For him they were attempts at legislation by varying degrees of force, qualities of charity, communality and pity which, if they come not from the freedom of the heart and soul, come not at all. He believed that mankind in attempting a purely material solution, whether bourgeois notion of a present heaven or socialist vision of a utopia to come, had devised for itself a self-destructive trap.

Consequently the primary fact in all Dostoevsky's analysis of the spirit of the nineteenth century was the ascension to power of the European middle class in the wake of the

Revolution. In one of his letters he has this to say:

> All the civilized world is entering upon bourgeoisdom, and its *avant garde* has already arrived there. Bourgeoisdom is the ideal toward which Europe is aspiring, is raising itself from its lowest points. Yes, dearest friend, it is time to come to the calm and humble acknowledgement that *bourgeoisdom is the definitive form of European civilization,* its majority its *état adulte.*[8]

In spite of his aspiration, Dostoevsky's recognition of this fact can scarcely ever be called calm or humble. Time and again he lacerated middle-class pretensions and deceits. Things for the Russian are never what they seem; this post-revolutionary middle-class society was far from being the thing of its personal, appetitive satisfactions and public rhetoric. 'Do you know,' he demands, 'that a great many people are ill because of their boundless confidence in their normalcy, and *eo ipso* they are infected with awful self-conceit, impossible narcissism, which sometimes reaches the level of one's infallibility.'[9]

It is, of course, natural for the novelist that he should locate the sickness of the times in the corruptions and contusions of the individual will. It is further characteristic of Dostoevsky that he understood the consequences of individual confusion in terms of mass delusion and the historical tragedy to which such delusion plays the necessary prelude. In the bourgeois code of progress, laisser faire economics and prosperity he saw merely a veneer. Civilisation for him, well before Freud, was only skin deep. Indeed he postulated a situation where flaying might become an acceptable practice:

> Civilization exists; its laws exist; there is even faith in them. Yet were a new vogue to appear, a multitude of men would promptly change. Of course, not all of them; still there would remain a tiny handful of them that you, my reader, and I should be surprised, and who knows where we ourselves should land—among the skinners or the skinned.
>
> Naturally, people will start shouting straight to my face that all this is trash, and that this much civilization did attain. Gentlemen what naiveté on your part! You are laughing? Well and what about France in 1793 (not to peep into more recent events)?

Hasn't there been firmly established there this very vogue of
stripping skins—and this under the guise of the most sacred principles of civilization;—this after Rousseau and Voltaire! You may
say that all this is not at all so; that this was very long ago. Still
please observe that, perhaps I am resorting to history solely for
the purpose of avoiding the discussion of current things.[10]

Dostoevsky's reference to the digressive irrelevance of
historical thought is one of the central and savage ironies of
this passage. Where the bourgeois believed in their own complacent, progressive determinism, he pointed to another and
much darker sequence of events to which their own ignorance
and vanity, their servitude to their appetites, had chained
them.

The point is that, to my way of thinking, the present period, too,
will end in Old Europe with something colossal, i.e. perhaps not
literally identical with the events which brought to an end the
eighteenth century, nevertheless equally gigantic, elemental and
dreadful, and also entailing a change of the face of the old world,
or at least, in the West of Old Europe.[11]

In a way that recalls the experience of Matthew Arnold, the
Russian felt himself almost living between worlds: a condition where 'the old has either been destroyed or is worn out;
the new is still born on the wing of fantasy, whereas in actual
life we behold something abominable which has reached
unheard of proportions'.[12] The source of the abomination he
felt to be located in what the nineteenth century had made of
the individual, and the basis for this psychological and spiritual error he saw as being the human failure of the aspirations
of the French Revolution.

For Dostoevsky the failure—the incipient disaster—of the
Revolution was summed up in the three unalterable slogans
he identified with bourgeois man. They stood in intentional
and ironic relation to the cries of liberty, equality and fraternity. These were, in strict order of utterance, '*Ôte-toi délà
que je m'mette*', '*J'y suis et j'y reste*', and '*Après-moi le déluge*'.
What they express is the attainment and possession of material
and political power and a complete irresponsibility in the

execution and distribution of the consequent gains. He thus believed that civilisation was based not on a true individualism but on an almost cannibalistic possessiveness. Given the nature of such individualism, all that could be expected was a constant friction of each man with his neighbour and the subsequent and inevitable disastrous civil strife that would emerge from such a class polarization when the excluded and resentful poor would rise against their greedy and irresponsible middle-class masters.

> But over there, in Europe, no bundle will ever be tied together; there, everything has become segregated in a manner different from ours—maturely, clearly and with precision; there groups and units are living their last days, and they themselves are aware of it; yet they refuse to cede anything, one to the other; they would rather die than yield.[13]

In accordance with this point of view Dostoevsky saw the materialism, splendour and glitter of the European capitals as merely a garish surface, a thin disguise of a deep individual and class discord. Like Mark Twain he was particularly embittered by Paris and, like another American visitor, Herman Melville, he was horrified by the poverty that existed in urban England. Thus he described London:

> I spent only a week in London, and what vast panoramas, what colourful settings, each with its individual personality, have imprinted themselves in my memory. At least that is the way London seems on the surface. Everything is so huge and garish in its individuality. And this individuality can be deceptive.
> Each object of garishness, each contradiction lives alongside its antithesis and obstinately walks hand in hand with it; they contradict each other and yet in no way evidently exclude each other. They all seem to defend themselves stubbornly, living in their own way and apparently not hurting each other. Yet simultaneously one finds here the same relentless, vague, chronic struggle between the individualistic basis of the whole Western world and the necessity of finding some way to live together, of finding some way to fashion a community and set up a house all in the same anthill; it may be an anthill but we had better get organised without devouring each other, or else we'll become cannibals! In this respect, however, you observe the same thing as in Paris: the same frantic struggle to preserve the status quo, to wring from oneself

all one's desires and hopes, to curse one's future, in which even the leaders of progress do not have enough faith perhaps, and to worship Baal.[14]

Dostoevsky located the anxiety and fear that lay just under the material complacency and splendour around him. He saw clearly the fatal inner contradiction of such individualism, and that French bourgeois civilisation was a parody of the ideals of the Revolution.

The Westerner speaks of fraternity as of a great motivating force of humankind, and does not understand that it is impossible to obtain fraternity if it does not exist in reality. What is to be done? Fraternity must be obtained at any cost.

But as it happens it is impossible to create fraternity, for it creates itself, comes of itself, exists in nature. But in French nature, and in Occidental nature in general it is not present; you find there instead a principle of individualism, a principle of isolation, of intense self-preservation, of personal gain, of self-determination of the *I*, of opposing this *I* to all nature and the rest of mankind as an independent, autonomous principle entirely equal and equivalent to all that exists outside itself. Well fraternity could scarcely arise from such an attitude. Why? Because in fraternity, in true brotherhood, it is not the separate personality, not the *I*, which should be concerned with its right to equality and equilibrium with everything else, but rather this everything else which comes of its own volition to the individual who is demanding his rights, should recognise him as possessing the same value and the same rights as it does, i.e. as everything else on earth.[15]

Thus Dostoevsky delineated the consequences for the independent autonomous self as it posits itself as the absolute entity to which all men and all things inevitably become both relative and reduced. Western individualism posits self-interest as truth. The nature of self-interest is to seek the satisfaction of appetite. Such an individualism makes all truth, or truths, relative to its own wilful needs and demands. For Dostoevsky, God, and his manifestation as man in Christ, is the truth which is absolute and to which the individual relates himself in order to seek salvation and to establish a true community. Thus, we are faced with two absolutely contradictory systems. On the one hand, there is the bourgeois relativism which is, or inevitably degenerates into, relationships based on power, since for them all perception and all truth is at best pragmatic and functional. Dostoevsky, on the other hand, posits an absolute truth and the search and attainment of grace. It is the absolute distinction between truth as a personal possession and the spiritual fact of being possessed by the truth.

Given this central fact, we can better understand the bitter and relentless analysis to which Dostoevsky subjected the bourgeois individual. He saw him as totally self-centred and, consequently, completely given over to deceit and self-flattery. This was true at every level of his being and activity, and was most of all apparent in the corruption of his heart and sympathetic powers. In his *Diary* there occurs a brilliant rendition of the bourgeois at one of their innumerable spas, taking the waters in a welter of goodwill and supposed pantheism—a vignette which provides a perfect example of this condition:

> But these people are freer than the rest because they are wealthier, and at least they can live as they please. Of course, they come in contact with nature only as far as politeness and *bon ton* will permit. To expand, to become dissolved in, or to open themselves fully to nature, to that golden ray of sun over there, which shines on us sinners, without discrimination from the blue sky—whether or not we are worthy of it—this no doubt would be unbecoming, at least in the measure you and I, or some poet, would like it at this moment. A small steel lock of *bon ton*, as heretofore, hangs over each heart and each mind.[16]

Thus the heart's real sympathetic power is closed, and compassion is made an object of self regard. Social intercourse becomes a sort of grease, which allows men to slide around the reality of one another. 'Liberalism', the rhetorical politics of such a selfhood, is really the ground for the personal melodrama of gestures based on 'enlightened' ideas, an activity so exhausting as to quite preclude the possibility of any action that stems from true faith or love. Like everything the heart is turned inwards and reflects only the self. This constant self-mirroring, Dostoevsky saw as stemming from the pomposity and rhetoric of a state of mind which has at its disposal 'a store of ready-made ideas, as of firewood for the winter', and a total disbelief in the actuality of any of the ideas which flowed through that mind. Tolstoy's Oblonsky in *Anna Karenina* is a complementary figure. Thus, the Parisians poured into the theatre to watch their own flattering and deceitful images. Life becomes the worst sort of art, and truth is perverted into appearance or style. Thus, 'this bourgeois is a strange person; he proclaims openly that money is the highest virtue and human obligation, and yet he loves to toy with nobility of character'.[17] Freedom and nobility in this wanton aesthetic collapse into parody, and the theatre and the street merge into a mass of posturing and dreadful actors. 'A good imitation of love,' says Dostoevsky, 'has the same value for a Parisian as love itself. Perhaps he even prefers the imitation.'[18] In such a society caricature and truth are one and the same.

For Dostoevsky, therefore, bourgeois society is a compound of deceit, materialism and chronic resentment. Reducing literature and thought to banality, it expels any possible self criticism and finds solace in anti-intellectualism and its own particular brand of pseudo-scientific positivism. 'Ours,' says Dostoevsky, 'is an age of *cast-iron* conceptions, positive opinions—an age which displays on its banner the motto: "To live by all means!"'[19] Their social thought, he believed, stemmed from a debased version of Darwin's evolutionary theory which successfully fused the ruthless and predatory exploitation of capitalism with a total and pleasing lack of personal responsibility. Their 'rational egoism' could see only as far as its own self-advantage, and material well-being. Thus, in order to shield further their guilts and consciences, they developed a philosophy based on a positivism and a seemingly scientific causality. For Dostoevsky, who called this 'rectilinear' thought, it was for them the safest way of proceeding from point A to B, while, at the same time, reducing and eliminating the actual nature of the human and spiritual.

Nearly always we perceive reality as we wish to perceive it, as we

K

wish to interpret it to ourselves. If, at times, we start analysing, and if in the visible we perceive not that which we sought to perceive but that which it is in reality, unhesitatingly we take that which we have perceived for a miracle. This happens quite often, and, at times I swear we would rather believe in a miracle than in the truth *which we do not want to see*.[20]

Bourgeois 'thought', then, is a methodology for handling reality and cashing in on it. Its basic necessity and premise is, in the teeth of its own rhetoric, to divorce reality from absolute and spiritual truth and make it relative to the demands they impose upon it. This is what Dostoevsky saw behind the supposed 'Idealism' of his time, among the Russian liberals.

I don't know if you will agree with me, but when our Russian idealist, an unquestionable idealist who knows that he is taken merely for such—so to speak, for a "patented" preacher of the "beautiful and the lofty"—suddenly finds it necessary to state or record his opinion on some matter (but of poetry—on some momentous and *serious* almost civic, matter), and to record it somehow in passing, but in order to express a decisive and weighty judgement, and one which by all means may be influential— unexpectedly by some miracle,—he turns into not only an ardent realist and prosaist, but even into a cynic. Moreover of that cynicism and prosaism, he is particularly proud. He records his opinions, and he almost cracks with his tongue. Ideals—let's toss them aside; ideals are humbug, poesy, verses; let's have in their stead nothing but 'realistic truth'. Yet he manages to over-salt it to the point of cynicism. The coarser, the drier, the more heartless it is—the more in his judgement, realistic it is. Why is this so?— Because, in a case such as this, our idealist, without fail, will be ashamed of his idealism... Concealed, profound inner disrespect for oneself does not even miss such men as Pushkin and Granovsky.[21]

Thus, at the very core of the bourgeois mind lies capricious freedom and the ultimately nihilistic equation of cynicism and truth. The basic action of such a mind is, of necessity, to reduce, contain and exploit reality. Of its very nature it must not only be cynical of anything but depraved human behaviour, but also hold to this depravity as a testament of faith. There is an implicit agreement that egotistic self-interest is what makes the wheels go round. Truth is, therefore, defined as admissible only as that which the self personally possesses and can use to its advantage. Dostoevsky believed that such a self, which opposes 'this *I* to all nature and the rest of mankind as an independent, autonomous principle entirely equal to all that exists outside itself', was not only unequal to the task of creating human communality, but that, fraught with hidden fears and anxieties and, indeed, unadmittedly self-disgusted, it was and would increasingly become crazily self-destructive.

Wholly characteristic of Dostoevsky's method of argument is the fact that he was never content merely to give both sides of the case. With the classic novelist's intelligence he compared the facts and practices of bourgeois life with their complacent ideology. Thus, in both his journalism and fiction, he delineated all the consequences, personal and historical, of man's loss of faith in himself as an immortal soul. Bourgeois man, subconsciously terrified of death, insists on interpreting himself as a creature whose very finitude demands as its consolation the maximum possible satisfaction of his appetites. Having severed himself from the absolute, he gives himself completely to the exploitation of the relative, and deems himself the centre of all things. God having been so killed, he believes himself ready to take his place. Vyacheslav Ivanov, in his book on Dostoevsky, brilliantly elucidates this point.

> It is true that, by practical experience acquired over thousands of years, man has been thoroughly taught not to adopt an independent attitude towards the world about him. Nevertheless, in the act of cognition—which after all, is the criterion of everything —he comes to know all things as objects wrought by himself. If, therefore, he has to seek the measure of things in himself, he is exposed to the temptation to regard himself as the sole creator of all standards. As soon as the Absolute had passed through the phase of being a metaphysical abstraction, and has become a mere conceptualistic phantom, the human understanding is irresistibly impelled to proclaim, as its final conclusion that all accepted values are universally relative. In these circumstances, it is no wonder, if the personality imprisoned in a subjectivist solitude, either yields itself to despair or falls a victim to the vain-glorious

delusion that it is dependent upon nothing. This is the danger that Dostoevsky has in mind when he writes, in the epilogue to *Crime and Punishment*, concerning a 'new, unprecedented, terrible pestilence', which 'is spreading over Europe from the depths of Asia'.

Here is a passage.

'Never before had men thought themselves so clever, never before had they believed so unshakably in their own wisdom, as did these sick creatures. Never before had men been so deeply convinced of the infallibility of their judgements, doctrines and principles. Whole districts, whole cities, whole nations caught the infection, and behaved like madmen. Everybody was in a state of high excitement, and nobody understood anyone else. Each man thought he alone was in possession of the truth, and was deeply distressed —beating his breast, weeping and wringing his hands at the sight of his fellows. Nobody knew on whom judgement should be passed, or what sort of judgement it should be; no two people could agree as to what was good or what was bad—who should be prosecuted and who should be acquitted. Men killed each other in a senseless fury.'[22]

A society so brought forth breaks into a multiplicity of individual units, each, at the price of every other unit, demanding satisfaction of its wants. Every individual, since he makes a personal demand and a wilful interpretation of the world, produces chaos in the subsequent and unremitting friction of private worlds. This is best seen in 'personal' relationships. Given such a relative and personal interpretation of the world, the other, in consequence, becomes reduced and, as a person, inadmissible. In such an interpretation the other becomes an object that is malleable or disposable as the need may arise. He is fluid and functional to the demands that are made upon him. He is also an object among objects, a commodity among commodities. Known only by his style or surface, the middle-class obsession with appearance, he is allocated only such reality as will allow interpretation of his conduct to suit the pragmatic needs of the moment. Thus, inevitably, every relationship becomes a power relationship, since the other self can have no reality beyond his function in the plans devised for him. Man in relationship with man is thus faced with the choice of dominating or being dominated. Society becomes the sum and structure of such relationships, and instead of brotherhood, corrupt systems of power are erected. Thus, public unity is created from the negations of personal hatred and private fantasies. The corruption of the individual leads to his seeking the self-justification of public accord. Individual nihilism leads dynamically outwards to group madness. What Dostoevsky bears witness to, is the relation between degenerate individualism and Fascist politics. Beginning with a system of atomistic individualism, we end, inevitably, with a massive, insane and authoritarian power structure. Thus, Dostoevsky saw Paris not as the city of artistic dreams but as the symbol of a 'colossal internal and spiritual regimentation coming from the very soul'.[23]

Dostoevsky, then, saw very clearly that this individualism, materialism and determinism were complementary. He saw, too, that the modern social structure and the modern organisation based on such premises would be largely a product of utilitarianism and espionage—a compound of lost souls who had politicised and rationalised their despair into a resentment against each other and, even more, against any attempt by a genuine individual to speak against them in the name of truth. Solzhenitsyn's present struggle is surely archetypal of precisely this situation. Hell, for him, is almost certainly what Dostoevsky prophesied—the closed circle populated by the cynic and the sycophant and ruled by a false god.

The depth of Dostoevsky's comprehension of an individualism based purely on materialism is of so profound a degree that it leads him to a prophetic understanding of its historical consequences. He saw the Russian liberals as an 'antiquated bundle of twigs' which 'is solid only on condition that the twigs are tied together, but just as soon as they are disjointed, the whole bundle falls apart into so many tiny blades which will be scattered by the first gust of wind'.[24] Or again, in the same passage, he talks of a forest fire raging and consuming

Russia. Nowhere was he more aware of the consequences of bourgeois individualism than in the corruption of the Russian youth, the nihilistic and revolutionary socialists of the 1860s by their liberal fathers, the romantic generation of the 1840s.

So that there is a definite ground to suppose that among our youth there is originating a movement diametrically opposed to the former one. Well, perhaps, this should have been expected. In point of fact: whose children are they? They are, precisely, the children of those 'liberal' fathers who, at the beginning of Russia's renaissance during the present reign, detached themselves *en masse* from the general cause, imagining that therein lay progress and liberalism ... the majority (of these liberals) was still made up of a mass of coarse petty atheists and great scoundrels—in substance, mere extortioners and 'petty tyrants', but braggarts of liberalism in which they managed to perceive nothing but a right to infamy. And just think what hasn't been said and asserted; what abominations haven't been set forth under the guise of honour and prowess! In substance, that was a vulgar stream into which an honest idea had been launched. And just then the liberation of the peasants had come, and along with it—the decomposition and 'segregation' of our educated society in every conceivable sense. People did not recognize each other, and liberals failed to recognise their kindred liberals. And after that —how many sad misunderstandings and painful disillusions. The most shameless reactionaries would sometimes suddenly come to the forefront as progressives and leaders, and met with success. What, then, could children of those days behold in their fathers? What reminiscences could they have maintained about their childhood and youth? — Cynicism, scoffing, pitiless assaults on the earliest, tender, holy beliefs of the children; and there-upon-not infrequently—the open debauch of fathers and mothers, with assurance and 'instruction' that thus it should be and that these are genuinely 'sane relations'. To this should be added a great many disintegrated fortunes, and, as a consequence, impatient discontent, high strung words screening mere egotistical, petty anger against material reverses. Well, at length, our youth managed to decipher and rationalize all this!

And since youth is pure, serene and magnanimous, it may, of course, have happened that some of them refused to follow such fathers and rejected their 'sane' instructions. In this way such a liberal upbringing could have caused altogether reverse consequences, at least in certain instances. These, perhaps are the young men and raw youths who are now seeking new paths; and they begin with a direct repudiation of that cycle of hateful ideas with which they had been faced in childhood, in the nests of their pitiful parents.[25]

While, in his diary, Dostoevsky hoped for the manifestation of the children's potential goodness to redeem their fathers' corruptions, in his creative work the 'repudiation of that cycle of hateful ideas' took quite another orbit. Their repudiation took the form, as we have already noted, of Raskolnikov's doctrine of the amoral superman, and, in that greatest of political novels, *The Possessed*, Dostoevsky artistically deduces the children's *rationalisation* of parental evil. He, unlike most thinkers, did not see revolutionary socialism as an alternative to decadent liberalism. He saw it, as Camus later sees it in *The Rebel*, as an ideological, theoretical and finally perverse attempt by the children to redeem the lost dignity of the self, and the sense of communality that had been destroyed by the behaviour of their fathers.

In spite of both his profound hope and sympathy for Russian youth, Dostoevsky perceived the true and terrible nature of their revolt. What he testified to was not the necessary and creative severance of one generation from another but the destruction of the fathers by their children as a consequence of their acting out and making manifest their parents' blasphemy; again we can refer to Raskolnikov's relation to Luzhin. Thus, for Dostoevsky, the relation between generations is not the theoretical, abstract and finally benevolent functioning of the rational will but rather the dreadful and organic consequences of the visitation and extension of the sins of the fathers in the lives of their children. The fathers were to be destroyed by a monster evolved from their own ideas. The consequent weird mixture of nihilistic and utopian social thought was not, therefore, a reaction against bourgeois thought and belief but rather the extension of these corrupt values beyond posture into manifest action. Thus it is, that since the fathers have corrupted religion and art, the children denounce them as irrelevancies. Since bourgeois 'fine feeling' is a mere screen for materialism, then the children implant materialism, empiricism and science at the very centre of their utopian philosophy. As the fathers have a woolly determinism, 'rectilinear' thought and a Darwin-derived evolutionary theory as the basis of their social thinking, so the children introduce the deadliest form of rationalism and historical causality as their hermetic and self-justifying historical philosophy.

In this analysis, of course, Dostoevsky is completely at odds with the Hegelian, and post-Hegelian—especially Marxist—philosophies of history. At the very base of this division is Dostoevsky's disbelief that the spiritual is no longer transcendental, and that what was once considered the spiritual has been thoroughly humanised and been translated and made immanent in the physical. For him this is the great illusion rather than the great truth of the nineteenth century.

We have already noted the inevitably destructive nature of bourgeois illusion. Following Dostoevsky's vital logic, we can now proceed to observe his analysis of the fatal illusions of their children, the revolutionary adolescents. Like many great novelists, Dostoevsky is preoccupied with the adolescent mind. This is no doubt in part due to the fact that the adolescent's mind is, of its very nature, in a state of dramatic crisis, torn as it is between childhood and maturity, faith and doubt—Camus refers to it as having a simultaneous need to experience faith and doubt—and the necessity of choosing one's role in a society which appears hostile and perhaps evil, while its modality swings between egotistic fantasy and a pervasive feeling of guilt and inferiority—tensions made much greater in a time of major social upheaval.

In his study of the Russian adolescent mind what primarily struck Dostoevsky was not so much the political nature and theories of the younger generation but the underlying private despair. The outbreak of suicide among them was, in his diary, a matter of constant concern. Thus, he discussed in October 1876 the case of a young girl:

Was she one of those well-known judges and deniers of life who are indignant against the 'absurdity' of man's appearance on earth, the nonsensical casualness of this appearance, the tyranny of the inert cause with which one cannot reconcile himself? Here we seem to be dealing with a soul which revolted against the 'rectilinearness' of the phenomena, which could not stand this rectilinearness conveyed to her since her childhood. The ugliest thing is that, of course, she died devoid of any distinct doubt or so called queries. Likewise, it is quite probable that she implicitly believed, without further verification, everything which had been imparted to her since childhood. This means that she simply died of 'cold, darkness and tedium' with, so to speak, animal and unaccountable suffering; she began to suffocate as if there were not enough air. The soul unaccountably proved unable to bear rectilinearness, and unaccountably demanded something more complex.[26]

Dostoevsky proceeds from this analysis of suicide as a consequence of 'scientific' logic to reveal a more complex state of mind.

To some observers all phenomena of life develop with a most touching simplicity and are not worth thinking about or being looked at. However, these same phenomena might embarrass another observer to such an extent (this happens quite often) that, in the long run, he feels unable to synthesize and simplify them, to draw them out into a straight line and thus to appease his mind. He then resorts to a different kind of simplification and *very simply* plants a bullet in his brain so as to extinguish at once his jaded mind, together with all its queries. Such are the two extremes between which the sum total of human intelligence is enclosed. But it stands to reason that never can we exhaust a phenomenon, never can we trace its end or beginning. We are familiar merely with the everyday, apparent and current, and this only insofar as it appears to us, whereas the end and the beginnings still constitute to man a realm of the fantastic.[27]

For Dostoevsky the essential value of a genuinely religious sense is that it demands no final security or solution but accepts mystery in this world. He considers that the desperate dilemma of the modern mind arises from an attempt, partly through vanity and partly through fear, to create absolute certainty for itself. Materialism and science, and the morality and politics so derived, seem to point to such a certainty, but in Dostoevsky's work we find the terrible irony of men who cannot live with uncertainty and yet who perish in the desert of false certainty that they create. Man in Dostoevsky's world cannot live within the confines and sterility of his phalansteries, Crystal Palaces, and similar Faustian structures. In recent psychology, for example the work of R. D. Laing, we have been told much of the relationship of schizophrenia and false security systems. Dostoevsky, a moral rather than clinical eye, saw, I think, even further than this. He was, in consequence, able to deduce the relationship between adolescent disturbance and its related political and social theory.

Thus it is that in characters such as Raskolnikov and Nicolai Stavrogin in *The Possessed* we can observe an acute disruption of personality which is primarily due to their agonised response to the conduct of their elders and the society created by them. Horrified by the all-too-human behaviour they perceive around them, they, by means of cynicism and suppressed rage, create personas which they intend to be superhuman, to be cleansed of the stench of the human. Thus in *Crime and Punishment* Razumihin, enraged by Raskolnikov's perverseness, cries that 'in any circumstances the first thing for all of you is to be unlike a human being'.[28] Thus, too, is it that in *The Possessed* Stavrogin is involved in everything and committed to nothing. Dostoevsky consistently pointed out that the consequence of this theoretical self-deification is a disconnection from one's fellow men and a solitary journey into a no-man's land of banality, despair and a final confrontation with evil as the reality of one's achievement.

Given this fact, we can, perhaps, better understand Dostoevsky's fictional world not as something merely strange and hysterical but as a place where he deduced the consequences of the logic of dehumanisation: how we commence in abstraction and end in madness.

Since we began with an example from *Crime and Punishment*, perhaps it is best to conclude our argument with it.

The passage chosen is Razumihin's attack on his own scientific and revolutionary generation.

Everything with them is 'the influence of environment', and nothing else. Their favourite phrase! From which it follows that, if society is normally organised, all crime will cease at once, since there will be nothing to protest against and all men will become righteous in one instant. Human nature is not taken into account, it is excluded, it's not supposed to exist! They don't recognise that humanity, developing by a historical living process, will at last become a normal society, but they believe that a social system that has come out of some mathematical brain is going to organise all humanity at once and make it just and sinless in an instant, quicker than any living process! That's why they instinctively dislike history, 'nothing but ugliness and stupidity in it', and they explain it all as stupidity! That's why they so dislike the *living* process of life; they don't want a *living soul*! The living soul demands life, the soul won't obey the rules of mechanics, the soul is an object of suspicion, the soul is retrograded! But what they want, though it smells of death and can be made of india-rubber, at least is not alive, has no will, is servile and won't revolt- And it comes in the end to their reducing everything to the building of walls and the planning of rooms and passages in a phalanstery! The phalanstery is ready, indeed, but your human nature is not ready for the phalanstery—it wants life, it hasn't completed its vital process, it's too soon for the graveyard! You can't skip over nature by logic. Logic presupposes three possibilities, but there are millions! Cut away a million, and reduce it all to the question of comfort! That's the easiest solution of the problem! It's seductively clear and you mustn't think about it. That's the great thing, you mustn't think.[29]

Notes to this chapter are on pages 233-4

WILLIAM MORRIS OR BERNARD SHAW: TWO FACES OF VICTORIAN SOCIALISM

James Redmond

We must have an ideal of a beautiful and good world. We must believe that to establish that beautiful and good world on earth is the best thing we can do, and the only sort of religion and politics that is worth bothering about. (The Simpleton of the Unexpected Isles, Act II.)

DURING THE 1880s and 90s William Morris and Bernard Shaw were very close acquaintances. They had a good deal in common in their political attitudes, and for several years they worked together for the advance of Socialism. Morris obviously took a liking to the young Shaw, for he went out of his way to encourage him at the beginning of his political and literary career. And among the hundreds of men Shaw talks about in print, Morris stands alone as the one Shaw admired without reserve—Morris was a prophet, Shaw often said, and a saint.[1]

Whenever Shaw spoke of William Morris (and he continued to speak regularly of him for sixty years after Morris was dead) his intention was always to associate his own thinking positively with Morris'. As a result of this, critics and historians have come to accept it as a commonplace truth that Shaw's political position is to be identified with the political position of Morris. Two careful scholars of the period have recently given new weight to the general belief that Shaw and Morris were—with respect to large political issues—very closely aligned. E. E. Stokes tells us that

> Bernard Shaw's twelve-year friendship with William Morris was the single most valuable personal contact in Shaw's long and varied life... Viewed in the historical and intellectual context of socialism, Morris and Shaw appear as the greatest socialist men of letters of the later nineteenth century in England.[2]

J. W. Hulse, in his shrewd and well-researched study of late Victorian Socialism, leaves us with the same picture of the Morris–Shaw relationship:

> Morris's Socialism might best be described as catholic, borrowing from the Middle Ages and from Russian nihilism, as well as from Mill and from Marx. And in this respect, Morris's most famous successor and disciple was Bernard Shaw... During the years when Shaw was defining his own position within the Socialist movement, he was in continual communication with Morris. The two men engaged in a substantial Socialist dialogue over the years, in addition to developing a rewarding interchange of ideas on art during the last months of Morris's life. Shaw's later intellectual development and the evolution of his political attitudes can in part be explained by the influence of Morris.[3]

There is, of course, a good factual basis for this alignment of Shaw's Socialism with Morris', but it is necessary to emphasise that what they shared was superficial and that beneath the surface they embraced utterly different kinds of Socialism.

It is a fact that Morris and Shaw saw themselves as belonging to the main stream of English Socialism. For example, they both respected Robert Owen as a practical pioneer of the kind of social reform they were working towards. Like Owen, they rejected the Christianity of their youth and to compensate spoke of their Socialist conviction in terms that were explicitly religious; and like him they marked their conversion to Socialism as the dividing-line between their immaturity and maturity.

Again, they were like Owen in that their Socialism was neither materialist nor altogether secular. Socialism for them was imaginatively identified with the coming of the millennium; and they spoke of their political faith, as naturally as he did, in phrases and concepts borrowed from the Judaic Pentateuch and the Christian Apocalypse. When they said their creative writing was a contribution to the new Bible of Socialism,[4] it was no more than what Owen and his followers had been doing when they offered—as they were always offering—new 'interpretations' of key Biblical passages in terms of the social conditions in contemporary England.

> What are the signs of the last days of misery on earth? 'And there shall be signs in the sun, and in the moon, and in the stars; and upon the earth, distress of nations, with perplexity; the sea and the waves roaring; men's hearts failing them for fear and for looking after those things which are coming on earth; for the powers of heaven shall be shaken.' 'And then shall they see the son of man (or TRUTH) coming in a cloud with power and glory. And when these things begin to come to pass, then look up and lift up your heads, for your redemption (FROM CRIME AND MISERY) draweth night.' 'THIS GENERATION SHALL NOT PASS AWAY UNTIL ALL SHALL BE FULFILLED.' What immediate and permanent consequences will follow from the Religion of Charity alone, unconnected with Faith? PEACE ON EARTH AND GOOD WILL TOWARDS MEN.[5]

The Christian rhetoric here is being employed for purposes which are explicitly post-Christian: the new God is Political Truth, the new cardinal sins are Crime and Misery, Exploitation and Poverty. Robert Owen, William Morris and Bernard Shaw (and in this they were very like Marx, of course) had a vision of the coming of Socialism which was explicitly parallel to St John the Divine's vision of the millennium. The pious, in the world to come, would be elevated, and the Devil with his followers would be cast into darkness. They did not define piety in the same terms—in fact my main purpose here will be to show that Morris and Shaw were often diametrically opposed in their views of what human qualities *are* pious— but there was one thing they all agreed about; the Devil, for all of them, was the Capitalism that had corrupted England for generations, nurturing sin and stealing souls, just like the old draconian serpent in the *Book of Revelation*.

It is interesting to compare Morris and Shaw because they

brought their very different personalities to the task of elab-
orating the Socialist vision of the new heaven on the new
earth, and because they revealed in the process some surprising paradoxes that have always caused confusion within the
Socialist movement. They were justified in thinking that their
creative writing was potentially crucial for the future of
Socialism, and the analogy with Christianity was so often
made because it was genuinely helpful. They were writing
the new Bible; professional economists were to be the new
theologians; and practical Socialists on the shop-floor were to
be the new worker-priests and missionaries, All three kinds of
Socialist would be necessary, but the new Bible would be at
the heart of Socialism, just as the old Bible had been the
centre of Christianity. Shaw kept emphasising that the utopian visions of Owen, Morris, and himself were of central
practical importance.

> ...in order to bring a social movement to a fruitful issue, it is
> necessary to propose—and to propose with entire conviction—ten
> impossible results for every possible one. Christianity had to pro-
> pose a Communist millennium to secure the feudalism of the
> Middle Ages... And, no doubt, as realised Christianity is to the
> Christianity of the Gospels ... so will the realised Socialism be to
> 'the New Moral World' of Robert Owen.[6]

Oscar Wilde wrote *The Soul of Man Under Socialism* after
having heard Shaw lecture on the subject, and in it he reiter-
ates the broad teaching of Ruskin and Morris. The intellectual
confusion of Wilde's essay depends largely on the fact that
much of what he steals from Morris is quite irreconcilable
with what he steals from Shaw, but there is one passage where
his two sources are in complete agreement:

> A map of the world that does not include Utopia is not worth
> even glancing at, for it leaves out the one country at which
> Humanity is always landing... Progress is the realisation of
> Utopias.

Unfortunately, Marx and Engels firmly established the attitude which is still common in Socialist circles, where the word
'utopian' is used almost exclusively as a term of abuse. This

is unfortunate because it covers up the important truth that in political life—very much as in religious life—practical action will be directionless if it is not guided towards some ideal concept, some theoretical goal. Religious morality must be based on some metaphysical system, and the metaphysical basis is better made as explicit as possible. Political morality must be based on some concept of an ideal community—and if the ideal is not spelled out in detail, the practical action will tend to be indecisive, full of compromise, confused, and even self-contradictory. The firm distinction between practical Socialism and utopian Socialism is an unhelpful one. No political policy that is wholly pragmatic can be a Socialist policy—as has been demonstrated every time Britain has had a Labour administration. Socialism cannot continue to exist in the absence of a vision of the future perfect society. Robert Owen's development shows that good-will, and pragmatic intelligence, are not enough. He came to preach about the 'New Moral World', because he realised that practical social reform must have its basis in an imaginative concept of a Socialist utopia.

Morris and Shaw are important for British Socialism because they each undertook the task of spelling out, letter by letter, their ideal Socialist community. It so happened that underneath their superficial agreements they differed radically on all of the crucial points; and they demonstrated permanent conflicts within the movement which remain hidden, though far from harmless, except when the utopian task is undertaken. A fair amount has been written about what Morris and Shaw had in common: what I shall do here is point to some of the ways in which their Socialist dreams were different, and suggest that these differences have more than local significance. In fact the ideal Socialism of Morris and the ideal Socialism of Shaw define the extreme positions between which lies the whole Socialist spectrum. Not only will there be a tendency towards both ends of the spectrum in each Socialist group, but the two tendencies will be present in every individual Socialist. (They were unusually well documented in Robert Owen at different stages of his career.) By comparing Morris and Shaw I also want to suggest that our habit of defining political attitudes in terms of ideas, rather than dispositions, can sometimes be seriously misleading. We know very well that political actions do not characteristically have their basis in reason—if they did, sensible men would not oppose each other politically any more than they do with regard to calculus or chemistry. But we sometimes lose sight of the fact that even what we call political thinking is governed by psychic at least as much as by rational forces.

From the beginning, the Greeks knew that a man's view of society is inseparable from his own psychological condition; that theoretical social systems are projections of psychic states, and not intellectual or logical in their essence. We ought to talk at least as much about political psychology as we do about political science. It was because this was what every Athenian schoolboy knew, that Socrates, when confronted with a question about moral harmony in the individual, could naturally, in *The Republic*, project the investigation into the wider terms of society:

> Justice, which is the subject of our inquiry, is, as you know, sometimes spoken of as the virtue of an individual, and sometimes as the virtue of a State.
> True, Adeimantus replied.
> And is not a State larger than an individual?
> It is.
> Then in the larger the quantity of justice is likely to be larger and more easily discernible. I propose therefore that we inquire into the nature of justice and injustice, first as they appear in the State, and secondly in the individual, proceeding from the greater to the lesser and comparing them.

Plato's point is surely valid—much of our discussion which is explicitly about politics is, like *The Republic*, implicitly and more importantly about individual psychology. This is

L

always kept in mind by Plato, and towards the end of his long dialogue he reminds us of it:

> Governments vary as the dispositions of men vary, and there must be as many of the one as there are of the other. For we cannot suppose that States are made of 'oak and rock' and not out of the human natures that are in them... States grow out of human characters. Then if the constitutions of States are five, the dispositions of individual minds will also be five?
> Certainly.
> Him who answers to aristocracy, and whom we rightly call just and good, we have already described. Then let us now proceed to describe the inferior sort of natures... Shall we follow our old plan, which we adopted with a view to clearness, of taking the State first and then proceeding to the individual?[7]

'Him who answers to aristocracy... we rightly call just and good.' The main reason for referring to *The Republic* here is that it is the classic expression of a political disposition which has been as important in modern Socialism as it was in previous movements. What Socrates calls Aristocracy we call Meritocracy, and Bernard Shaw gave vigorous modern expression to the Socratic concept of intellectual dominance both politically within the State and psychologically within each citizen. In *Back to Methuselah*, his ideal Socialist future has a physical setting taken from fourth-century Athens, and his ideal humans are abstractions of Socratic-Shavianism. William Morris, on the other hand, also under the banner of Socialism, rejected this emphasis on intellect, law-and-order, repression and self-abnegation: instead he advocated the liberality and passion and loving lawlessness that in England had been proclaimed most memorably by William Blake.

Shaw consciously offers a return to the Socratic idea of an abstract, heavenly Athens, and Morris intentionally elaborates Blake's New Jerusalem in an England which is green and pleasant again, and wholly immersed in an utterly non-abstract, sensually appreciated, Nature.

When we contrast the utopian visions of these two Victorians, it becomes clear that their differences have nothing to do with rational factors—that they depend not upon any *intellectual* contradiction in the Socialist movement, but upon differences in the authorial dispositions. Political convictions vary as the dispositions of men vary, and British Socialism has from the beginning embraced a wide variety of dispositions. An extraordinary amount of energy was expended by Morris and Shaw and their contemporaries in a desperate attempt to create a united Socialist front, but the attempt failed, as every subsequent attempt has failed. To look closely at the opposition of Morris to Shaw is to see why Socialism can never be united in a stable way, to see why the dream of a whole world as a unified communist community is unrealisable. There may well be as many kinds of Socialism as there are individual Socialists, just as there are perhaps as many kinds of Christianity as there are Christians. In each case— with Socialist conviction every bit as much as with Christian faith—the condition is so complex, so enmeshed with the individual personality, that it cannot be abstracted, or reduced to the formulae of dogma. The ideological aspect of Socialism or of Christianity can be shared by millions, but the more crucial aspects are personal, and must remain individual. Socialist parties, like Christian Churches, can only be rather loose collections of people who are all aware of their being obliged to compromise if they want to belong. There is a great deal of overlapping, but the opposite ends of the Socialist spectrum have very little in common.

William Morris' ideal of Socialism was expressed in most of his work during the last twenty years of his life, but most elaborately in *A Dream of John Ball* and *News from Nowhere*. In these works he portrays an ideal medieval England in a state of communist anarchy, where all potential problems disappear because men and women are free to love one another and themselves: the ideal is individual-orientated, and the concept of the State has been forgotten.

Bernard Shaw's ideal was developed over his unusually long

career as a writer, but it was most clearly set out in his three plays which portray communist utopias: *Back to Methuselah*, 1920; *The Simpleton of the Unexpected Isles*, 1934; and *Farfetched Fables*, 1950. Shaw's ideal solves all potential problems by eliminating all human emotion, and by suppressing all human appetite. His ideal is community-centred, and it is the individual human who disappears, very much as in *The Republic*. Plato puts the central problem in dramatically forceful terms:

> Adeimantus interposed a question: How would you answer, Socrates, said he, if a person were to say that you are making these people miserable ... the city in fact belongs to them, but they are none the better for it; they are no better than mercenaries who are quartered in the city and are always mounting guard?
> Our aim in founding the State was not the disproportionate happiness of any one class, but the greatest happiness of the whole. ... And so I say to you, do not compel us to assign to the guardians a sort of happiness which will make them anything but guardians, or clothe our husbandmen in royal apparel, and set crowns of gold on their heads, and bid them till the ground as much as they like, and no more. Our potters also might be allowed to repose on couches, and feast by the fireside, passing round the wine-cup, while their wheel is conveniently at hand, and working at pottery only as much as they like; in this way we might make every class happy—and then, as you imagine, the whole State would be happy. But do not put this idea into our heads; for, if we listen to you, the husbandman will no longer be a husbandman, the potter will cease to be a potter, and no one will have the character of any distinct class in the State. We mean our guardians to be saviours of the State.[8]

In theoretical and in practical politics, there is one basic question from which all the others derive—are we to think of the well-being and happiness of the individual citizens, or are we to think only of the security, efficiency and stability of the State? Plato and Shaw, in talking about their ideal systems, are very explicit about their own position; communal harmony must depend upon each individual being *moulded* for his social function, and to the extent that the natural impulses of any citizen would lead to an impairment of his functional efficiency, those impulses must be thwarted. The terms 'happiness' and 'fulfilment' are used only with regard to the community *as an idea*. Individual happiness or satisfaction must be subordinated to the concept of 'the general good'.

Plato and Shaw, in fact, imagine an ideal state where the perfection of life depends, not upon the realisation of all human goals, but upon the repression of the basic human instincts, desires, and appetites. This conviction—that only rigorous repression will lead to genuine happiness—is so ubiquitous in modern political thought because (through Plato) it is a central element of our Hellenic as well as of our Hebraic inheritance. Robert Owen held the conviction firmly during his experiment in New Lanark, and acted upon it with unusual efficiency: industrialists who came to visit were always impressed by the successful war Owen was waging against sin among his workers: by imposing fines, and by employing various kinds of moral blackmail, he claimed to have reduced the number of illegitimate births and the amount of heavy drinking, and automatically increased his workers' efficiency *as workers*. Socrates and Shaw would have applauded the whole endeavour whole-heartedly; but Owen himself was to drift away from his early, repressive approach, and looking back to the New Lanark experiment he was to speak with sadness, and some shame:

> The people were slaves at my mercy; liable at any time to be dismissed; and knowing that, in that case, they must go into misery, compared with such limited happiness as they now enjoyed.[9]

Like so many Socialist leaders in Eastern Europe today, Robert Owen in his New Lanark days was sincere in his commitment to the idea of his people having 'limited happiness' through partial slavery. For the Victorians, perhaps even more than for others, the essence of a political disposition was most clearly revealed in its attitude to the sexual lives of the citizens. John Stuart Mill seized on the political importance of one of Owen's remarks about sexual morality:

> Robert Owen's definitions of chastity & prostitution (*Chastity, sexual intercourse with affection. Prostitution, sexual intercourse without affection*) . . . take as firm a hold of the mind as the vulgar ones which connect the ideas of virtue & vice with the performance or non-performance of an arbitrary ceremonial.[10]

Socrates and Shaw restrict sex and—if their ideal can be achieved—they abolish it. To the extent that sex is allowed, of necessity, to take place, it must be kept scientifically efficient; it is something one does as a duty to the community, in the interests of 'the general good'; all personal involvement, all affection must be excluded. Robert Owen's definitions point to the heart of the distinction between Shaw and Morris. When Owen punished fornication in New Lanark, he was a Socialist close to Shaw's heart. But his definition of chastity as sexual intercourse *with* affection, and prostitution as sexual intercourse without affection was to become one of the major tenets of the Socialism of William Morris.[11] I shall be contrasting Shaw and Morris in simplified black-and-white terms, but Robert Owen, in the inconsistency of his attitudes to the main issues, is more typical of the mixed nature of the average Socialist position; a mixture of puritan zeal and free-thinking tolerance, intellectual disciplinarianism and sentimental liberalism: Morris and Shaw have paradigmatic functions for British Socialism because they represent, in unusually clear terms, constant opposing elements in the ethos of Socialism.

William Blake was the genius who, for the nineteenth century, most forcefully expressed the case against rationalism, organisation, efficiency, repression, and a community-centred, meritocratic Socialism; and he was most violent in his dismissal of the abstract concept of 'the general good':

> He who would do good to another must do it in Minute Particulars:
> General Good is the plea of the scoundrel, hypocrite & flatterer,
> For Art & Science cannot exist but in minutely organized Particulars
> And not in generalizing Demonstrations of the Rational Power. . .
> . . . O Reasoners of Albion![12]

Socrates thought of the State as being the only meaningful unit, and he set out to repress any existence an individual might have apart from his social function—the farm-labourer must live *in order to* labour on his farm; the potter must not think of himself as having a level of existence separate from the one in which he compulsively makes pots according to a grand social scheme that the individual need not understand and must not question.

The issue, at first glance unimportant, of what kind of clothing each citizen should wear, is in fact at the heart of the matter. Socrates insists that to allow a worker to clothe himself in finery would be disastrous to the harmony of the State. Shaw's utopians are stripped as naked of clothes as they are of flesh and blood and appetites. Socrates and Shaw are very shrewdly aware of the psychology of clothing, and for the same reason William Morris dresses his dustman in the 'royal apparel' that Socrates feared might turn his husbandman to rebellion:

> I looked over my shoulder, and saw something flash and gleam in the sunlight that lay across the hall; so I turned round, and at my ease saw a splendid figure slowly sauntering over the pavement; a man whose surcoat was embroidered most copiously as well as elegantly, so that the sun flashed back from him as if he had been clad in golden armour. ... I thought that this Mr Boffin, in spite of his well-known name out of Dickens, must be at least a senator of these strange people. ... Dick laughed, 'Yes, yes,' said he, 'I see you take the allusion. Of course his real name is not Boffin: ... we only call him Boffin as a joke, partly because he is a dustman, and partly because he will dress so showily, and get as much gold on him as a baron of the Middle Ages. As why should he not if he likes?'[13]

Morris wants a society where a dustman may be mistaken for a senator—a society, that is, where no individual becomes identified with his function, where there is a firm recognition that each individual is an integral unit in himself, and has an identity which, on one level, is independent of his relationships with other individuals or with the State. For Socrates and Shaw, the individual must be neutralised and subjected to classification for the convenience of the community. For Blake and Morris, human beings are not suitable material for such classification, and can be categorised only through a destructive process of cramping, and stretching and amputation, and betrayal of their most valuable quality—their unique individuality. For the meritocrats, Socrates and Shaw, men must be bred, and trained, and ruthlessly *moulded* for their roles in society, and no job, least of all the job of governing, should be entrusted to an amateur. For Blake and Morris, all men should think of themselves as being 'amateurs', for no job should be allowed to become a man's definition. For Socrates and for Shaw the existence and the essence of an individual citizen are co-extensive, and they are to be defined by his function. For Blake and Morris, existence precedes essence, and the individual's first duty is to determine his own essence, to realise himself:

> "Know thyself!" was written over the portal of the antique world. Over the portal of the new world, "Be thyself" shall be written. And the message of Christ to man was simply "Be thyself". That is the secret of Christ.

This is Oscar Wilde *(The Soul of Man under Socialism)* characteristically, putting the point in dubious terms, but whether or not 'Be thyself' is in fact the secret of Christ, it was certainly the slogan of the strain of British Socialism represented most vigorously for the Victorians by William Morris.

In political terms we have a contrast between Socialist totalitarianism, based exclusively on intellect and efficiency, and Socialist anarchy based on sentiment and individual fulfilment. A good many general ideas are held in common, but the different dispositions of the writers have led to extreme divergence of effect. What Morris and Shaw reveal, in fact, is an ambivalence which has characterised Socialism from the beginning to the present day. The word 'socialism' was first used consistently in the 1830s, and it soon became fixed to the Owenites—it was used to mean the opposite of 'self-seeking', the opposite of 'self-interest', the opposite of 'self-centredness'. The great appeal of Socialism was in its offer of an alternative to the individualism which had proved so rapacious and destructive in the long initial phase of machine-capitalism. Of the qualities which Morris and Shaw hated in the life of Victorian England, the most odious of all was selfish competitiveness. In 'Art Under Plutocracy', for example, Morris speaks of the progress of Socialism as being opposed by 'men whose apparent self-interest binds them', and he finally equates Socialism with all that is fine in humanity: 'I hold that the condition of competition between man and man is bestial only and that of association human'. Bernard Shaw, in his prefaces, articles, letters, and hundreds of public speeches, used the same vocabulary for the same purpose of vilifying Victorian capitalism—with the bitterest irony he poured contempt on the ideal of 'Free Competition' based on supposed self-interest.

The one basic point about which all Socialists agreed was their opposition to the image of a society where it was every man selfishly for himself. But of course there have always been two distinct and opposite ways of being unselfish. One is to love one's neighbour as oneself, and the other extreme is to hate oneself, or part of oneself, as one hates the Devil. Loving altruism, or self-disgust; universal benevolence, or self-repression; Eros against decay, as Norman Brown puts it in his study of the permanent conflict; Life against Death.[14] These are the two faces of Socialism; there has always been this same human paradox in Socialism that also characterised Christianity and the other great idealistic movements.

Christianity, of course, was the movement which dominated all Socialist thinking in the nineteenth century. Owen, Morris, and Shaw could be quite violent in their anti-Christian polemics, but they turned automatically to the Christian tradition as a source of metaphor and example: they spoke of great Socialists as being 'saints' of the new, and true, religion, but these saints were no more homogeneous than the Christian saints had been. The paths to a sanctified life vary as the dispositions of men vary. In Christianity there were the saints who loved everything in God's creation, and there were the saints who mutilated their bodies in self-hatred. St Francis of Assissi loved the birds, the flowers, the worms, and even the stones; and St Simeon Stylites taught his followers that true human happiness could be achieved only through continuous denial, fasting, self-abnegation, and mortification of the flesh. Where Francis taught love for all living things, Simeon taught withdrawal, suppression, contempt for man's individuality, and a bitter loathing of man's physical existence.

They are both pillars of the Church, and they represent permanent, though opposite, human impulses. Francis in his affectionate innocence was a walking token of what Jesus put very directly: 'Whoever shall not receive the kingdom of God as a little child shall in no wise enter therein'. Simeon, on the other hand, was a walking token of an equally orthodox Christian impulse, for St Paul has always been as influential as Jesus in the formation of Christian attitudes, and Paul obviously sees children as being ignorant, unruly brats who must be thwarted and reformed until they put away childish things and become men, who must also in their turn be thwarted and reformed. Where Jesus is nearly always advocating love, Paul for most of the time is deprecating sin. St Simeon was very Pauline in that he was much possessed by thoughts of death and by impatient longing for his own death. St Francis was Christ-like in his adoration of life, even in the meanest of living things. The attitude to qualities of childhood is most indicative, and whereas Jesus delights in the innocence and vitality of childhood, Paul demands reverence for the quiet wisdom of old age. In a passage of seminal importance for the entire Millennialist-Utopian movement,

God reveals to St John the Divine the crucial duality of His own essence. St John had a vision of the end of the thousand years:

> And I saw a new heaven and a new earth, ... And I John saw the holy city, new Jerusalem, coming down from God out of heaven ... And he said unto me, It is done. I am Alpha and Omega, the beginning and the end.[15]

Francis and Simeon approached God in opposite directions, but to similar effect, for God was to be found in both directions. These two saints figured large in the consciousness of literary men in the Victorian period and when they were invoked, as by Tennyson for example, it was for their relevance to nineteenth-century England. Tennyson's St Simeon Stylites is presented as an awful image of withdrawal and solitary suffering (conditions of potentially fatal attraction to the poet himself) carried to their inevitable conclusion in morbid disease:

> Who may be saved? who is it may be saved?
> Who may be made a saint, if I fail here?
> Show me the man hath suffered more than I.
> ...   I die here
> Today, and whole years long, a life of death.
> Bear witness, if I could have found a way
> (And heedfully I sifted all my thought)
> More slowly-painful to subdue this home
> Of sin, my flesh, which I despise and hate.

Tennyson's Francis is the saint whom Victorian poets and thinkers held in greatest veneration:

> Are we devils? are we men?
> Sweet St Francis of Assisi, would that he were here again,
> He that in his Catholic wholeness used to call the very flowers
> Sisters, brothers—and the beasts—whose pains are hardly less than
> ours![16]

John Ruskin spoke of St Francis as having inspired all that was best in European painting, and as being the force behind the innovating genius of English Romanticism:

> It is good to read of that kindness and humbleness of St Francis of Assisi, who spoke never to bird nor cicala, nor even to wolf

and beast of prey, but as his brother; and so we find are moved the minds of all good and mighty men, as in the lesson that we have from the Mariner of Coleridge, and yet more truly and rightly taught in the Hartleap Well, ... and again in the White Doe of Rylstone.[17]

St Francis was taken up as a symbolic champion by the line of English Romantic writers with whom Morris identified. St Francis was for Wordsworth, Coleridge, Ruskin, Tennyson and their admirers, the image of the redeemer who would come to rescue England from the heartlessness and horror of the age. He would teach Englishmen what he had taught his fellow-Italians in the thirteenth century—to love the birds, and the flowers, and one another, and themselves. When William Morris and Burne Jones gave up the idea of entering the priesthood, it was only so that they might fight the same campaign in secular terms—it was still to be a 'crusade against the heartless coldness of the times'.[18] St Francis was the saint of love for them, and his antipode was St Simeon, the saint of solitude, and suffering, and death.

Like all good Christians, and all good Socialists, both Francis and Simeon stood for *selflessness*. Francis loved all of God's creation before himself; in fact he could love himself only *through* his love for others. Simeon was self-less in the sense that he obliterated his own personality and worked for his own physical destruction. Christianity could embrace these extraordinary opposites, and in this, as in so many other respects, Socialism is the legitimate heir of Christianity.

Their contrasting Socialist utopias reveal that Morris was working with the nineteenth-century image of St Francis in mind, and that Shaw was in some respects the St Simeon of Victorian socialism. They can each be taken to represent extreme points in the scale on which we all take moving positions.

In whatever ways we differ in evaluating the lives we find ourselves living, we are all of the opinion that life is just not good enough. Human dissatisfaction with life is constant; it seems that as a species we are born with an incurable distaste for the present. Christianity and Socialism are entirely motivated by—and are elaborate, formalised statements of—our dissatisfaction with human life. In whatever terms we express this dissatisfaction, there are only two directions in which we can turn for comfort. From the unacceptable present we can run backwards or forwards; backward towards childhood and beyond, or forward towards death, and beyond death. God is Alpha and Omega, and for societies, *or for individuals*, paradise lies back beyond the beginning of life, or forward beyond the end.

Christianity had the first paradise in Eden, and the second paradise of the millennium; the good Socialist society was either to be a return, in Morris's words, to the primitive communism which preceded civilisation, or it was to be, as in Shaw's utopian plays, a new heaven into which civilisation must *wither*. In personal terms—to use the most hackneyed lines from two poets who were influential in the development of social thinking among the Victorian literati—the individual must direct his longings either to that heaven from which we come trailing clouds of glory, or to that easeful death, with which Keats was rather *more* than half in love.

Like so many artists in the nineteenth century, Morris followed Blake in choosing to run backwards—his utopias return England to an idealised Middle Ages, and in personal terms they return Morris to a land of idealised youthfulness, where all the inhabitants are free of the restrictions of adult morality. In *News from Nowhere* the inhabitants are called Youngsters and they live a carefree, childlike life, characterised by what Freud was later to call polymorphous perversity: their senses are freshly sharp, and are freely gratified with no suggestion of guilt. They do not read books, and they have no reverence for abstract knowledge or abstract thought. There is no educational system to suppress their individuality; there is no marriage to entrap them.

Shaw went forward from the present; his utopia is placed in the future 'as far as thought can reach', and his ideal men are called Ancients. Not only are their senses obliterated, but the ideal aspires to the disappearance of human physical existence; men are to become wholly abstract, etherialised forms in a whirlwind of pure thought.

Both Morris and Shaw introduce contemporary human beings into their paradise, so that the contrast will underline the utopian qualities. Morris's narrator in *News from Nowhere* is aware of being, in comparison, old and clumsy, and inhibited, and perverted by his artificial learning as much as by his money-orientation. His hosts are young and lovely and sensuous: they are generous with their possessions and with themselves. They have no sense of economy—they spend freely with no thought for tomorrow. Their bliss is child-like: 'Let us rejoice', they say, 'that we have got back our childhood again'.[19]

Shaw introduces contemporary men into the last part of *Back to Methuselah* in order to contrast them with his Ancients. They are, in comparison, crudely childish, irrational and tedious. The words used to describe them are those Swift used for his Yahoos—they are 'loathsome', 'disgusting' and 'dangerous'. The Ancients neither eat nor, perhaps thanks to Swift, do they excrete. They do not have sex; they are, like Shaw, the opposite of spendthrifts. They live by Shaw's credo that self-control and self-conservation are the highest human qualities. Shaw's most important concept is that of Vital Economy and John Tanner tells us for Shaw that: 'Political Economy and Social Economy are amusing intellectual games; but Vital Economy is the Philosopher's stone'. Shaw's Ancients are as mean with themselves as Morris's Youngsters are generous. The Ancients, like Shaw, loathe the idea of 'spending'; and here, as always in the work of any writer brought up in Victorian England, the pun on the word 'spend' is meaningfully rich. Sexual energy is being sublimated into abstract rational energy. Shaw claimed that *Back to Methuselah* is the longest and the best play ever written (an excellent example of Shaw's command of the half-truth) and its final scene is given over to explicit repetitions of his Platonic sermon:

> *Martellus*: The body always ends by being a bore. Nothing remains beautiful and interesting except thought, because the thought is the life.
>
> . . .
>
> *She-Ancient*: The body was the slave . . . but the slave has become the master; and we must free ourselves from that tyranny. It is this stuff (indicating her body) this flesh and blood and bone and all the rest of it, that is intolerable.
>
> . . .
>
> *Lilith*: They have redeemed themselves from their vileness, and turned away from their sins. Best of all, they are still not satisfied . . . after passing a million goals they press on to the goal of redemption from the flesh, to the vortex freed from matter, to the whirlpool in pure intelligence that, when the world began, was a whirlpool in pure force . . . I will not supersede them until they have . . . disentangled their life from the matter that has always mocked it.[20]

Against this tradition of European thought, Blake expressed his revulsion with equal vehemence: 'Damn braces. Bless relaxes'. 'The road of excess leads to the palace of wisdom'. 'Prudence is a rich, ugly, old maid courted by Incapacity'.[21] As Blake opposes Plato, and as Francis stands as a balance to the excesses of Simeon, William Morris enlivens the aridity and sterility of Shaw's final vision of Socialist utopia. Blake and St Francis in their most innocent, childlike, moments of universal love could pass among Morris's Youngsters. Neither Plato in his most ethereal communion with ideal forms, nor St Simeon on his highest pillar, was further removed from common humanity than Shaw's Ancients.

These two faces of Victorian Socialism are aspects of the two faces of the human species. To contrast Morris' Socialism with Shaw's is to remind oneself that our species, individually or collectively, is torn constantly in two opposite directions; by the pleasure principle, and by the repressive impulse.

A good deal has been written about the intellectual affinities and the ideological links between Morris and Shaw. But it is useful to remark that their different psychological makeup led them to spell out in detail such very different socialist utopias, and it is necessary to see that to minimise the great differences between the politics of Morris and Shaw is to reduce Socialism to the level of superficial slogans to be used for electioneering. We shall not understand the Socialism of Owen, Morris, Shaw, or their nineteenth-century confreres if we refuse to take them seriously when they speak about the *religion* of Socialism.

Notes to this chapter are on pages 234-5

LAND REFORM AND CLASS CONFLICT IN VICTORIAN BRITAIN

H. J. Perkin

DISRAELI TOLD the House of Lords in 1880: 'If I were asked to mention the two subjects which most occupy the thought of the country at the present moment, I should say one was the government of Ireland, and the other the principles upon which the landed property of this country should continue to be established'; and he reminded them of his 'conviction—and it is a profound conviction—that the politics of this country, so far as internal affairs are concerned, will probably, for the next few years, mainly consist in an assault upon the constitutional position of the landed interest'.[1] After the renewed agrarian violence of the previous winter, Ireland's troubles were manifest, but it would have been beyond even Disraeli's political prescience to have foreseen the campaigns of Henry George or the burgeoning of the Socialist societies of the eighties. He was merely expressing a feeling widespread at the time that a crisis was impending in 'the land question' which would not be confined to Ireland. The *Manchester Guardian* talked of 'the prominent position which the land question has now reached', and prophesied that 'the stirring of the national mind which is already visible on this subject will before long translate itself into a call for action'.[2] *The Times* observed, 'Among the many questions with which the Liberal Government will have to deal in the new Parliament, those connected with land are by far the most important', and

M

advised extreme caution.[3] Gladstone, with that enigmatic waywardness which at once encouraged and confused his followers, had declared that the State was in principle perfectly entitled to buy out the landowners if it became expedient to do so.[4] Bright, whose venerable elder statesmanship no one could call revolutionary, told his Birmingham constituents that 'the time is near in my opinion when the great landed monopoly of this country will be assailed, and when it will be broken into and broken up'.[5]

The prospect of a general attack on the land system induced what Justin McCarthy called 'the landowners' panic'[6]—the first of the resignations which would eventually carry most of the Whigs out of the Liberal into the Conservative party. It was not so much 'land quacks', in Lord Derby's phrase, that they feared. Land nationalisation had been advocated for a hundred years, from Thomas Spence to Herbert Spencer, without result, and Henry George had not yet crossed the Atlantic. Rather was it 'a new thing, and one of much significance . . . that thoughtful men and good citizens see much to be amended in the land laws'.[7] The danger lay in the appeal of land reform to classes already well-represented in the Commons, amongst whom there were many who looked forward with enthusiasm to alterations in the land laws which they believed would produce far-reaching changes in the distribution of property, and therefore in the structure of society. The Lords, under Disraeli's strategical direction, prepared to choose the least unpopular ground on which to meet the challenge of the Commons.

In the event, of course, nothing came of it. Apart from the legislative spring-cleaning of 1925, designed to adapt the forms of land law to the realities of land-ownership, there has never been a fundamental reform of the land system.[8] The collision between Lords and Commons—expected for a further five or six years—was averted by the break-up not of the 'landed monopoly' but of the Liberal party over Irish Home

Rule. The land reformer who said that 'the people of this country can only grasp one, what may be called first-class, political question at a time',[9] backed the wrong one. The importunate irrelevance of Home Rule dragged the Radicals and land reformers from the high road just as their Canaan came in sight, to pass another generation in the wilderness. By then it was too late. Yet the land reform agitation deserves a place in history larger than the footnote it is usually accorded. It is the aim of this chapter to claim for it a place nearer to the centre of the socio-political development of Victorian Britain and to discover what light it can throw into the fog which still clings around two of its major themes, the relations between the aristocracy and the middle classes, and the fission and incipient decline of the Liberal party.

I

What were the reasons for the impending crisis in the land question in 1880? No doubt the example of Ireland and the 'great depression' helped to precipitate it. The Irish question was pre-eminently one of land, and Cobden had prophesied that the end of prosperity would revive discontent with the land system in Britain. The landlord made an accessible scapegoat, but though they gave the opportunity and provided some of the steam, Ireland and the depression were not the main drive behind the agitation. The main drive must be sought, where it has traditionally been found, in the hostility of the middle classes towards the landed aristocracy. The clash of interests between landlord and manufacturer was as familiar to Disraeli, Carlyle, Roebuck and their contemporaries as it is to the historian.[10] They saw its influence in all the political battles of a restlessly legislative age. The most celebrated actions were fought over the corn laws and factory reform, but the skirmishing can be followed, under their own banners or those of Church and Dissent, through the struggles over parliamentary reform, taxation policy, education, Church establishment, tithes, game laws, reform of the civil service, the universities and the army, and even rural squalor and the health of towns. Since every one of these touched on the land question or the influence of landowners, the land question was permanently in the field and might at any time become the centre of the battle. That it should do so around 1880 could be explained by the growth of urban democracy and the need of the middle classes for a louder drum to recruit the new electors. Its failure could equally be explained by the reluctance of the working-class voter to distinguish between landlord and capitalist, and the consequent abandonment of the attempt.

This has been the traditional view of both orthodox and Marxist historians; the land reform movement was an aspect —since it failed, an unimportant aspect—of the conflict between land and capital. As long as the conflict lasted, that is, until the rise of a politically aggressive proletarian movement forced land and capital into defensive alliance, land reform was charged with life and power. When the conflict ceased, land reform atrophied. For the traditional orthodox view, here is C. R. Fay: 'The thing of which John Bright was persuaded, that landlordism is the common foe, was tenable only in the days of Bright. It was impossible in the days of Thomas Spence; for industrialism was then too young to be self-conscious. It was impossible in the days of Henry George; for by then socialism had passed beyond land reform altogether.'[11] For the traditional Marxist view, here is Marx himself: 'The whole thing [all land reform since Baron Colins] is ... simply a socialistically decked-out attempt to save capitalist rule and actually re-establish it on an even wider basis than its present one'.[12]

The main difficulty about both these views is their conception of the middle class as a monolithic grouping around the capitalist manufacturers and merchants. This it was not. No class is monolithic in its reactions. The Victorian middle class was less monolithic than most, partly because many of its members were tied by birth, marriage or friendship to the landowning class, partly because many of them looked forward to acquiring estates and becoming themselves landowners, most of all because it was not one class but several. The assumption that the new, raw capitalists of the Industrial Revolution were the true middle class, and that all the rest were a *petite bourgeoisie* trailing along in their wake, lies behind both traditional views. Against it may be set the existence of two influential groups which originated and directed middle-class opinion quite as much as they. The first was a group of businessmen who belonged to an older and less radical commercial world—old-established merchants, especially in the East and West India trades, bankers, brewers, even some manufacturers. Superficially their incomes were of the same type as those of the newer capitalists, but, even before the spread of the industrial company, tended to be more stable, to give their earners more leisure, and to approximate more and more closely to the character of interest. Such men felt a close affinity with the *rentier* and the landlord, and could not be stirred into specious activity against them. Some of them, like most merchants of Liverpool and certain West Riding manufacturers, had a longstanding sympathy with the Tories, and though the rest mainly supported the Liberals, they were as a group a conservative rather than a radical force in politics. They were, moreover, a group which in the economic nature of things was bound to grow, since the development of larger units and the spread of the public company favoured the type of businessman whose income contained an apparently unearned element, as against the owner-manager. They were a nucleus around which middle-class conservatism could grow.

The other group was the professional class, a class which, though neglected by historians, has had an influence on the development of the last hundred years out of proportion to its numbers. The neglect is explained by the great diversity of social origin, family connection and political allegiance to be found amongst professional men. This in turn was reinforced by the peculiarity of their economic interest, which enabled them with greater ease to take up a wide variety of 'progressive' or 'advanced' political attitudes. It will be found that much in Victorian middle-class opinion which has been attributed to the industrialists was due to, or more consistently pursued by, professional men. In particular, they played a leading part in the later stages of the land reform agitation which goes far towards explaining its character, its temporary success, and its ultimate failure.

It is hoped that a study of the land reform movement will show how, beginning as a manifestation of general middle-class hostility, it became the catalyst which helped to resolve the middle class into its elements, and to unite a large part of the business class in a new combination with the landowners. Far from being a stratagem which the capitalists abandoned with reluctance when forced into alliance with the landlords, land reform was one of the most important factors alienating them from the Liberal party. It was not socialism so much as capitalism itself which by the 1880s had passed beyond land reform altogether.

II

The hostility of a large part of the middle class towards the landowners was for most of the century real enough. The myth of middle-class rule had no foundation in contemporary middle-class opinion. The *Westminster Review*, observing in 1833 that 'the landed interest must always exercise great sway in public affairs, for that class alone have much leisure to meddle in them', had called the Reform Act 'an unreal mockery, if the power of the wealthy landowners be not clipped by depriving them of the means of living upon the public wealth'.[13] John Bright told the Commons in 1848: 'This House and the other House of Parliament are almost exclusively aristocratic in their character. The administration is therefore necessarily the same, and on the Treasury Board aristocracy reigns supreme'.[14] John Stuart Mill noted in 1871 that 'the landlords, and those who looked forward to being landlords, have had the command of Parliament up to the last Reform Act, and still wield enormous power'.[15] At all three dates the middle class was vociferously aware that the landowners were the ruling class, and most of them deplored it.

At the heart of their hostility lay the denial of the economic necessity of the landowning class. Brought up on the gospel of work and the horror of waste common to the Evangelical and the Benthamite, they could not separate unearned luxury from the idea of sin. It was the idleness rather than the wealth of the 'lounging class' that offended them.[16] 'We are literally nearly all workers,' boasted Edmund Potter, the world's leading calico-printer, of his little Pennine town, 'we have scarcely a resident amongst us living on independent means—leading a strictly idle life'.[17]

Capitalists worked, landlords did not. Chamberlain's jibe at those 'who toil not, neither do they spin' was the common coin of the age.[18] The classical economists from Adam Smith onwards—themselves professional men—have been accused of indecently exposing the landowners to the charge of uselessness. By drawing an arbitrary line between rent and profit, they justified middle-class prejudice against the 'land monopoly'. 'Wages and profit,' wrote Nassau Senior, 'are the creation of man. They are the sacrifice made, in the one case of ease; in the other, of immediate enjoyment. But a considerable part of the produce of every country is the recompense of no sacrifice whatever; is received by those who neither labour nor put by, but merely hold out their hands to accept the offerings of the rest of the community.'[19] In the unflattering role they gave the landowner the economists were merely expressing the instinctive opinion of the middle class. The typical landowner had inherited his estate. The typical capitalist, before the days of large unearned incomes from industrial shares, was the active entrepreneur without whose skill and energy, profit, rent and wages would all cease. Like the professional man, he did not need abstruse reasoning from the labour theory of value to convince him that he was contributing much to society, the landowner little. He knew that idleness for him meant bankruptcy, for the landowner nothing worse than boredom. In this conviction lay the moral superiority of the middle class.

Land reform offered the middle class the opportunity of prosecuting their hostility to the extreme point of abolishing the landowners as a class. Whereas the other reforms—parliamentary, fiscal, administrative, educational, ecclesiastical— aimed at the superstructure of aristocratic power and privilege, land reform aimed at the foundations, at the great estates themselves. Break up the great estates, the argument ran, and the whole edifice of idle wealth and luxurious privilege would crumble away. This was the test of how far hostility was prepared to go. Though the middle class might agree that the power of the landed class ought to be diminished, they were not unanimous in seeking its liquidation. Rather were they deeply divided, between those, a small minority, who prescribed for the great estates a swift death, painless or otherwise; those who wished to remove all the obstructions to a gradual death from natural causes; and those who, though often hostile to landed pretensions, did not wish them to die at all. The land question became critical because it appealed to the deeply rooted prejudices of the middle class. It failed to achieve political effect because the only practical programme of reform to achieve wide popularity, 'free trade in land', was one which promised, what it could doubtfully perform, the silent and painless erosion of the great estates.

III

What all land reformers, and indeed most of the middle class, could agree on was simple enough: land had got into too few hands. How few was not at first clear. The figure of 30,000 landowners given currency by the 1861 Census of England and Wales was patently wrong, if only because more than half of these were women. It was to scotch this absurdity and quieten the 'great outcry raised about what was called the monopoly of land' that Lord Derby called in the House of Lords in 1872 for the returns which came to be known as the New Domesday Book. They showed that there were rather more than a million proprietors in the British Isles (excluding the metropolis) of which about 300,000 owned more than one acre.[20] Low as these figures were compared with most European countries,[21] reformers were not convinced. They examined the returns, which had been prepared on a county basis by the poor law officials of the Local Government Board, and found them to be full of errors and duplications, a landowner being counted as many times as he held estates in different counties, and as many times in the same county as the officials knew him under different spellings of his name. Thus the Duke of Buccleugh counted as 14, 28 dukes as 158, and 525 peers as more than 1,500 owners.[22] Reformers therefore published their own estimates, deducting for errors, duplications, corporate owners, glebe lands and charities and favoured a figure of less than 200,000 individual owners of 1 acre or more. Even this, they claimed, understated the case, for it included large numbers of small, non-agricultural properties on the outskirts of towns. Sir Arthur Arnold calculated that 7,000 persons owned four-fifths of the United Kingdom, while G. C. Brodrick estimated that 4,000 proprietors of 1,000 acres or more owned more than one half of England and Wales, and that nearly half the enclosed land was held by an aristocracy of only 2,250 families.[23] Whatever the figures, Britain compared with most parts of the Continent was a country of large estates where, except in isolated pockets like Cumberland and the Isle of Axholme, peasant proprietors were practically non-existent.

The concentration of property, it was asserted, was not fortuitous. 'The means by which large masses of property have been acquired in this world are principally two, force and fraud', the *Westminster Review* had declared in 1844.[24] Just as seventeenth-century Parliamentarians used history as a weapon against the Crown, so nineteenth-century land reformers used it against the landlords. The peers and squires, they asserted, had once been mere tenants of the land, in which their royal overlord and the cultivating sub-tenants had enjoyed valuable concurrent rights. By a long and nefarious process they had turned lordship into ownership, and deprived both king and peasants of their rights. Feudal dues, the king's immemorial rent-charge in the land and the main source of taxation, had been systematically evaded over centuries and finally abolished between 1645 and 1660. 12 Charles II, c 24, the statute by which feudal tenures had been turned into freehold, and vestigial feudal incidents exchanged for an excise on beer paid chiefly by the non-landed, became for reformers the symbol of the iniquity of landowners. The wrong had been aggravated by 'the great land tax fraud' by which, as Cobden put it, the people had been 'cheated, robbed and bamboozled upon the subject of taxation'.[25] On this view, the needs of war had in 1692 forced Parliament to restore the old burden in the shape of the four-shilling land tax. This in its turn had been evaded by legislative trickery and administrative chicanery until, instead of meeting most of the needs of the State, it bore a mere 4 per cent of its expenses.[26]

The peasants had been robbed by a parallel process. They had first had their ties with the soil loosened by the substitution of a spurious commercial freedom for the security of manorial custom. Then, when economic conditions were favourable, they were driven out by enclosures and the throwing together of farms, for wool at one period, corn at another. Thus had the English peasantry been divorced from the soil and millions of acres 'taken from the public property of the poor and added to the private property of the rich'.[27]

It was also agreed that the evils resulting from the mal-distribution of land reached far beyond those immediately involved in its cultivation. 'The land laws of this country', wrote James Beal, the Radical estate-agent, 'are at once the root, the cause and the protector of the greatest social evils with which we are afflicted, and demand, far more than the Corn Laws, a public agitation in favour of their abolition.'[28] The least of these evils was the undermining of the family life and parental authority of the landowners themselves by the practice of settling the estate upon an unborn eldest son. The heir was tempted into extravagance and debt,[29] whilst the younger sons were either turned out to make their own living or provided for by the patronage system. As the veteran free trader, Colonel T. P. Thompson, put it,

> This is clearly the end and the aim of primogeniture, that £10,000 a year is to be concentrated in the hands of the eldest son, that it may act as a battering-ram for procuring £1,000 a year for each of the others . . . by entry into the public pantry, and appropriation of the victuals that is [sic] therein.[30]

The political and economic consequences were equally deplorable. In spite of two Reform Acts, the Ballot Act, and the reform of the civil service, Lord Derby in 1881 could still place political influence first amongst 'the objects which men aim at when they become possessors of land', and 'the money return' last of all.[31] It was still widely believed that bribery, tenant-bullying and place-hunting were the characteristic contributions of the landed interest to political life. The economic grievance lay in the indebtedness of the large estates and their alleged failure to improve agriculture. The Earls of Derby and Leicester were quoted to show that food production could be vastly increased. The land was allegedly undercapitalised since it was in no-one's interest to invest in it: not the landlord's, since under the settlement system he was a mere life-owner without the means or the motive to improve; nor the tenant's, since outside Scotland few had even the limited security of a long lease. and to improve was to invite a rise in rent. It was admitted that some settlements provided exceptional powers to lease and mortgage, and that in 1856 and 1877 Parliament had (subject to Chancery control) enlarged the powers and lightened the burdens of limited owners. But the reformers' logic was inexorable: in spite of the Settled Estates Acts, in spite of those 'eleemosynary statutes' the Drainage Acts (by which, it was said, a landlord could get the State and the tenant to improve his land, and make a profit out of the transaction), the land had not been improved.[32] As long as settlement remained, the needs of landowners' families would come before those of agriculture.

Most grievous of all were the social consequences. There was scarcely a social problem, from rural hovels and village pauperism to the slums, drunkenness and moral degradation of town life, which reformers did not place at the landlords' door. The landlords had divorced the people from the soil, and therefore they were responsible for the consequences: the loss of prosperity and self-respect, the dependence on an insecure wage, the lack of steps in the form of allotments and smallholdings by which the landless man could climb to a farm, and 'all the vast and unnumbered social sores connected with pauperism and rural degradation'.[33] Reformers were willing to except 'the *noblesse oblige* sort of property' and to agree that the worst slums were owned by small rather than large landlords. It was the system itself they attacked.

Finally, it was agreed that the need for reform was urgent. The maldistribution of land was, they believed, rapidly worsening, and the process of squeezing out the small owner accelerating. The growth of industry, commerce and population was inflating rents and with them the landlords' share of the nation's income. Unless the trend was reversed and the land more evenly distributed, nothing could prevent the landlords from achieving a stranglehold on the community.

IV

On the diagnosis and prognosis of the disease all land reformers could agree. On the remedy there was the most profound disagreement which extended to the heart of the question, the principle of property itself. There was an unbridgeable cleavage between the minority who favoured some form of public ownership of land or rent, and the majority who clung to the principle of private property. Though there were schemes, such as Mill's for taxation of the unearned increment of rent or Chamberlain's piecemeal municipalisation,[34] which aimed to attract both, they served rather to convince opponents of the dangerous connection between all land reform than to unite reformers. Nor was there much more agreement amongst those who favoured public ownership. They were divided into fragmentary groups seeking nationalisation, municipalisation, or the appropriation of rent: nationalisation with or without compensation, at once or by stages lasting up to a century, of land alone with or without the 'improvements', or of land, mines, railways, and even indeed all the means of production—for at this point land reform shaded into Socialism; municipalisation with voluntary or compulsory purchase; and State appropriation of varying proportions of rent, from the four-shilling tax at valuation, through the unearned increment tax, to complete confiscation.[35] That means divide even more than ends is a commonplace amongst revolutionaries. If Marx rejected land reform as a capitalist deviation, the land nationalisers who followed Alfred Russell Wallace came to reject the Georgist single tax as confiscatory and unjust.[36]

On the other side was a deficiency rather than an embarrassment of means. The end was the replacement of the great estates by a wider distribution of property, ultimately perhaps by a nation of property-owners, home-owners and peasant proprietors. Given the rooted suspicion of State intervention and the firm attachment to private property general amongst the Victorian middle class, how was this end to be achieved? It might be possible to prevent further maldistribution by putting a stop to the enclosing of wastes and commons. Part of the re-awakening of the land agitation in the 1860s was the reaction to the attempts of London landlords to appropriate commons like Hampstead Heath, Clapham and Wandsworth Commons for building development. A public outcry led to the founding of preservation societies, a Select Committee, and to the Metropolitan Commons Act (1866) to prevent further encroachment. A ten-year battle ensued, in and out of the courts, until the veto was in 1876 extended to the rest of the country.[37] But the preservation of commons could not rectify the existing maldistribution. Nor could other schemes do more than mitigate its effects. Tenant right, or compensation for improvements unexhausted when the tenant quit his farm, had been advocated by Philip Pusey from 1847 onwards, and embodied in an ineffective Act (1875) fitted with an escape clause. Moved by the bad harvests of the later seventies and taking advantage of the land agitation, the Farmers' Alliance sprang up in 1879 to demand an effective Act, and got it in 1883.[38]

Leasehold enfranchisement, a movement attracting such diverse figures as Cardinal Manning and the ex-stonemason Henry Broadhurst, aimed at giving the tenant the option of buying the freehold, so as to prevent at the termination of a lease the transfer to the landlord of the tenant's improvements, especially buildings. An association was formed, a Bill sponsored in 1885, and a series of Select Committees on Town Holdings obtained between 1886 and 1892, without legislative result. The complications of the system of building leases, with any number of intermediate lessees between the freeholder and the actual occupier, and the lack of sympathy for a scheme which in the view of other reformers transferred value created by the community from rich landlords to wealthy tenants in the West End of London and elsewhere, were against it.[39] The allotments and smallholdings movement had a wider appeal and a tradition of philanthropic endeavour going back to the 1830s. Jesse Collings' scheme in the 1880s, modelled on the Bright clauses of the Irish Land Act of 1870, proposed to substitute for paternalism State-aided purchase. It was the only sectional scheme offering much hope of substantially modifying the distribution of land but, like the others, it was subordinate to the main movement for land reform, and overlapped it both in aims and personnel.[40]

The only scheme which commanded wide support inside and outside Parliament was one which not only accepted the principle of private property in land but aimed to enhance it. At the same time it offered, without any State intervention beyond a few minor changes in the law, an ultimate redistribution of the land amongst a much larger proportion of the population. This ingenious programme was known as 'free trade in land'.[41] It was the one variety of land reform which attracted supporters from every class, even from amongst the landowners themselves. At no point was it inconsistent with free trade or *laisser-faire*. Indeed, it claimed Cobden's blessing as the essence of free trade applied to the land market. Far from depriving the businessman of his hope of purchasing an estate, it increased that hope by promising to cheapen the cost of acquiring it. Meanwhile, it promised painlessly to break up inefficient and unwieldy estates, and silently to erode the privilege and influence of the large landowners.

How was this paradox to be accomplished? By the abolition of the devices by which, it was claimed, the great estates were artificially held together. John Bright defined free trade in land as follows:

It means the abolition of the law of primogeniture, and the limitation of the system of entails and settlement so that life-interests may be for the most part got rid of, and a real ownership substituted for them. It means also that it shall be as easy to buy and sell land as to buy or sell a ship... It means that no legal encouragement shall be given to great estates and great farms, and that the natural forces of accumulation and dispersion shall have free play, as they have with regard to ships, and shares, and machinery, and stock-in-trade, and money. It means, too, that while the lawyer shall be well paid for his work, unnecessary work shall not be made for him, involving an enormous tax on all transactions in connection with the purchase and sale of land and houses. A thorough reform in this matter would complete, with regard to land, the great work accomplished by the Anti-Corn Law League in 1846.[42]

Primogeniture and entail were more the symbol than the substance of complaint. Few landed estates passed by intestacy, and entail, by which in theory an estate could be made to pass to a long though limited series of life-owners, could be barred by the cheap and foolproof method provided by the Fines and Recoveries Act of 1833. The villain was strict settlement, the device by which, through successive resettlements at the marriage of the eldest son in each generation, an estate could be kept out of the market ostensibly for ever. A sort of treaty between the families of the bride and bridegroom, it created or confirmed a life-estate in the land for the bridegroom's father and provided that it should pass on his death to the son, and on the latter's death to the eldest son of the marriage. Meanwhile the estate had to provide an income or a start in life for every member of the family, including jointures for the widows of the life-owners, dowries for the daughters, and portions for the younger sons, in each generation.[43] In this way, it was said, the estate would be kept together, at the expense of a large burden of debt, and in defiance of the natural forces making for its dissolution.

The system of conveyance by private deeds out of which settlement had grown was the chief obstacle to the cheap and speedy transfer of such land as did reach the market. To assure a good title and guard against secret transfers and charges a purchaser, mortgagee or long leaseholder had to investigate the title for sixty years past. This begot delays and expense. Since solicitors were, until 1881, paid by piece-rate, according to the searches they made and the length of the documents they examined or engrossed, the expense bore no relation to the value of the property, but only to the complications of the title. The legal cost of transferring small properties was disproportionately high and might, in some cases, exceed the purchase price. A premium was thus given to large transactions, and small purchasers discouraged.

The only complete solution was the abolition of private conveyance and its replacement by the public registration of title. This had been advocated by the 1829 Real Property Commissioners, and since then by a succession of eminent lawyers, Select Committees, Royal Commissions and Lord Chancellors. Registration of deeds, as in Middlesex, Yorkshire, Scotland and Ireland, and in the ineffective voluntary registration Acts of 1862 and 1875, was useless. What was needed was compulsory registration, the title to land inhering in an entry in the register, with its reference to a cadastral map, confirmed by a certificate in the owner's possession. Nothing less, it was urged, could provide an indefeasible, marketable title, and make land transactions as cheap, simple and speedy as those in other commodities. But ownership had to be a simple relationship, and settlement, with its countless concurrent and future interests in the land, stood in the way. As the celebrated conveyancer, Joshua Williams, admitted, 'I do not think that the registration of titles will succeed unless you please to abolish settlements altogether'.[44] The landlords, it was pointed out, could not have their cake in secret and binding dispositions of land and eat it in cheap transfer and ready mortgages.

The advocates of free trade in land had revolutionary expectations. If primogeniture, entail, settlement and private conveyance were abolished, 'land would be thrown open to

N

free competition, the overgrown estates would soon be broken down, and a great portion of the soil would gradually come into the possession of the working classes'.[45] Such a belief could be held only by those who supposed the existing system of landholding to be incompatible with the laws of supply and demand operating in a free market, and the great estates to be contrary to nature and political economy, requiring the 'pressure of feudal law' to keep them in being. Over most of the world outside the British Isles, it was argued, the staying power of the peasant and his ability to wring more from the soil at less cost except in patient labour had left him in possession. The natural distribution of the land was the widest compatible with earning a modest family living from it, and only the political self-interest of the landlords prevented its realisation.

V

In origin free trade in land was a by-product of that most characteristic political manifestation of the middle class, the Anti-Corn Law movement. In the words of the *Westminster Review* in 1846,

> 'Free trade in land' would be the boon demanded by the land-owners, if they knew their own interest, in compensation for the repeal of the corn laws—a free unrestricted power of alienation, which would turn our overflowing commercial capital from foreign loans and railways into English farms—which would transform our nobility into a commercial aristocracy, and enable the farmer and the tradesman to become the proprietor, instead of the tenant, of his farm and of his shop.[46]

The land question was never far from the minds of the Leaguers from the start. The first Anti-Corn Law Tract ended with some 'remarks on the land tax fraud', and the exigencies of debate constantly forced the question of land to the front. When the repealers did not raise it, the protectionists did. It was Peel who justified the corn laws by the 'extraordinary burdens on land', and sent the repealers burrowing into

history for the legendary sins of the landlords.[47] It was 'Dowry'
Knatchbull who ineptly shone the limelight on strict settlement.[48] And it was the agriculturists' plea of the necessity for
protection which the League met by demanding in the interests of agricultural efficiency a thorough reform of the land
laws.[49] Indeed, as far as the middle class was concerned, land
reform dated from the corn law agitation.[50] Earlier land reformers, Paine, Ogilvie and Spence, and even Cobbett, whose
Legacy to Labourers (ironically dedicated to Peel) had appeared as recently as 1834, were ignored until resuscitated by
the Georgists in the 1880s.

Whilst the campaign lasted, the Leaguers were almost as
incensed about land laws as about corn laws. Many expected
the League to develop into the party of the middle-class, in
whose programme free trade in land would have a prominent
place. From their point of view repeal came too quickly and
too easily. As James Beal put it, 'The sudden conversion of
Lord John Russell and Sir Robert Peel to the policy of Free
Trade prevented the development of the Anti-Corn Law
League campaign to the broader area of Free Trade in Land,
which was the next inevitable stage in the agitation'.[51] It
rapidly became clear that victory had, temporarily at least,
sated the middle class, and it was not prepared to press its
advantage against the landowners. This was the measure of
Peel's statesmanship. Land reform was a weapon held in
reserve, and it had not been needed. The class which had so
unstintingly supported the League was not united behind
Bright's attempt to harness its motive power to a radical programme of free trade, smaller taxes, a cheaper foreign policy,
a wider franchise, and free trade in land.[52] In spite of the
efforts of Cobden and Bright land reform languished for
nearly twenty years. It maintained a flickering interest only
in the bills of Locke King against primogeniture and of Philip
Pusey on tenant right. The reason, as Cobden clearly saw, was
the apathy of the merchants and manufacturers, an apathy

based on their ambivalent attitude to land. As he told Bright
in 1851, 'Public opinion is either indifferent or favourable to
the system of large properties kept together by entail. If you
want a proof, see how every successful trader buys an estate,
and tries to perpetuate his name in connection with "that ilk"
by creating an eldest son.'[53] Their indifference was likely to
increase as commercial and industrial incomes grew larger, as
their incomes assumed a more complex character, and the
distinction between profit and rent grew more blurred.

Until his death Cobden continued to look to the merchants
and manufacturers to lead the attack on 'feudalism'. 'With
many faults and shortcomings, our mercantile and manufacturing classes', he wrote in 1862, '...are after all the only
power in the State possessed of wealth and political influence
sufficient to counteract in some degree the feudal governing
class of this country. They are, indeed, the only class from
whom we can in our time hope for any further beneficial
changes.' He tried to wink at their 'timid and servile conduct
towards the aristocracy', but he more and more despaired of
galvanising them into effective action:

> We have the spirit of feudalism rife and rampant in the midst of
> the antagonistic development of the age of Watt, Arkwright and
> Stephenson! Nay feudalism is every day more and more in the
> ascendant in political and social life. So great is its power and
> prestige that it draws to it the support and homage of even those
> who are the natural leaders of the newer and better civilisation.
> Manufacturers and merchants as a rule seem only to desire riches
> that they may be enabled to prostrate themselves at the feet of
> feudalism. How is this to end?[54]

Then suddenly, in the last few months of his life, there
were signs of resurrection in the land question. The revival
may be dated from his own last speech at Rochdale in November 1864: 'If I were five-and-twenty or thirty, instead of
unhappily twice that number of years, I would take Adam
Smith in hand, and I would have a League for "free trade in
land" just as we had a League for free trade in corn'.[55] Land

reform, we know from his letters, was never far from his mind. The previous year he had had to defend Bright and himself against *The Times'* attack on 'the two Gracchi of Rochdale'. Why did he choose so late a date to suggest a League? Perhaps he was responding to a new atmosphere favourable to land reform. The reviews of the middle sixties suddenly rediscovered the land question and the merits of peasant proprietorship. Neither the ideas nor even the books reviewed were new: they included W. T. Thornton's *A Plea for Peasant Proprietors* (1848), J. S. Mill's *Principles of Political Economy* (1848), F. W. Newman's *Lectures on Political Economy* (1851), and Herbert Spencer's *Social Statics* (1851).[56] Perhaps the new interest was a belated response to Cobden and Bright's patient education of the public mind on the land question. At all events, from this time onwards a public opinion began to form around the land-reforming ideas of these men, and of Thorold Rogers, Henry Fawcett, Nassau Senior, Sir Henry Maine, Shaw Lefevre, Cliffe Leslie, and their fellows. Some of them, notably Fawcett and Shaw Lefevre, led the agitation of 1865 against the enclosure of commons, and founded the first preservation societies. It was men like these, professional authors, journalists, academics and lawyers, who were to play the leading part in reviving land reform and organising the wave of public opinion which swept on to the abortive crisis of the early eighties.

Professional men, of course, are society's intellectuals, and it is not surprising to find them producing the ideas which society discusses. They have, however, been too readily viewed as individuals or, if grouped at all, grouped into family connections without sufficient emphasis that such connections are normal in any social class. It is instructive to look at them as a class, and ask what it is that marks them off from their neighbours. They are as a class peculiar in one respect, that they are not tied by economic interest to any particular economic system. Whereas the landowner and the business-

man see their incomes, their way of life and their very existence, tied to the economic system which produces them, the
professional man is aware that in any organisation of society,
provided it does not fall below the moral and technical
standards of existing civilisation, his services will be necessary,
valued and rewarded. He is not therefore under the same
economic pressure to maintain the system, and is free to in-
dulge in criticism and reform. Neither, of course, is he under
pressure to change it. He is, compared with the landowner
and the businessman, released from the narrower constraints
of economic interest, and is freer to exercise his judgement
according to other, non-economic criteria. What in others
requires a considerable insight or effort of will, comes easily
to him. He is apt, therefore, to see politics in moral terms
rather than those of economic interest.[57]

The moralisation of politics—the appeal in political questions to abstract justice and social ideals—is the characteristic
contribution of the professional class to public discussion.
That it should have become an important factor in Victorian
political life is not unexpected. First, the professional class
was growing rapidly and achieving a wider influence because
of the changing character of society. Industrialism and urban-
isation did not merely increase the weight of the business and
proletarian as against the landowning and cultivating classes.
Together with the ensuing rise in living standards they increased the demand for the professional services of administra-
tors, teachers, lawyers, doctors, architects, engineers, ministers
of religion, journalists and authors. As the balance of population tilted decisively in favour of the towns, the professional
class came into its own. Secondly, in its tendency to see politics
in moral terms it was for a long time swimming with the tide
of middle-class opinion. Hostility against the landowners was
highly moralistic. Like any interest or group which feels
excluded and aggrieved, the early Victorian business class was
apt to seek comfort in moral condemnation of its opponents.

As long as the tide of hostility flowed against the landlords uninterrupted by cross-currents deriving from the changed economic interests of businessmen, the moral view of politics prevailed. One of the functions of the professional class was to carry over this fruitful if exasperating attitude from an age in which it worked for the businessmen into one in which it worked against them. Land reform was one of the vehicles in which this was achieved.

It is not pretended that all professional men were land reformers, or all land reformers professional men. Land reformers were drawn from all classes, even from the landed class itself.[58] To see politics in similarly moral terms is not necessarily to reach the same position. Land reform itself had professional men amongst its opponents, the economist Mc-Culloch, the historian Froude and the lawyer Underhill, for example. Others, like the lawyer-historians Pollock and See-bohm, saw small value in it and rejected the assumptions of free trade in land. The professional class was too small to affect politics by itself, and the moral attitude encourages pros-elytisation. Nevertheless, the professional class was strongly represented amongst land reformers, more strongly amongst land-reforming Members of Parliament than in the Commons as a whole, while amongst the Radicals they formed a sub-stantial group and occasionally a majority.[59] Inside and outside Parliament professional men played a leading role in the agitation, strikingly so in the more extreme kinds of reform. Mill's Land Tenure Reform Association, which went beyond free trade in land to advocate taxation of the unearned incre-ment of rent, was founded in 1870 chiefly by professional men, in association with six members of the (first) International Working Men's Association. Amongst the moving spirits were Mill himself, Fawcett, Thorold Rogers, Cliffe Leslie and J. E. Cairnes, all academic economists, Alfred Russell Wallace the naturalist, and the journalist John Morley, the exceptions being Dilke the Radical landowner, and P. A. Taylor, of the well-known silk-manufacturing firm of Courtaulds.[60] Wallace founded in 1881 the Land Nationalization Society.[61] The Land Reform Union (later the English Land Restoration League) which split off from it in 1883 to organise Henry George's second lecture tour of Britain, exhibited a similar combination of professional and working men.[62] It was the same formula—in some cases the same men—which produced the Socialist societies of the eighties, and has since played so large a part in the origin and development of the Labour party. The moral attitude to politics was apt to lead some professional men further left than land reform.

Free trade in land found support in every class: amongst working men, like George Odger and his friends of the first International and the Land Tenure Reform Association, for whom it was first of many steps; amongst some Whig land-owners or their heirs, like Lords Carington, Lymington and Blandford, for whom it was the one step to prevent all others; it even found a sort of sympathy amongst some Tory land-owners who favoured a modified form which would safeguard the principle of family estates while frustrating criticism. Its main strength, however, lay in the middle class, and even there in the professional rather than the business group. The first body to inherit Cobden's legacy was the Cobden Club— that Fabian Society of progressive Liberalism. Its membership was so wide that its annual dinners looked like the Liberal party in conclave. But the majority were merely annual diners, and the burden of propaganda was carried by a small group of enthusiasts amongst whom professional men were predomi-nant: dons like G. C. Brodrick, Warden of Merton College, Cliffe Leslie and Thorold Rogers, the lawyers Shaw Lefevre, MacDonell and Wren Hoskyns, and the agricultural expert James Caird. Mill, Rogers and Cliffe Leslie formed a link with the Land Tenure Reform Association. The Cobden Club published the handbooks of the movement: *Systems of Land Tenure in Various Countries* (1870), the main contributors, apart from foreigners, being Wren Hoskyns, Cliffe Leslie, Judge Longfield of the Irish Landed Estates Court and Sir George Campbell of the Indian Civil Service; Sir Arthur Arnold's *Free Land*, G. C. Brodrick's *English Land and English Landlords*, and W. E. Baxter's *Our Land Laws of the Past*—all except the last, a small pamphlet, by professional men.[63] Other leading publicists were the journalists Charles Bradlaugh and Justin McCarthy, Professors J. S. Blackie, E. S. Beesley and J. S. Nicholson, the lawyers Joseph Kay, T. E. Scrutton and Osborne Morgan, and the estate agent James Beal.

This is not to deny the importance of the Radical businessmen: Bright, Chamberlain, Collings, Baxter, J. W. Barclay, William Fowler, and the rest. Indeed, the decisive step in the development of the agitation was the inclusion of free trade in land in the Radical programme of the seventies. In Chamberlain's attack on the Liberal leadership in 1873 Free Land took its place besides Free Church, Free Schools and Free Labour in 'the motto of the new party'.[64] From this point on, the history of free trade in land was bound up with that of the Radicals. Through them it achieved its footing in Parliament, and by its connection with them it unwittingly condemned itself to failure. Who then were the Radicals? According to a contemporary view they represented, like land reform, a reaction of capital against land. For Charles Mackay, a progressive political journalist, they were 'a narrow-minded and often uneducated plutocracy' sprung from the Manchester School of a generation earlier.[65] A French observer saw in them 'a campaign of the English bourgeoisie against a privileged class whose rights they covet'.[66] Such an over-simplification ignores the evidence of the Radicals themselves. From the beginning their rebellious anger was aimed not at landlords alone but at 'the power of wealth' in general. Chamberlain's broadsides were fired indiscriminately at 'wealthy landowners and millionaire manufacturers'.[67] If he were appointed Chancellor, the City, Gladstone thought, would be terrified of his views of 'ransom'.[68] Goldwin Smith's original complaint that the Liberal party was swerving from its proper aim 'to put an end to class government and establish a government of the nation' was provoked as much by 'the terrible influence of capital over labour' as by the pretensions of the aristocracy: 'These millionaires were in fact on the point of becoming, in conjunction with the landowners, our absolute masters'.[69] The conjunction was inherent in the Radical programme. The appeal to the working-class voter, the emphasis on welfare measures and State intervention, and the demand for 'ransom' in the shape of graduated taxation, were a calculated attack on the rich as such, irrespective of their source of income. Only 'free land' singled out the landlord for attack. The rest of the programme, with the possible exception of Church disestablishment and reform of the House of Lords, could be viewed as inimical to both landowner and businessman. Businessmen supporting the programme were clearly an aberration from the norm, and regarded by their fellows as cranks and demagogues. Chamberlain and his friends had—according to the point of view—betrayed or risen above the interests of their class. Their dictum, that 'politics is the science of human happiness',[70] was an explicit statement of the moral attitude. Such an attitude was natural to the professional men who formed the largest occupational group amongst the Radicals. To the businessmen it was a luxury afforded only at the expense of their immediate class interests.

VI

In the later seventies the increasing confidence of the Radicals was one of the causes converging to force a crisis in the land question. Depression and bad harvests combined to raise complaints from businessmen and farmers at the high level of rents at a time of falling prices. For the Irish peasant they meant not hardship but ruin, and landlord-tenant relations took an ugly turn. The land reformers in Britain and Ireland rose to meet their opportunity with a crescendo of public discussion in the press and on the platform. In this atmosphere the Conservatives, with an instinct which was part of their traditional equipment for dealing with reforms which had become inevitable, determined to forestall worse measures by bringing in their own. The Agricultural Holdings Act (1875) and the Settled Estates Act (1877) having failed to abate the rising storm, a bolder programme was attempted. The Lord Chancellor, Lord Cairns, had given notice of four land Bills when, in April 1880, the Conservative Government was defeated at the polls. The Liberal press demanded that Gladstone should deal 'first and boldly with the land question', and this he promised in the House to do, only asking time for the Government to consider it fully.[71]

No comprehensive reform was attempted by the Government. Gladstone had small faith in the efficacy of free trade in land to perform its promises, and his overriding concern was to prevent the defection of the Whigs. He had early warning before the end of the year in the resignation of the Duke of Argyll over Irish land policy. Apart from the Irish Land Act of 1881, the only Government measures were marginal: the Ground Game Act (1880) enabling the tenant farmers to take hares and rabbits concurrently with the landlord, and the Agricultural Holdings Act (1883) to prevent the landlord from contracting out of his obligation under the 1875 Act to compensate the tenant for improvements. Instead, the Government encouraged Lord Cairns to carry on with the Tory Bills already introduced, and these were enacted. Two of them were technical improvements in conveyancing and litigation, while the third introduced the modern system of remunerating solicitors by a maximum percentage of the price of the land transferred. The fourth was the Settled Land Act of 1882, which set out the main principles governing settled

land ever since.[72] In effect it put the entire management of
the land, as if it were his own freehold, in the hands of the
tenant-for-life, subject to certain safeguards protecting the interests of other beneficiaries. It even allowed the outright sale
of the land, provided that the purchase money, after meeting
charges on the estate, was secured on the same terms and for
the same purposes as the land it represented. It did not please
the reformers, who were not to be satisfied with anything less
than the complete abolition of settlement, primogeniture and
entail, and regarded the Act as an attempt to encourage
settlement by increasing its convenience.

Outmanoeuvred and frustrated, the agitation grew more
strident and extravagant. The early eighties saw the founding
not only of the Land Nationalization Society and of the Georgist movement but also of a multitude of Socialist clubs and
societies, from Hyndman's Social Democratic Federation to
the Fabian Society, all including amongst their objects the
public ownership of land. The less extreme reformers, through
the Free Land League of 1885, intensified their demands, and
leasehold enfranchisement grew from an idea into an organised movement. The 'advanced' Liberals, looking ahead to the
rural labourers' vote, espoused Collings' scheme for allotments
and smallholdings. By the 1885 election, with Hartington
and Chamberlain taking opposite sides on most questions, the
main division in politics was seen to be not that between
Liberal and Tory, but between 'advanced' Liberals and the
'moderates' or Whigs. Chamberlain was confidently introduced as 'your coming Prime Minister'.[73] Hartington gloomily
forecast that the future Liberal party would be Radical, and
that there was nothing for the Whigs but to disappear or turn
Tory.[74] The land question played a more prominent part than
in any election before or since, and the Radicals claimed that
'three acres and a cow' had won the English counties. The
election won, and the caretaker government turned out on
Jesse Collings' smallholdings amendment—against which a

significant group of Whigs voted with the Tories[75]—the Liberal party seemed poised once more for a Radical advance and an attack on the land question. At this point Gladstone launched his Home Rule 'thunderbolt', and land reform was lost in the rift which split the party and unexpectedly left Chamberlain, Collings and their friends on the Whig side. From that landslip it was never to recover.

The 1886 split had the same significance for land reform as for the Liberal party in general. Though both had triumphs still to come, for both it proved the real beginning of the end. Yet at the time it seemed to clear the way for a new advance, unhampered by the Whigs, and progressive Liberalism was now much freer to experiment with democratic and social reforms, amongst which land reform promised to occupy a prominent place. The loss of Chamberlain and his friends, though they continued to pursue moderate land reform, was regretted, but the defection of Hartington and the 'moderates' had been a calculated risk, and was not wholly unwelcome. The party could now continue its accustomed advance towards the left, its expected evolution into the party of the Radicals. At Manchester in 1889 the National Liberal Federation adopted a substantially Radical programme which included enfranchisement of leaseholders, security for tenants' improvements, increased powers for obtaining land for allotments, abolition of restrictions on the transfer of land, and even the taxation of ground rents and mining royalties along Georgist lines. The famous 'Newcastle programme' of 1891 went further still, embracing the abolition of primogeniture and entail, and the compulsory purchase of land for local purposes. The Tories were sufficiently sensitive of the electoral appeal of land reform to pass, in the Allotments Act (1887) and the Smallholdings Act (1892), modified versions of Collings' and Chamberlain's schemes—without, of course, the essential element of compulsory purchase. It seemed that once Irish Home Rule was achieved, comprehensive land reform would be the next legislative concern of a future Liberal government.

No such comprehensive reform was ever achieved, or even attempted. The harassed Liberal minority government of 1892-5 was too obsessed with Ireland to pay it much attention. When the Liberals returned to power in 1906, they had the means to achieve it, but the will was lacking. The Smallholdings Acts of 1907 and 1908 merely extended the provisions of the 1892 Act, though in a manner more offensive to property, since compulsory purchase for letting by local authorities was potentially more voracious of land than State-aided purchase by the smallholders themselves. The nearest the last Liberal government came to effective land reform was in the land taxation clauses of the 1909 Budget, which Lloyd George inserted under pressure from the Land Valuation Parliamentary Campaign Committee, formed in 1906 amongst Liberal MPs of Georgist leanings. More than any other Budget proposal, these taxes on unearned incremental land values and undeveloped land and minerals precipitated the collision with the House of Lords and so the constitutional crisis.[76] It was Lloyd George himself who, in 1922 at the insistence of the Conservatives in his Coalition, repealed the land tax clauses of 'the People's Budget'. Non-socialist land reform as a political possibility petered out with World War I and the quarrel as to its conduct which began the final break-up and decline of the Liberal party.[77]

VII

Why did the land reform movement fail? Partly because in the only variants acceptable to the propertied members of the Liberal party it came so near to success. The reforms of the early 1880s were a sufficient instalment of free trade in land to test its main assumptions and prove them false. Life-owners did not use their new powers to flood the market with estates. The 'natural drift' of property towards the small owner did not assert itself. Peasant proprietors did not triumphantly emerge as the fittest survivors of agricultural depression. State-aided purchase under the 1892 Act and State-aided leasing under those of 1907-8 were an admission that the free market was failing to produce smallholdings or to change significantly the distribution of property.[78] If in the twentieth century there has been a considerable increase in owner-occupation, it has been amongst existing farmers rather than new peasants from the working classes; and if a break-up of some great estates, it has been the fortuitous by-product of taxation policy rather than the deliberate result of land reform.

Ultimately, however, the failure of the movement was due to Liberal equivocation—a flirtation with land reform rather than a marriage, and one which was disastrous to other Liberal prospects. Equivocation was inherent in the indecision of the late Victorian Liberal party as to its future purpose and appeal. It was both a symptom and a cause of the process by which the party was alienating many of its traditional supporters without permanently gaining new ones. It failed to answer with a clear voice the question, to whom was Liberalism, to whom was land reform, supposed to appeal? In the policies it pursued it increasingly asked its propertied supporters to rise above their economic interests, while not offering to meet more than part-way the economic aspirations of the working classes. The tension between these two appeals was too great for the party's survival. It is not too much to say that equivocation over land reform was the most damaging example of the policies which undermined the Liberal party and prepared the way for its decline. The agitation, which began in the class conflict between the businessmen and the landowners, ended by helping to bring about their *rapprochement* in the same political party and so had a profound if paradoxical effect on the social structure of politics.

However difficult it is to measure, it is clear that in the last quarter of the nineteenth century a geological shift was taking place in the political allegiance of the landed and business classes, and in the ability of the Liberal party to command their support. Sir Robert Ensor saw a symbol of this change in the transformation of the City of London from a Liberal into a Conservative stronghold.[79] John Roach in a stimulating article on the Liberal intelligentsia has said, 'In the history of Victorian politics more attention might be given to the change which converted a large part of the educated classes from the Liberal side to the Conservative'.[80] It is a change which demands explanation, all the more so since it runs counter to theoretical expectations, both orthodox and Marxist. That it should have been the Conservatives, the traditional party of the majority of landowners, rather than the Liberals, the party (notwithstanding its landowning wing) of the majority of Victorian businessmen, which survived into the twentieth century as the party opposed to Labour, is one of the more surprising quirks of modern British history. The decline of the Liberal party had its origins in the drift of landowners, businessmen and others to the Conservatives which began well before 1886, and of which the Unionist defections were only the most spectacular example.

Unfortunately, such a shift in the traditional allegiances of important social groups defies accurate statistical measurement. Both Ensor and Roach illustrate it by individual examples—Goschen, Henry Sidgwick, Sir Henry Maine, J. F. Stephen, Robert Lowe, and Lord Lytton. Such examples can be multiplied by anyone familiar with the period. The problem is how far they support inferences about the behaviour of whole classes. J. A. Thomas's statistics of the economic interests of MPs provide useful information about some of the most politically active members of the various classes.[81] There are considerable difficulties in using his figures, which are discussed in the Appendix to this paper, where a method of counteracting the effects of the electoral swing is developed. The resultant analysis shows that up to the early 1880s a

Liberal government commanded the support of two-thirds or more of the businessmen in the Commons, and a Liberal opposition more than half. By the 1890s, the position was reversed: it was the Conservatives who had two-thirds of businessmen MPs when in office, and half when out of it. Over the same period Liberal landowning MPs shrank from a substantial minority to a negligible one. This analysis confirms the view that between the 1870s and the 1890s the Liberal party was steadily losing ground in its share of the Parliamentary representation of both landowners and businessmen, that the losses were greater amongst 'City men' than amongst, say, merchants, and that the only important group of which the Liberal share increased was the professional class.

Given that such a drift did occur, why did it come about? Ensor rightly rejected 'the fashionable Marxian answer', that the capitalists were forced by a proletarian challenge into the arms of the landowners and their party. 'In the political field,' he wrote, 'the working-class stirrings of the 'eighties came to very little all told; and if in the trade union field they were less negligible, they wore no revolutionary aspect.' Nor does there seem to have been any likelihood of the working-class itself capturing the Liberal party and driving out the businessmen. Ensor's own answer was that 'the source of alarm was agrarian, not proletarian; it was Irish, not British'. Irish agrarian violence evoked in the businessman's breast 'a moral horror at unprevented and largely unpunished crime'; a 'feeling that in Ireland justice had been overborne by force'; and 'a peculiar kind of patriotic impulse'. No doubt it did. But were businessmen so much more sensitive than other Liberals to morality, justice and patriotism? Were those who remained behind indifferent to these appeals? Did the Liberal party condone Irish violence? And if the businessman was repelled by violence in the eighties, why did he remain unmoved by the threat of it in Ulster in 1912? Though Irish affairs indeed contributed to the defections, there is no need to rely for the

P

explanation on such nebulous emotions.

May not the main cause be found in emotions much nearer the head and pocket: in fear for the power and influence of the propertied classes, and for the institution of property itself? Roach has laid bare the misgivings of 'old Liberals', like Sidgwick, Stephen, Maine, Lowe and Lytton, at the implications of Liberal policy: it seemed to them to be paving the way for a tyrannical, equalitarian democracy which would despoil the rich and abrogate national and imperial responsibilities in an orgy of selfish hedonism. It was not so much working-class stirrings which evoked this fear. As yet the new voters predominantly supported the traditional parties. The danger lay in what many considered those irresponsible middle-class politicians, inside and outside the Liberal party, who played upon their greed and envy, and aimed to buy their votes with an insidious bribery which could only whet their appetites for more. 'Ransom' (graduated taxation) and 'socialism' (expensive welfare measures) would weaken the defences of property and open the breaches to more extreme equalitarianism. The Georgists and Social Democrats, the land nationalisers and Fabians, would not need to win a victory at the polls if their 'friends' inside the Liberal party could be persuaded to transform it into an instrument of their policies.

To many it seemed that the Liberals were caught up in a 'creeping conspiracy' against property which threatened landowner and businessman alike. Land reform had a special place in this 'conspiracy'. It was the continuous strand linking the Liberals with the extremists to their left. It began with land reform for Ireland which by 1881 had begun to undermine the rights of property owners there. Who could say it would not spread to Britain, where free trade in land, leasehold enfranchisement, compulsory purchase, and the taxation of ground rents, would lead insensibly to the single tax, if not to outright nationalisation? Home Rule itself could be construed as part of the conspiracy. Not only was it accompanied by a

Bill to buy out the Irish landowners at twenty years' purchase
for £120 million—a scheme which might have been drawn
up by Wallace. Gladstone himself admitted that the crucial
problem was the position under an Irish Nationalist government of 'the minority', which in 1886—whatever it became
by 1912—meant not so much Ulster as the landed class
throughout Ireland.[82] As Salisbury put it, 'By the Land Act
of 1870, by the Ballot Act of 1872, by the Land Act of 1881,
and last of all by the Reform Act of 1884, the power of the
gentry in Ireland is absolutely shattered'.[83] Their subjection
without safeguards to a Dublin government of their enemies
was to invite spoliation or worse. Home Rule was an instalment of the Radical plan 'to smash up the landowners'.[84]
Salisbury put it succinctly: 'We are on an inclined plane
leading from the position of Lord Hartington to that of Mr.
Chamberlain and so on to the depths over which Mr. Henry
George rules supreme.'[85]

For the plausibility of this view of the direction in which
Liberalism was tending, Liberals themselves, and especially
those on the left wing of the party, must bear some of the
responsibility. The moral appeal in politics is apt to appear
humbug to those whose interests are threatened. Many Liberals allowed themselves to be carried by it into arguments
against the privileges of property which seemed capable of
indefinite extension in the direction of equalitarianism. Land
reformers especially were open to the temptation to press their
arguments beyond what was necessary to support their moderate, unrevolutionary schemes. They could be accused of
speaking with two voices, one for the upholders of private
property, and one for its detractors. Mill himself was up-
braided by the *Edinburgh Review* in 1871 for offering his
schemes to land nationalisers and socialists as a step towards
their goal, and to others as a bulwark of private property.[86]
His Land Tenure Reform Association and its successors, as
we have seen, seemed to act as a bridge, in doctrine and per-

sonnel, between the Liberals and the Georgists, and more extreme reformers beyond them. According to Hyndman, in 1885, the Radicals were doing the Social Democrats' work for them, and Chamberlain was 'too clever a man not to know that the very arguments which he uses against the landowners will be turned against himself as a capitalist and the class to which he belongs'.[87] Even though Chamberlain left the party, his programme and the arguments remained.

How were capitalists likely to react to such a danger? As we have seen, they ceased as a class to be interested in land reform when the Corn Laws were repealed. By the last quarter of the nineteenth century there were many reasons why their apathy should have turned into a more active revulsion. As the structure of industry and commerce changed with the growth of business units and the spread of joint-stock organisation, the distinction drawn by the classical economists between profit and rent, between earned and unearned wealth, was no longer relevant. Arguments against the one were arguments against the other. Moderate land reform might lead to more extreme kinds, and these in turn to varieties of socialism. Other Radical measures, above all graduated death duties (introduced by Harcourt in 1894) and graduated income tax (introduced by Asquith and Lloyd George in 1907 and 1909), made no distinction between land and other property. The propertied classes would stand or fall together. The defection of the Whigs, whether over Ireland or the more general danger to property, was a danger signal to many businessmen. It deprived them of their surest anchor against a drift to port and the equalitarian rocks. Some of them preferred to abandon ship.

What of those businessmen and landowners who were left? There were enough of them to prevent a thorough-going land reform, the capture of the party by the left wing, or its transformation into a predominantly working-class party. Many remained out of loyalty, habit, or an attachment to free trade.

But the hard core were believers in the high principles of Liberalism, with its concern for the underdog, for social justice as they conceived it, and for a state of society in which hard work and enterprise were rewarded and privilege was not allowed to become gross exploitation. That is, they were motivated less by economic interest than by sentiment, generous impulse, personal ambition or eccentricity. Like the Radicals and land reformers before them, they stood out from their fellows as aberrations from the norms of the classes to which they belonged. They were becoming exponents of the moral view of politics. The increasing prominence of professional men in the Liberal party was symptomatic of the trend. Only amongst this interest in the Commons did the Liberals maintain much more than their share of the representation. When last in office under Victoria the party could claim a majority only of this interest, and in the Cabinet professional men nearly equalled the rest. By 1906, for the first time in any Cabinet, they equalled the landowners and businessmen and could, with a trade unionist, outvote them.[88] It is significant for the evolution of the parties that when in 1911 the Conservatives came for the first time to choose a businessman, Bonar Law, as their leader, the Liberals were led by a barrister, Asquith, closely seconded by a solicitor, Lloyd George.

If this analysis is correct, the late Victorian defections left the Liberal party with its roots less firmly bedded in the subsoil of economic interests. By the beginning of this century it had become that rare and noble political plant, a party mainly devoted to the moral view of politics, and dangerously isolated from the hard facts of economic motivation. Its subsequent history pathetically proclaims that such a rarefied idealism does not pay. It lost the permanent, solid support of the propertied classes without gaining that of the working-class. Though in 1906 the cry of 'free trade in danger' temporarily rallied some traditional supporters, the great Liberal majority was from one point of view a dwarf standing on the shoulders of a giant. Working-class votes were lent, not given, for the moralist in politics (as with Labour party intellectuals today) is never wholly trusted. When the Liberals ceased to serve working-class interests, working-class politicians were ready with an alternative allegiance. The Liberal party, crumbling on both wings, decayed to a high-minded and admired but unsupported remnant. To its decline the agitation for land reform, which to Disraeli in 1880 had seemed to threaten the constitutional position of the landed interest and with it, perhaps, the extinction of the Conservative party, had made a peculiar and perverse contribution.

APPENDIX

A MEASURE OF THE DRIFT OF BUSINESS AND OTHER MPs FROM THE LIBERAL TO THE UNIONIST PARTIES, 1868-1914

In his analyses of the socio-economic composition of *The House of Commons, 1832-1900* and *1906-1911* (Cardiff, 1939 and 1958), Dr J. A. Thomas gives useful statistical tables of the economic interests of the MPs in each Parliament from the Great Reform Act to World War I. These he tries to use to show, *inter alia*, when the business interests in the House of Commons began to outweigh the landed interest, which he takes to be as early as the 1850s. This conclusion does not follow from his figures which, being of 'interests' rather than MPs and not allowing for the overlap either between land-owners and businessmen or between the various business in-terests (he gives only one category for landowners and eleven for business interests in the first book and no less than sixty-eight in the second), total far more than (usually more than double) the number of MPs in each Parliament. Whether or not we accept that, down to World War I at least, most land-owners were likely to be landlords first and businessmen second and certainly to come to the defence of land against any radical attack, the landed interest was in a clear majority amongst MPs until the Parliament of 1880, and in a minority only from 1885 onwards.

His figures can, however, be used for a more interesting purpose, to illustrate the drift of both landowners and businessmen from the Liberal to the Conservative and Unionist and Liberal Unionist Parties in the late nineteenth and early twentieth centuries. The difficulty in this analysis is that some method must be devised to counteract the effect of the electoral swing, which normally gave each Party a larger number of MPs from every interest when in a majority in the House than when it was in a minority, the number increasing with the size of the majority.

The effect of the electoral swing can be eliminated by constructing an associative index (AI) on the following formula:

$$\frac{\text{Liberal members of interest}}{\text{Unionist members of interest}} \times \frac{\text{Unionist MPs}}{\text{Liberal MPs}}$$

The index, as it is greater or less than unity, shows by how much the Liberal share of each interest is greater or less than the Liberal share of the MPs of the two Parties. (Liberal Unionists are included with Unionists. Other Parties, notably Labour and the Irish Nationalists, are for simplicity's sake excluded from the calculation.) If the index for an interest is 1.0, the Liberals have the same share of it as they have of the combined Liberal and Unionist MPs; if it is 2.0, they have twice the share of the interest as of MPs, and so on. In Table 1, the first row of figures for each interest gives the Liberal percentage of the category, the second the associative index. (Working-class MPs have been omitted, since until the 1900 Parliament they were comparatively few and almost entirely Liberal, and from 1906 predominantly Labour. A small number of farmers, auctioneers and land agents and other miscellaneous occupations have also been omitted. Newspaper proprietors in the nineteenth century were still primarily journalists, and have been attached to the Professions. 1910 refers to the Parliament elected in December of that year.)

TABLE I

Liberal Proportion of Each Interest in the House of Commons, 1868-1910

		1868	1874	1880	1885	1886	1892	1895	1900	1906	1910
Land	%	47.4	33.9	48.6	47.5	25.1	23.8	17.0	16.7	51.7	23.5
	AI	0.63	0.72	0.66	0.67	0.69	0.36	0.48	0.43	0.37	0.31
Business	%	71.8	57.3	69.7	61.1	40.9	49.9	32.0	32.3	71.6	52.5
	AI	1.73	2.05	1.58	1.22	1.39	1.15	1.09	1.03	0.93	1.11
Professions	%	72.7	61.5	77.2	68.7	45.6	56.0	40.8	44.3	82.1	57.7
	AI	2.04	2.24	2.36	1.63	1.75	1.47	1.60	1.60	1.76	1.37
Armed Forces	%	44.4	24.8	41.3	28.6	11.8	14.7	7.5	11.1	40.8	24.3
	AI	0.56	0.46	0.49	0.30	0.28	0.20	0.19	0.27	0.26	0.32

The table shows that the Liberals always had a minority of the landed MPs, whether in or out of office, and that their share fell off sharply from 1886 onwards, becoming very small by the Edwardian age. Their share of the related category of military and naval MPs (a rather small category) was still smaller, and fell off earlier, from 1880 onwards, to become almost negligible before the end of the century. Their share of the business MPs began as a large majority, more than twice their share of combined MPs in the 1874 Parliament, and fell steadily to the end of the century, when it was close to unity, and remained so in the Edwardian age (but see the next paragraph). Only in the case of MPs from the professions did the Liberals succeed in maintaining a predominant share of the interest; omitting lawyers, who were relatively equal in the two Parties, the Liberal share was overwhelming.

A more refined analysis of the business interest is still more illuminating. If we take finance (bankers, insurance and finance company directors) to represent the growing financial and corporate end of the spectrum of capitalism, and merchants to represent the declining traditional and more individualist end, we get the following result:

TABLE 2

		1868	1874	1880	1885	1886	1892	1895	1900	1906	1910
Finance	%	71.7	51.1	61.4	54.0	31.1	38.0	21.7	20.9	64.1	42.1
	AI	1.77	1.47	1.11	0.87	0.93	0.70	0.65	0.57	0.66	0.74
Merchants	%	82.9	72.7	81.0	77.4	57.2	66.2	46.8	39.3	87.1	66.7
	AI	3.39	3.74	2.97	2.55	2.75	2.25	2.04	1.40	2.50	2.00

It will be seen that the Liberal share of the financial interest began as strongly as that of the wider business interest, but fell off sharply from 1880, and by the end of the century reached levels approaching, though not yet reaching, those of the landowners.[89] Their share of the merchants, overwhelmingly predominant at the start of the period, also declined to the end of the century, though it was still much greater than unity in 1900, but recovered strongly in the era of the Tariff Reform movement, to reach levels greater even than the Liberal share of the professions. Table 2 illustrates how Liberalism continued to hold attractions for the traditional businessman of the owner-managing phase of capitalism—a declining breed by the twentieth century—while it increasingly alienated the newer corporate businessman of high finance capitalism—the breed fittest to survive in the twentieth-century economy.

Notes to this chapter are on pages 235-9

NOTES AND REFERENCES

Robert Owen of New Lanark: His Critique of British Society
John Butt (pp13-32)

1 *A Supplementary Appendix to the First Volume of the Life of Robert Owen*, Vol IA (1858), xxi-xxii
2 R. Miliband, 'The Politics of Robert Owen', *Journal of the History of Ideas*, XV (1954), 235ff; cf also Chushichi Tsuzuki, 'Robert Owen and Revolutionary Politics' in *Robert Owen Prophet of the Poor* (ed S. Pollard and J. Salt), 1971, 13-38
3 Cf my introduction to *Robert Owen Prince of Cotton Spinners* (1971), 10-12
4 Cf my introduction to reprint of *Life of Robert Owen by himself* (1971), xxv
5 *Ibid*, 12-23
6 *Ibid*, 22ff
7 W. H. Chaloner, 'Robert Owen, Peter Drinkwater and the Early Factory System in Manchester', *Bulletin of John Rylands Library*, 37 (1954) 78-102
8 Cf my 'Robert Owen as a businessman' in *Robert Owen Prince of Cotton Spinners*, 169ff; Birmingham Public Library, Boulton & Watt MSS, Letterbook 1793-6, Boulton & Watt to Robert Owen & Co, 18 Dec 1795
9 'Robert Owen as a businessman' 170ff; A. J. Robertson, 'Robert Owen and the Campbell Debt 1810-22', *Business History*, XI (Jan 1969), 23-30; my introduction to *Life*, xi-xix
10 'Robert Owen as a businessman', 172
11 *Ibid*, 179; A. J. Robertson, 'Robert Owen, Cotton Spinner: New Lanark, 1800-25' in Pollard & Salt, 159
12 *Life*, 86-9
13 Introduction to *Life*, xxiii
14 'Robert Owen as a businessman', 199-201 and 211-13
15 *Ibid*, 188ff
16 *Life*, 80-1
17 F. Podmore, *Robert Owen*, I, 60 and 75n
18 Cf S. Pollard, *The Genesis of Modern Management* (Pelican edn) 1968, 231ff; T. C. Smout, 'The Landowner and the Planned Village', *Scotland in the Age of Improvement*, ed N. T. Phillipson and R. Mitchison, Edinburgh (1970), 75ff
19 Brotherton Library MS Tour Book of John Marshall 1807, f67

20 Glasgow City Archives, Sederunt Book of the Glasgow Cottonmasters' Association
21 Cf M. Browning, 'Owen as Educator' in *Robert Owen Prince of Cotton Spinners*, 52-75; H. Silver, 'Owen's Reputation as an Educationist', in Pollard & Salt, 65-83; Introduction to *Life*, xxviii ff
22 M. Browning, 64-9
23 R. Owen, *A New View of Society* (Everyman edn) 1966, 121
24 *Ibid*, 121-2
25 *Report to County of Lanark*, Glasgow (1821); *Life*, 233-4, 236, 238
26 *Life*, 125, 126, 151; *A New View of Society*, 83
27 Introduction to *Life*, xxxi; S. Pollard, 'Robert Owen as Economist' *Co-operative College Papers*, 14 (1971) 23ff; on Malthus cf *An Essay on the Principle of Population* (Pelican edn) 1970, passim; on Ricardo cf *Principles of Political Economy*, ed R. M. Hartwell (Pelican 1971) passim
28 J. H. Treble, 'The Social and Economic Thought of Robert Owen' in *Robert Owen Prince of Cotton Spinners*, 26ff; *A New View of Society*, 85, 181-2
29 *Life*, 103
30 *A New View of Society*, 69-70
31 *Life IA*, 74
32 *A New View of Society*, 122; Ricardo's *Principles of Political Economy*, 310ff
33 *Effects of Machinery on Manual Labour and on the Distribution of the Produce of Industry* (1832); *A New View of Society*, 156ff
34 Cf *Report to County of Lanark*
35 S. G. Checkland, 'The Birmingham Economists 1815-50', *Econ Hist Rev* (1948) 1-19
36 *Life*, 233
37 Introduction to *Life*, xxxiii; W. H. Oliver, 'Owen in 1817: The Millennialist Moment' in Pollard & Salt, 166-87; J. F. C. Harrison, *Robert Owen and the Owenites in Britain and America: The Quest for the New Moral World* (1969) 92ff
38 Harrison, 197ff; W. H. Fraser, 'Robert Owen and the Workers' in *Robert Owen Prince of Cotton Spinners*, 84ff; cf also my 'Robert Owen and Trade Unionism' in *Robert Owen Industrialist Reformer Visionary 1771-1858* (Robert Owen Bicentenary Association pamphlet, 1971) 15-19
39 Harrison, 122ff; R. B. Rose, 'John Finch, 1784-1857: a Liverpool Disciple of Robert Owen', *Trans Historic Soc of Lancashire and Cheshire*, CIX (1958); James Murphy, 'Robert Owen in Liverpool', Ibid CXII (1961)
40 Harrison, 238-9; W. Pare, *Co-operative Agriculture* (1870)
41 Harrison, 244; cf also his 'Social Reform in Victorian Leeds: the work of James Hole, 1820-95', *Thoresby Society Publications*, Leeds 1954; James Hole, *History and Management of Literary, Scientific and Mechanics' Institutes* (1853)
42 Harrison, 245ff; Holyoake, *The Co-operative Movement Today* (1891); cf also his *Sixty Years of an Agitator's Life* (1902) 2 vols. His influence on Bradlaugh is discussed by D. Tribe, *President Charles Bradlaugh* (1971) 25ff and on Tom Mann in *Tom Mann's Memoirs* (1923) 17
43 W. Lovett, 'The Life and Struggles of William Lovett' (ed R. H. Tawney, 1967) vii ff, xiii, 43, 49; Harrison, 248ff
44 Cf my introduction to *Robert Owen Prince of Cotton Spinners*, 11, 12; Harrison, 197, 199, 225

45 Cf J. Saville, 'J. E. Smith and the Owenite Movement, 1833-4' in Pollard & Salt, 115-44; my 'Robert Owen and Trade Unionism', 18; W. H. Fraser, 91ff

46 Cf my 'Robert Owen in his own Time 1771-1858' and H. Silver, 'Robert Owen as Educationist', both in *Co-operative College Papers*, 14 (1971) 15-22 and 55-62

47 Cf B. J. Rose, 'Owen as Co-operator', *Ibid*, 37-48

48 H. Martineau, *Autobiography* (1833), I, 231

O'Connor, O'Connell and the Attitudes of Irish Immigrants towards Chartism, 1838-48

J. H. Treble (pp33-70)

1 R. O'Higgins, The Irish Influence in the Chartist Movement, *Past and Present* No 20, p83. See also J. A. Jackson, *The Irish in Britain* (1963) pp 118-19. 'In the Chartist period, the Irish produced three great leaders in John Doherty, Bronterre O'Brien and Fergus O'Connor. In local movements throughout the country Irish support was readily forthcoming. . . Tacit support for Chartism was widespread among the Irish.' In this chapter I am only concerned with Irish political alignments in Yorkshire, Lancashire and Cheshire

2 A. Macintyre *The Liberator* (1965) pp53-4 and 76

3 For Deegan, see *Northern Star* 23 February 1839

4 For Doyle's nationality, see *Manchester Times* 3 August 1839 and for Brophy's background, see *Northern Star* 30 April 1842

5 Asa Briggs (ed) *Chartist Studies* (1959) pp70n, 78n

6 For Hoey, see *Leeds Mercury* 29 August 1829; for James Duffy, see *Manchester Times* 18, 25 January 1840; and for West, see *Northern Star* 23 April 1842

7 The title was bestowed on him by T. Steele, the 'Head Pacificator' of the Loyal National Repeal Association, C. Gavan Duffy *Four Years of Irish History* 1845-9 (1883) p126

8 For the main outlines of this dispute, see *Freeman's Journal* 27 May, 13-15, 22, 28, 29 June, 4 and 9 July 1833

9 *Leeds Times* 9 January 1836

10 *Ibid* 2, 9 April, 21, 28 May 1836

11 *Ibid* 7 May 1836

12 *Ibid* 16 April 1836

13 *Liverpool Mercury* 29 January 1836

14 *Freeman's Journal* 14 September 1841. These points were made in a letter which T. M. Ray, Secretary of the Loyal National Repeal Association, was instructed to write to Repeal societies in Britain, warning them against any fraternisation with the Chartists

15 D. Read and E. Glasgow, *Feargus O'Connor: Irishman and Chartist* (1959) p48

16 *Northern Star* 5 January 1839. Letter III. These letters which first appeared in 1837 were republished in the *Northern Star* in 1838-9. In Letter VI O'Connor pointed out that Ireland's degradation need not continue

since he was prepared to take over the mantle of leadership which O'Connell in his view had discarded. 'Irishmen,' he proclaimed, 'I have a life at your service; but no tongue or single note to purchase triumph by cunning and deceit, no desire to elevate myself at the expense of your independence.' *Northern Star* 16 February 1839

17 *Freeman's Journal* 5 June 1839. Letter of Daniel O'Connell to Birmingham Chartists, dated 30 May 1839. O'Connell on this occasion tried to draw a distinction between 'the rational and sober-thinking portion of the Chartists' and those who advocated physical force methods. He made a plea for the moral force advocates to rally round 'their old, well-tried leaders, the Attwoods, the Scholefields, and the Muntzes' to form a new radical body in favour of household suffrage; the ballot; triennial parliaments; abolition of property qualifications; and electoral districts of equal size. Such a move would receive his blessing. Little, however, came of this or subsequent attempts to produce an association friendly to Ireland and committed to parliamentary reform. The short-lived Complete Suffrage Movement, which O'Connell supported, would not commit itself to repeal of the Act of Union. For other offers by O'Connell to co-operate with 'the moral force Chartists', see *Freeman's Journal* 12 March 1841; *Manchester Times* 25 April 1840. For his relations with the Complete Suffrage Union, see *Freeman's Journal* 11 May, 16, 30 August 1842 and *Leeds Times* 4 November 1843

18 *Manchester Times* 25 April 1840

19 D. Gwynn *Daniel O'Connell* (1930) p266

20 J. T. Ward *The Factory Movement 1830-55* (1962) pp190-1

21 The exchange of views between O'Connell and Stephens on the Factory Reform question took place in November 1837, although the correspondence was not published until January 1839. *Freeman's Journal* 11 January 1839

22 *Manchester and Salford Advertiser* 5 January 1839

23 *Northern Star* 5 January 1839. See also Oastler's speech in Manchester:- "The question was, for what had Mr Stephens been dragged to the dock? and he was about to answer it from Mr O'Connell's mouth, because he was 'a bloody-thirsty villain', so said the death's-head-and-cross-bones O'Connell. . . O'Connell and the Birmingham council, and the Scotch traitors [Rev Patrick Brewster], and the whig government, had raised a hue and cry against Stephens, in order that they might then dare to take him." *Manchester and Salford Advertiser* 5 January 1839

24 *Northern Star* 5, 12 January 1839

25 D. Read and E. Glasgow, *op cit* p73

26 *Life and Struggles of William Lovett* (Preface by R. H. Tawney) (1967) pp150-65. These addresses to the Precursor Society only succeeded in producing recriminations between the two sides. This exchange took place in the autumn of 1838

27 *Northern Star* 23 February 1839

28 *Ibid* 2 March 1839

29 For the strike, see *Leeds Mercury* 29 August, 5, 12, 19 and 26 September, 3 October 1829

30 *Ibid* 10 August 1839

31 *Manchester Times* 18, 25 January 1840, *Sheffield Iris* 14 January (3rd edition), 21 January 1840

32 For Richardson's claim, see *Northern Star* 23 February 1839. For Irish activity in Manchester see *Manchester and Salford Advertiser* 29 June 1839 where a claim that the Chartists 'had established one [branch] in the very hotbed of O'Connell's precursors and that society was fast increasing in efficiency and numbers', was recorded. For Irish speakers supporting the idea of a 'Sacred Month', see *Ibid*, 27 July 1839. For Irish orators at Preston giving their support to the National Convention, see *Northern Star* 23 February 1839

33 D. O'Connell to N. Maher, 23 October 1838, W. J. Fitzpatrick [ed] *Correspondence of Daniel O'Connell* (1888) II p156

34 *Liverpool Mercury* 31 May 1839. Smyth did, however, acknowledge that 'there are some honest men among the Chartists who are well disposed towards Ireland . . . but alas! for their cause, their influence is not great'

35 *Freeman's Journal* 14 December 1838; 22 May 1839. The quotation is taken from the first reference. For an attack on O'Connor, made some two years earlier, by 'Erinensis' of Huddersfield, see *Leeds Times* 5 November 1836. 'The Irishmen of this town', 'Erinensis' wrote, 'love liberty as dearly (if not more so) as those who taunt them with being lukewarm; but, let me ask, who would value our acts, if we were mean and base enough to attend at meetings where our benefactor, O'Connell . . . is abused and vilified by a renegade Irishman and a designing Tory . . . [a man who, moreover], is a slave to his love of notoriety and not of justice.' In the same edition the *Leeds Times* pointed out that O'Connell had 'no business' to denounce O'Connor 'and reckon on his taking it coolly like a whipped schoolboy'.

36 *Freeman's Journal* 30 January 1839. 'The torch-light preacher' referred to was Rayner Stephens

37 *Ibid* 26 October, 10, 15, 23 November, 14, 20, 28 December 1838. The quotation is taken from a letter H. Colquhoun, Secretary of the Manchester Precursors, to T. M. Ray and published in *Freeman's Journal* 23 November 1838

38 *Ibid* 10, 27 November, 14 December 1838; 30 January, 5 February, 8 March, 2, 19 April, 22 May, 1 June 1839

39 *Northern Star* 23 February 1839, speech of Richard Marsden of Preston to the National Convention

40 *Freeman's Journal* 26 January 1839

41 See for instance his speeches against a Chartist alliance, reported in *Freeman's Journal* 7 September 1841 and *Manchester Times* 18 January 1840. On other occasions, however, O'Connell did try to differentiate between 'moral force' and 'torch and dagger' Chartists and to persuade the former group to co-operate with middle-class radicals. See Footnote 17

42 A. Macintyre *The Liberator* (1965) pp43, 51-7

43 For the Repeal campaign see K. B. Nowlan, *The Politics of Repeal* (1965); J. H. Treble The Irish Agitation in J. T. Ward [ed] *Popular Movements c.1830-50* (1970)

44 *Freeman's Journal* 29 September 1840

45 *Ibid* 22 December 1840 and 26 January 1841

46 *Ibid* 16 April 1841. The precise total forwarded to Dublin from Liverpool in the period 5 January-13 April was £37.18s.10d. [£37.94]

47 *Ibid* and 3, 10 March 1841

48 *Ibid*, 29 August, 15, 26 September, 7, 14 November, 4 December 1840;

9 February, 16 April 1841; *Manchester Times* 24 October, 5 December 1840

49 *Freeman's Journal* 13 August, 19 October, 17 November, 4 December 1840; 3 February, 25 May, 30 June, 4 August 1841. *The Tablet* 7, 14 August 1841

50 *Freeman's Journal* 2 September 1843; *Leeds Times* 30 September 1843

51 *Freeman's Journal* 8 August, 15 September 1843

52 The first Repeal Rent subscriptions from Bolton were sent to Dublin in November 1841. *Ibid* 12 November 1841. The movement, however, only really gathered momentum in the town in the following year; by April 1842 2,000 signatures had been collected for a Repeal petition. *Ibid* 12 April 1842. For Barnsley, see *Northern Star* 3 June 1843

53 J. H. Treble, 'The Place of the Irish Catholics in the Social Life of the North of England 1829-51' (unpublished University of Leeds PhD thesis, 1969) pp320-33

54 *Freeman's Journal* 22 July 1840. The words are T. Duggan's who was at this point in time the leader of the Manchester Repealers

55 *Ibid* 4 December 1840. From a letter of James Whitty of Bradford to Dublin

56 For this type of argument see speech of E. Hayes at Leeds, *ibid* 5 February 1842; report on the Leeds Repeal organisation, *ibid* 2 September 1843; speech of W. O'Neill Daunt, *Leeds Times* 23 September 1843

57 *Freeman's Journal* 5 February 1842, speech of E. Hayes at Leeds

58 *Liverpool Mercury* 1, 8, 22 June 1832; *Catholic Magazine*, Vol II, No 20 (September 1832) pp592-5; *Manchester Guardian* 8 September 1832

59 J. H. Treble, The Attitude of the Roman Catholic Church towards Trade Unionism in the North of England 1833-42, *Northern History* V (1970) pp93-113

60 J. H. Treble, 'The Place of the Irish Catholics in the Social Life of the North of England 1829-51' (unpublished University of Leeds PhD, 1969) p128

61 *Ibid* pp322-4

62 *Liverpool Mercury* 28 June 1839 and 31 May 1839, from a letter of George Smyth

63 *Freeman's Journal* 20 November 1841, from a letter of George Smyth

64 *Ibid* 12 July 1843. From letter of Rev D. Hearne of Manchester to D. O'Connell: 'A deputation of Chartists called on me a short time back, to ask me to allow the Repealers to join them in a petition against the arms bill. I refused to sanction any connection with them. I have had to dismiss a Repeal collector for his having taken a subscription from Feargus O'Connor.' See also *Northern Star* 3 May 1845 and J. Gillow *Bibliographical Dictionary of the English Catholics* (1885) III, p233: 'By the right use of great zeal, and considerable practical talent, he [Rev D. Hearne] not only saved his parishioners from the evils of Socialism, Chartism, and the like, but also rendered them sober, united, and peaceful.'

65 For clerical attitudes to Chartists who were Catholics, see J. H. Treble, 'The Place of the Irish Catholics in the Social Life of the North of England 1829-51' (unpublished University of Leeds PhD, 1969) pp298-302. For a Catholic Chartist's complaint of clerical hostility in Scotland, see *Northern Star* 23 July 1842. On the other hand there were a few places

 224   NOTES AND REFERENCES

where little or no antagonism was displayed by priests towards Chartism.
See for instance the reception of Chartists at the Jesuit-run Stonyhurst
College, near Blackburn, *ibid* 1 January 1842

66 I found no reference in either the Leeds Diocesan Archives or the northern press which would suggest that the North of England Vicars-Apostolic
imposed spiritual sanctions against Catholics who were Chartists

67 *Northern Star* 19 December 1840

68 D. Read and E. Glasgow, *op cit* p92

69 *Leeds Times* 23 January 1841; *Freeman's Journal* 25 January 1841

70 *Freeman's Journal* 25 January 1841. O'Connell later addressed a 'closed'
gathering of the Leeds Parliamentary Reform Association, *ibid* and *Leeds
Times* 30 January 1841

71 D. O'Connell to P. V. FitzPatrick 26 January 1841 in W. J. Fitzpatrick
[ed] *op cit* II p256

72 *Freeman's Journal* 6 April 1841

73 *Ibid* 11 May 1841. Letter of John Kelly of Manchester to Dublin. 'We
have completely defeated the Chartists; they called a meeting of the Irish
Chartists in Manchester in their Association Rooms, for the express purpose of passing a vote of censure on Mr O'Connell, but the Repealers
attended, and had a chairman appointed, and a vote of thanks and
confidence passed to Mr O'Connell.'

74 *Leeds Mercury* 18 January 1840

75 *Manchester Times Extraordinary* 14 January 1840

76 *Leeds Mercury* 4 February 1843 quoting *Manchester Guardian*

77 *Leeds Times* 18 January 1840

78 *Anti-Bread Tax Circular* 21 April, 26 August 1841

79 For a full analysis of the relations between the League and the Chartists,
see Lucy Brown 'The Chartists and the Anti-Corn Law League' in Asa
Briggs [ed] *op cit* pp342-71

80 *Northern Star* 5 January 1839

81 N. McCord *The Anti-Corn Law League* (1958) p99

82 A. Briggs [ed] *op cit* p355; *The Tablet* 18 July 1840; *Northern Star* 3
November 1840

83 *Manchester Guardian* 5 January 1842; *Manchester Times* 8 January 1842;
Freeman's Journal 11 May 1841

84 *Freeman's Journal* 29 June 1841; *Manchester Times* 8 January 1842

85 *Freeman's Journal* 11 May 1842; *Manchester Times* 12 March, 2 April
1842

86 Quoted N. McCord *op cit* p101

87 *Ibid* p102; *Manchester Guardian* 5 January 1842; *Northern Star* 8 January
1842

88 *Manchester Guardian* 9 March 1842; *Northern Star* 12 March 1842; *Manchester Times* 12 March 1842; *Manchester and Salford Advertiser* 12 March
1842. The *Manchester Times* devoted a leading article to the Hall of
Science affair.
'Reasons may be asked for the evident want of confidence which Mr.
O'Connor's countrymen here have in him. His somewhat dubious proceedings previous to, during, and after he vacated his seat in parliament,
have contributed to this. His late pro-tory policy has also aided to produce the effect. But the main reason, we believe, is to be found in his
constant, unremitting, and industrious abuse of Mr. Daniel O'Connell.

That gentleman is looked up to by ninety-nine out of every hundred of his oppressed fellow-countrymen as their champion, their leader, and friend.' *Manchester Times* 12 March 1842

89 Edward Watkin was a prominent organiser of the Anti-Corn Law League in Manchester. For O'Connor's allegations of complicity between the town's immigrant leaders and the Anti-Corn Law League, see *Northern Star* 12 March 1842. In court O'Connor spoke of bribery of the Irish by 'persons of wealth and station' who desired his assassination. Some of those who were hired for this end received '1s. for their work, and 1d. for admission; while another part received 2s. 6d. and 1d. for admission.' One man, however, had been given £5 to throw him off the platform among those Irish in the audience with 'hatchets, pokers, stones of immense size, and missiles of various description, and whose especial duty it was then to assassinate me.' See *Manchester and Salford Advertiser* 12 March 1842. At a Repeal of the Union meeting William Duffy subsequently denied that 'the Irish inhabitants of Manchester are the hired Swiss in the pay of the Anti-Corn Law League' and argued that the Chartists themselves had broken up the meeting to avoid public exposure of their pro-Tory and anti-O'Connell stance! See *Manchester Times* 2 April 1842. Daniel O'Connell was, however, furious at the Manchester Repealers' open repudiation of his 'moral force' doctrines, asserting that 'nothing could be more outrageous or criminal than the attack made on the meeting assembled at Manchester.' *Freeman's Journal* 25 March 1842. Later he had a series of resolutions inserted in the Manchester press deprecating the Hall of Science fracas and declaring that 'we will not receive the co-operation of any man who engaged in violent proceedings.' *Ibid* 5 April 1842. The Rev D. Hearne followed a similar line of attack, for which he was thanked by groups of Yorkshire and Lancashire Chartists. *Northern Star* 26 March, 2 April 1842

90 *Northern Star* 12 March 1842
91 N. McCord, *op cit* p99
92 *Northern Star* 8 January 1842
93 *Freeman's Journal* 22 December 1840, 3 March 1841. At Manchester the local Repealers resolved that 'although we revere and respect his [Emmet's] memory, we view with horror the principle that brought him to an untimely end; therefore, we call on all Irishmen to refrain from attending such a meeting.' Emmet was executed after playing a leading part in the unsuccessful Irish Rebellion of 1803
94 *Ibid* 14 September 1841
95 *Ibid*
96 *Ibid*
97 *Ibid* 28 September 1841, letter of T. Gately of Birmingham
98 *Ibid* 6 October 1841, letter of H. Coddington of Stockport
99 *Manchester Guardian* 29 September 1841. This meeting was attended by English representatives from the Anti-Corn Law League, including Edward Watkin who seconded this resolution. Admission to this gathering was by ticket only so that Chartist interventions were reduced to a minimum
100 *Northern Star* 29 January 1842
101 *Ibid* 29 January, 5 February 1842
102 *Ibid* 5 February, 23 April 1842

Q

103 The Hall of Science fracas at Manchester which occurred after this new Chartist campaign for an Anglo-Irish *entente* had been launched was but one indication of how little impact the inclusion of the demand for the Repeal of the Act of Union in the Second National Petition had had on immigrant opinion

104 *The Tablet* 28 January 1843

105 *Northern Star* 27 May 1843

106 *Ibid* 3 June 1843

107 *Ibid* 10 June 1843. At the same meeting at which the Rev Coppinger spoke, the Rev Egan, another Catholic priest, advised Hull Repealers 'not to be led into any secret societies, to have nothing to do with plots, or to commit any breach of the laws, but peaceably, constitutionally, and temperately assist the Irish people to establish the national independence of their country.'

108 *Ibid* 3, 10 June 1843

109 *Leeds Times* 10 June 1843. This letter was dated 31 May 1843. There was inevitably a slight time-lag before these instructions became widely known. The *Leeds Mercury* (10 June 1843), quoting from the same letter, had a slightly different wording to the version published in the *Leeds Times*. According to the *Mercury* Ray wrote thus: 'We can countenance no connexion with Chartists, but, above all, with their leaders, who hold out the abhorrent doctrine of physical force, and some of these people, we have every reason to suspect, are in the pay of the Tories, and are now coming amongst the repealers to create confusion, and commit us into the hands of our enemies.'

110 *Northern Star* 17, 24 June 1843; *Freeman's Journal* 20 June 1843; *Leeds Mercury* 1 July 1843. At Bolton, however, there seems to have been a successful Chartist-Repealer meeting after Ray's instructions were issued. See *Freeman's Journal* 4 July 1843

111 Thus of one such gathering at Leeds it was reported that 'the few "cast off" Chartist Repealers' who attended, 'were not even countenanced by the presence of that proportion of Irishmen which we are accustomed to observe in public meetings having an object purely British, - so effectually does the precaution of O'Connell seem to have operated here in deterring the Irish from any union with the English Chartists.' *Leeds Mercury* 1 July 1843. The *Leeds Times* on the other hand described the same meeting in glowing terms. This latter report was almost certainly inaccurate. See *Leeds Times* 1 July 1843

112 *Northern Star* 12 October 1844. See also *ibid* 5, 26 October 1844

113 *Ibid* 28 September 1844, leading article

114 *Ibid* 12 April, 10 May 1845, leading article

115 For further details on this point see J. H. Treble, 'The Place of the Irish Catholics in the Social Life of the North of England 1829-51' (unpublished University of Leeds PhD, 1969) pp337-50

116 Smith O'Brien Papers [National Library of Ireland], Vol 438, No 1867, Richard O'Gorman to Smith O'Brien, 29 March 1847. O'Gorman reported seeing 'today a sort of requisition calling on Feargus O'Connor to come over and lecture—I believe that acquisition will be numerously signed.'

117 Minute Book of the Council of the Irish Confederation 12, 19 May 1847. [Ms 23 H43-44, Royal Irish Academy, Dublin]

118 *The Nation* 15 August 1847 quoted Sir C. Gavan Duffy *Four Years of Irish History 1845-9* (1883) p450

119 *Northern Star* 8 August 1846. Mr Smith of Bradford was in favour of such
an address on the grounds that if they could not impress the Irish people
'they could [make an impression] upon the Irish in England, who were
already favourable to them; upwards of fifty Irish Repealers were members of the Land Fund at Bradford.' There is no other evidence available
to check this last claim, although at this point in time it would, if valid,
represent a minor breakthrough for a local Chartist body
120 *Ibid* 18 September 1847. A resolution exhorting Irishmen, 'wherever
practicable', to establish branches of the Irish Democratic Confederation
[henceforth cited as IDC] was passed in London in late September 1847.
Ibid 2 October 1847
121 *Ibid* 18 September 1847
122 *Ibid* 16 October 1847. Segrave accepted all the points made in the address
'excepting that passage which states that the Old and Young Irelanders
are our friends, as being from the same persecuted land.'
123 *Ibid* 20 November 1847. At a meeting of the Barnsley Branch of the IDC
sentiments favourable to the *Nation* were then being uttered. "Mr Segrave
was proud to learn that the conductors of that journal had thrown aside
their unholy and unjust prejudices by offering the hand of friendship to
the oppressed people of England and Scotland. He would say with the
Northern Star, 'Let bygones be bygones', and if the *Nation* is desirous to
form a holy brotherhood of the democracy of the United Kingdom, the
day is not far distant when the liberty of all will be achieved."
124 I found no reference in the columns of either *The Nation* or the *Northern
Star* during 1847 of any Irish Confederate Club in the North of England
holding any form of joint meeting with local Chartists
125 *The Nation* 15 January 1848. Leach delivered a forceful speech in favour
of the Charter on this occasion
126 *Ibid* Mitchel at the outset stressed the points of divergence between
English Chartists and Irish Confederates. 'I say that if the people of
England, who are suffering as well as ourselves under this intolerable
government, offer us a hand to help us to get rid of our common enemy,
we will help them to strike down theirs. (Cheers). But our means must
be somewhat different. They may go to their parliament with their three
miles of petition—I say let us not send one inch of a petition to that
parliament. (Loud cheers). They ask extended franchises for returning
members to their own English parliament—I say we want no franchise for
the purposes of that parliament at all.'
127 *United Irishman* 26 February 1848
128 *The Nation* 29 January 1848. Treanor described John O'Connell in the
following terms: "The man upon whom it is said the 'mantle of Moses',
or, rather, the cloak of his father, has descended, but who possesses
neither the mind, the talent, the power, or the honesty of that great man,
and yet, like the jackdaw in the plume of the peacock . . . apes the manners, the power, and the language of him whose name he bears. Divest
him of that name and what is he? A fourth-rate parish demagogue; an
empty, frothy agitator, 'a knave in politics', a government tool without
power, without talent, a mere atom on the face of creation, a tyrant and
a coward."
129 *Ibid* 12, 19 February, 4 March 1848
130 Smith O'Brien Papers, Vol 442, No 2377. Smith O'Brien to James Smyth,

Secretary of the Manchester and Salford Confederate Club, 28 February 1848. Smith O'Brien, however, promised to attend this Repeal rally if his parliamentary duties permitted. He felt that the proposed meeting should include supporters of the Loyal National Repeal Association as well as Irish Confederates

131 Minute Book of the Council of the Irish Confederation [Royal Irish Academy, Dublin, MS23 H43-44] 8 March 1848. Originally Smith O'Brien, T. Chisolm Anstey, T. Meagher, C. Gavan Duffy, John Martin, T. McGhee, O'Gorman (Senior) and Dillon were appointed to attend. Later the deputation's composition was altered because of the need of the Confederation to be represented at a forthcoming demonstration of Dublin 'traders and citizens'. Meagher, Doheny, McGhee and West were to be asked to go to the Manchester rally. *Ibid* 11 March 1848. Three days later, anticipating a clash between the citizens and government at the Dublin rally, the Council decided to send Meagher alone. At the same time they expressed their 'deep regret that the proposed deputation is necessarily prevented from being in Manchester on St Patrick's day', and asked 'our English and Irish friends in Manchester and Birmingham' to believe 'that it is not against the English people but against the so called English government, we entertain hostility and that no earthly power shall ever influence us to regard our English allies with other the friendliest feelings [sic]'. *Ibid* 14 March 1848. To allay Smith O'Brien's fears, he was informed by T. Halpin, Secretary of the Irish Confederation, that 'the Secretary [of the Manchester Confederates] (Mr. Jas. Smyth, a Confederate) states that the Chartists have promised not to introduce their doctrines at the Meeting, a promise which he believes they will keep'. Smith O'Brien Papers, Vol 442, No 2391. T. M. Halpin to Smith O'Brien 9 March 1848. Smith O'Brien however opted for the Dublin meeting

132 *Northern Star* 25 March 1848. Feargus O'Connor addressed the meeting in his own flamboyant style. 'If I were asked what brought you here tonight and if I were to receive a true and consistent answer, the answer should be—to receive absolution from me. (Cheers). For thirteen years I have been advocating the very union which you have tardily confirmed'. The meeting was a huge success despite an address from the Catholic clergy of Manchester and Salford, exhorting their flocks 'to refrain, for the present, from taking part in any processions or promiscuous bodies where large bodies of men assemble'. See *The Tablet* 25 March 1848

133 For the history of the Repeal movement after February 1848 see K. B. Nowlan, *op cit* pp171-231

134 *Liverpool Mercury* 25 July 1848, leading article

135 *Manchester Guardian* 22 March 1848

136 *Leeds Times* 8 April 1848, leading article; *The Nation* 8 April 1848. It has not been possible within the confines of this paper to discuss in any detail the relationship between the followers of the Loyal National Repeal Association on the one hand and Irish Confederates and English Chartists on the other. It can be broadly argued that in certain of the northern towns—Leeds and Stalybridge for example—the Repeal Association lost its hold over a sizeable proportion of its immigrant following as early as the autumn of 1846. In other areas—Manchester and Liverpool for instance—Conciliation Hall controlled the political outlook of the majority of immigrants until 1848 itself, although even before that point in time the

Confederation had made some inroads into John O'Connell's support. Down to 1848, however, both Confederates and Repealers remained anti-Chartist. After the February 1848 Revolution in France Confederates and Repealers began meeting together. Furthermore there is some indication that Repealers were now prepared to abandon their former animosity towards Chartism and to attend Chartist meetings. These points will be fully developed in my forthcoming book on *Irish Immigrants in the North of England 1829-51*

137 *The Nation* 29 April 1848

138 *Leeds Times* 1, 8 April 1848; *The Nation* 1 April, 6, 27 May 1848; *Manchester Guardian* 31 May 1848; *Liverpool Mercury* 27 June, 25 July 1848

139 *Liverpool Mercury* 25, 28 July, 1 August 1848

140 *Ibid* 22 August 1848; *Leeds Times* 26 August, 2, 9 September 1848; *Manchester Guardian* 19, 23 August 1848

141 This is an expanded version of a paper delivered at the University of Strathclyde on 23 March 1971 to a Robert Owen Bi-centenary Conference. I am very much indebted to my colleagues, Professor S. G. E. Lythe, Mr B. F. Duckham and Dr W. H. Fraser of the University of Strathclyde, for their helpful criticism of this paper. I am also grateful to the Carnegie Trust for Scottish Universities for financial support for my research programme. I would like to thank the Council of Trustees of the National Library of Ireland for permission to quote from the Smith O'Brien Correspondence and the Royal Irish Academy for allowing me access to the Minute Book of the Irish Confederation

Dickens and the Self-Help Idea
Robin Gilmour (pp71-101)

1 'Dickens: the Two Scrooges', *The Wound and the Bow* (rev edn, 1952), 26

2 'Manners, Morals, and the Novel', *The Liberal Imagination* (New York, 1950), Doubleday Anchor edn, 200

3 *The Autobiography of Samuel Smiles*, ed Thomas Mackay (1905), 222

4 *Life and Labour* (1887), 238-9; quoted in Kenneth Fielden, 'Samuel Smiles and Self-Help', *Victorian Studies*, XII (1968), 155. This is an excellent study of Smiles' social thinking, and I am additionally grateful to Dr Fielden for the helpful advice he has given me with the background of self-help

5 *Thrift* (1875), 94

6 Quoted in George Ford, 'Self-Help and the Helpless in *Bleak House*', in *From Jane Austen to Joseph Conrad*, ed Robert C. Rathburn and Martin Steinmann Jr, (Minneapolis, 1958), 95. See also *Speeches of Charles Dickens*, ed K. J. Fielding (Oxford, 1960), 117, 281, 400

7 *Autobiography*, 222

8 *Speeches*, 406. There is an extremely useful discussion of Dickens' attitude to work in Chapter V of Alexander Welsh's recent study, *The City of Dickens* (Oxford, 1971)

9 *Speeches*, 405

10 *Speeches*, 48
11 *Self-Help* (1859), 314, 325, 328
12 *Mid-Victorian Britain* (1971), 247
13 'I had read it often, and knew its many striking passage almost by heart' (*Autobiography*, 222)
14 References are to the edition of the novel in Everyman's Library
15 H. Taine, *Notes on England* (Second edn, 1872), 175-6
16 *Victorian People* (Penguin edn, Middlesex, 1965), 142
17 John Forster, *Life of Charles Dickens*, ed A. J. Hoppe (2 vols, 1966), I, 25-6. Hereafter cited as *Life*
18 *Dickens: from Pickwick to Dombey* (1965), 355
19 *Irish Essays* (1882); reprinted in *Dickens: the Critical Heritage*, ed Philip Collins (1971), 269
20 F. R. and Q. D. Leavis, *Dickens the Novelist* (1970), 88
21 *loc cit*
22 *Household Words*, 30 March 1850
23 For a full discussion of the part self-help plays in the scheme of values of *Bleak House*, see the article by George Ford cited in note 6 above
24 I cannot agree with Trevor Blount ('The Ironmaster and the New Acquisitiveness', *Essays in Criticism*, XV, 1965, 414-27) that 'the Ironmaster merely represents . . . the old privilege translated into different terms' (418). This seems to me to do less than justice to the complexity of Dickens' position here, and essentially to falsify his picture of the ironmaster: see Anne Smith's effective rebuttal, 'The Ironmaster in *Bleak House*', *Essays in Criticism*, XXI (1971), 159-69
25 *Works*, ed E. T. Cook and Alexander Wedderburn (1903-12), XXXVII (1909), 7; letter of 19 June 1870, to Charles Eliot Norton
26 Introduction to *Little Dorrit*, 'New Oxford Illustrated Dickens' (1953), xiv
27 That Dickens was passing through something of a personal crisis at this time is evident from Forster's discreet, but fascinating and revealing account of this period in *Life*, Bk VIII, ch 2
28 Humphry House, *The Dickens World* (Second edn, 1942), 156
29 John Lucas, *The Melancholy Man* (1970), 302
30 *Life*, 22
31 'The Heroes and Heroines of Dickens', *Review of English Literature*, II (1961), 18

The Unschooled Philosopher: An Unlikely Impression of John Stuart Mill

D. R. Gordon (pp102-32)

1 Preface to 1870 edition of *St. Paul and Protestantism*, reprinted in Matthew Arnold: *Dissent and Dogma* (ed R. H. Super), (Michigan 1968) 126. For Arnold, 'Hellenism does not address itself with serious energy enough to morals and righteousness'. Mill has even taken away its beauty and charm by strident attacks on the Church of England
2 Bertrand Russell, 'John Stuart Mill' in J. B. Schneewind (ed): *Mill* (1968) 1-21

3 Edward Alexander, *Matthew Arnold and John Stuart Mill* (1965) 5. Despite what is carefully argued in Mr Alexander's excellent first chapter, 'representative figure' is depreciatory; it also inaccurately describes a *precursive* figure such as Mill

4 R. P. Anschutz, *The Philosophy of J. S. Mill* (Oxford, 1953) 5

5 'Probably rightly' because the nature of originality is, nowadays, itself rarely examined; it is indeed partly what is at issue in this essay

6 Mill, *Autobiography* (ed Jack Stillinger) (Oxford, 1971) 18. This is the best edition of the *Autobiography* currently in print, incorporating as it does, much material from the original draft. cf Jack Stillinger, *The Early Draft of John Stuart Mill's Autobiography* (Urbana, 1961)

7 Stillinger, 18

8 *Ibid*

9 *Ibid*, 33-4. Professor Stillinger inserts in a footnote a longish passage (of which this is a part), which was, apparently, first marked for deletion by Harriet Taylor

10 *Ibid*, 105

11 *Ibid*, 124-5; my italics

12 *Ibid*, 125-6

13 Perhaps Carlyle should also be mentioned: 'I believe that the early success and reputation of Carlyle's French Revolution, were considerably accelerated by what I wrote about it in the Review.' *Autobiography*, 129

14 Quoted in Basil Willey, *Nineteenth-Century Studies* (1955), 142

15 Quoted in Professor Stillinger's Introduction to the *Autobiography*, xvii

16 *Autobiography*, 83. In this and ensuing quotations, Mill's constant use of qualifying expressions such as 'or thought I saw' or 'I thought' etc is emphasised by my italics which are not in the original. Mill uses one or two similar signs of reservation, and equally significantly, in Chapter One of *Utilitarianism*, in the course of debating whether in morality, 'Foundations' or moral principles should come first

17 *Ibid*, 83-4

18 *Ibid*, 83

19 *Ibid*, 85-6

20 *Ibid*, 86

21 *Bentham*, reprinted in the *Collected Works of John Stuart Mill*, Vol X, *Essays on Ethics, Religion and Society* (Toronto, 1969), 92

22 *Autobiography*, 89

23 *Ibid*, 87

24 *Ibid*, 88

25 *Ibid*, 89

26 *Ibid*, 90. Mill's point about Wordsworth is that he does not merely express outward beauty but 'states of feeling, and of thought coloured by feeling, under the excitement of beauty'

27 *Ibid*, 92

28 Matthew Arnold, *Letters to Clough*, quoted in E. Alexander, op cit, 29

29 *Autobiography*, 158

30 For example, *System of Logic*, 7th edition in two volumes (1868) Vol II, 553. All later references to the *Logic* will be to this edition

31 *Autobiography*, 130

32 *Collected Works of John Stuart Mill*, Vol XII and XIII: *The Earlier Letters of John Stuart Mill* (Toronto, 1963), 236

33 *Op cit,* 712
34 Hugh S. R. Elliot, *The Letters of John Stuart Mill,* 1910, Vol I, 181. In this letter there are further interesting remarks on Moral Psychology and Ethology
35 F. A. Hayek, *John Stuart Mill and Harriet Taylor 1951,* 199, Mill adds, '*But I am not fit* to write on anything but the outskirts of the great questions of feeling and life. . .'
36 *Autobiography,* 146
37 *Ibid,* 150
38 *Logic* Vol II, 551
39 *Ibid,* 551
40 *Ibid,* 554-5
41 *Utilitarianism,* in *Essays on Ethics, Religion and Society,* 206
42 *Auguste Comte and Positivism,* in *Essays on Ethics,* etc, 300
43 *Utilitarianism,* 206
44 'Sedgwick's Discourse', in *Essays on Ethics,* etc, 74
45 *Earlier Letters,* 207-8
46 *On Liberty,* Everyman Edition (1910), 115
47 *Utilitarianism,* 217
48 *Ibid,* 212
49 *Ibid,* 213
50 *Ibid,* 213
51 'Sedgwick's Discourse', 74
52 Maurice Cowling, *Mill & Liberalism* (Cambridge, 1963). This powerful assault on Mill is not so much a defence of 'true' liberalism as an attack on Mill for pretending to be what he was not
53 Jeremy Bentham, an *Introduction to the principles of Morals & Legislation* (ed W. Harrison), (Oxford 1948), 125. cf also H. L. A. Hart, 'Bentham' *Proceedings of the British Academy* vol XLVIII (1962), 297-320, and K. Britton, 'Utilitarianism: The Appeal to a first Principle' *Proceedings of the Aristotelian Society* vol 60 (1959-60), 141-54
54 *Remarks on Bentham's Philosophy,* in *Essays on Ethics,* etc, 7
55 *Bentham,* 94. On the notions of happiness as fullness of life and as satisfaction of desire cf A. Kenny, 'Happiness' *Proceedings of the Aristotelian Society* vol 66 (1965-66), 93-102 reprinted in Joel Feinberg (ed), *Moral Concepts* (Oxford 1969), 43-52, and I. Berlin, *John Stuart Mill and the Ends of Life* (1959)
56 *Ibid,* 93
57 *Ibid,* 89-90; my italics
58 *Remarks on Bentham's Philosophy,* 13
59 *Bentham,* 95
60 *Ibid,* 111
61 *Ibid,* 110
62 *Logic,* Vol II, 554
63 *Utilitarianism,* 207
64 Samuel Clarke, 'Discourse on Natural Religion', in L. A. Selby-Bigge, *British Moralists* (Oxford, 1897) Vol II, 5-6. Clarke's is a classical illustration. For him, moral truths 'are so notoriously plain and self-evident, that nothing but the extremist stupidity of Mind, corruption of Manners, or perverseness of Spirit can possibly make any Man entertain the least doubt concerning them . . . as if a man that understands Geometry or

Arithmetick, should . . . contend that the Whole is not equal to all its parts. . .' Clark's position is not, in fact, as bad as this passage might lead one to suppose
65 F. H. Bradley, *Ethical Studies* (Oxford, 1876) Essay III. cf Britton *loc cit*, Professor Britton says that in the 1838 essay on *Bentham*, Mill remained a utilitarian, in part because he held 'that moral principles are reached through experience and rational reflexion and are therefore liable to revision in the light of new experience or new reflexion'. This, as Professor Britton would certainly urge, is not much of a utilitarianism.
66 It ought to be better known than it is that Mill takes his teaching on specific consequences (in the *Remarks*) almost word for word from John Austin's *Province of Jurisprudence Determined*, Lecture II. Unfortunately, he does not take that teaching meaning for meaning. Austin is speaking of the consequences of a specific act, rather than of a class of actions. Admittedly his language is that of 'specific consequences' and Mill takes this seriously. But what could the *general* consequences of a specific act be? It is at this point that Mill speaks about the entire moral bearings of an action.
67 *Logic* Book VI, Chapter X, 509
68 *Ibid*, 508
69 For a comprehensive account of this process, see W. D. Hudson (ed) *The Is-Ought Question* (1969). This is a formidable debate; the essential first step has been to recognise that it is not values that are mysterious but facts, eg the fact that Jones promised to pay Smith five dollars. This assertion has the mysterious property that it can be shown to generate, in a few steps, and with plausible logic, the value judgement that Jones ought to pay Smith five dollars. cf in the above volume, J. R. Searle, 'How to derive 'Ought' from 'Is'.'

Dostoevsky's Anti-Utopianism
A. J. Noble (pp133-55)

1 Saul Bellow, 'Foreword to Dostoevsky's *Winter Notes* on Summer Impressions', *Winter Notes on Summer Impressions*, trans Richard Lee Renfield (New York 1965), 25
2 F. M. Dostoevsky, *Crime and Punishment*, trans Constance Garnett (1958), 129
3 Ibid, 131-2
4 F. M. Dostoevsky, 'Spiritism. Something about Devils. Extraordinary Craftiness of the Devils, if only These Are Devils', *Diary of a Writer*, trans Boris Brasol (New York 1954), 192
5 Dostoevsky, 'The same rule—only in a new version', *Diary of a Writer*, 852
6 Dostoevsky, 'The Most Enormous Military Mistakes Sometimes May Not Be Mistakes at All', *Diary of a Writer*, 855
7 Dostoevsky, 'Spiritism. Something about Devils. Extraordinary Craftiness of the Devils, if only These Are Devils', *Diary of a Writer*, 192-3
8 F. M. Dostoevsky, Letter quoted by Konstantin Mochulsky, *Dostoevsky:*
R

His Life and Work, trans Michael A. Minihan (Princetown 1967), 232

9 Dostoevsky, 'Am I an Enemy of Children?', *Diary of a Writer,* 931-2

10 Dostoevsky, 'About Stripping Skins in General and Various Aberrations in Particular—Hatred of Authority Coupled with Lackeyism in Thought', *Diary of a Writer,* 604

11 Dostoevsky, 'Never Was Russia More Powerful Than at Present—Not a Diplomatic Decision', *Diary of a Writer,* 724

12 Dostoevsky, 'The Best Men', *Diary of a Writer,* 488

13 Dostoevsky, 'Meditations about Europe', *Diary of a Writer,* 250

14 Dostoevsky, 'Chapter V, Baal', *Winter Notes on Summer Impressions,* 89

15 Dostoevsky, 'Essay on the Bourgeoisie', *Winter Notes on Summer Impressions,* 110-11

16 Dostoevsky, 'What Gives Relief at Spas: Mineral Water or Bon Ton?', *Diary of a Writer,* 406

17 Dostoevsky, 'Essay on the Bourgeoisie', 105

18 Dostoevsky, 'Chapter VIII, *Bribri* and *Ma Biche*', *Winter Notes on Summer Impressions,* 142

19 Dostoevsky, 'Belated Moral', *Diary of a Writer,* 536

20 Dostoevsky, 'From the Book of Predictions by Johann Lichtenberger in the Year 1528', *Diary of a Writer,* 697

21 Dostoevsky, 'Idealists—Cynics', *Diary of a Writer,* 379-80

22 Vyacheslav Ivanov, 'Dostoevsky's Philosophy of Life', *Freedom and the Tragic Life* (New York 1957), 24-5

23 Dostoevsky, 'Baal', *Winter Notes on Summer Impressions,* 88

24 Dostoevsky, 'Segregation', *Diary of a Writer,* 245

25 Dostoevsky, 'Isolated Phenomena', *Diary of a Writer,* 271-2

26 Dostoevsky, 'Two Suicides', *Diary of a Writer,* 469-70

27 *Ibid,* 468-9

28 Dostoevsky, *Crime and Punishment,* 145

29 *Ibid,* 216-17

William Morris or Bernard Shaw: Two Faces of Victorian Socialism

James Redmond (pp156-76)

1 eg, 'A decent nation would have buried [William Morris] in Westminster Abbey; but he himself would not have rested there as he does in the little grave at Kelmscott which has made the place the shrine of a saint...'
Shaw, 'Morris As I Knew Him', in *William Morris: Artist, Writer, Socialist,* ed May Morris (Oxford 1936), vol I, xxxvi ff

2 E. E. Stokes, 'William Morris and Bernard Shaw', *The Journal of the William Morris Society,* I, i (1961), 13f

3 J. W. Hulse, *Revolutionists in London* (Oxford 1970), 110, 122

4 eg, '[Those works which express Morris's] vision of the life to come on a happy earth . . . survive as the best books in the Bible of Socialism.
Shaw, 'Morris As I Knew Him'
'I have written *Back to Methuselah* as a contribution to the modern Bible.'
Shaw, 'Voluntary Longevity', Preface to *Back to Methuselah*

5 Robert Owen, 'A Further Development of the Plan for the Relief of the Poor, and the Emancipation of Mankind', 1817. Printed in the Supplementary Appendix to the first volume of *The Life of Robert Owen: Written by Himself* (1858), 134

6 Shaw, 'Socialism at the International Congress', *Cosmopolis III*, September 1896, 659

7 *The Republic*, Books II and VIII

8 *Ibid*, Book IV

9 Robert Owen, *The Revolution in the Mind* (1849), 21

10 J. S. Mill, 'On Marriage and Divorce', in *John Stuart Mill and Harriet Taylor: Their Correspondence and Subsequent Marriage*, ed F. A. Hayek (1951), 74, 291

11 See, eg, the ninth chapter of *News from Nowhere*, and the relevant paragraphs of *The Manifesto of the Socialist League*, which is reprinted in E. P. Thompson's *William Morris, Romantic to Revolutionary* (1955)

12 *Jerusalem*, plate 55, 11, 56ff

13 *News from Nowhere*, ch iii

14 Norman O. Brown, *Life Against Death: The Psychoanalytical Meaning of History* (1959)

15 Revelation, 21

16 'Locksley Hall Sixty Years After'

17 *Modern Painters*, Pt III, sec I, ch xii

18 Georgina Burne-Jones, *Memorials of Edward Burne-Jones* (1904), vol I, 84

19 *News from Nowhere*, ch xvi

20 *Back to Methuselah*, Part V

21 *Proverbs of Hell*

Land Reform and Class Conflict in Victorian Britain

H. J. Perkin (pp177-217)

1 *Parliamentary Debates*, 3rd Series, vol 256, 619 and 618

2 13 February and 31 March 1880

3 5 May 1880

4 Speech at West Calder, 27 November, *The Times*, 28 November 1879

5 *Manchester Guardian*, 25 March 1880

6 *The Nineteenth Century*, August 1880

7 Sir John MacDonell, *The Land Question* (1873), 2

8 The abolition of the law of primogeniture and the virtual assimilation of the law of real property and that of personalty in 1925 were, however, amongst the aims of the largest group of Victorian land reformers

9 W. E. Baxter, *Our Land Laws of the Past* [1881], 3

10 Cf Asa Briggs, *Victorian People* (1954), 29

11 *The Corn Laws and Social England* (1932), 143. The quotation continues the argument that 'between socialism and land reform there is no natural affinity', but this does not alter its implication concerning the failure of land reform

12 K. Marx and F. Engels, *Selected Correspondence* (Moscow, 1956), 416: Marx to F. A. Sorge, 20 June 1881

13 January 1833, 'Causes of the Distress of the Landed Interest'
14 G. M. Trevelyan, *Life of Bright* (1913), 166
15 *Dissertations and Discussions* (1875), vol IV, 251: Speech on Land Tenure Reform, 15 May 1871
16 Cf G. C. Brodrick, *English Land and English Landlords* (1881), 355
17 Edmund Potter, *A Picture of a Manufacturing District* [Glossop] (Manchester, 1856), 24
18 J. L. Garvin, *Life of Chamberlain* (1932-51), vol I, 392. It was applied, for example, nearly twenty years earlier, to the same class in the same way by the *Westminster Review*, July 1864, 'The Tenure of Land'
19 *Political Economy* (1872 ed), 89. Cf Adam Smith, *The Wealth of Nations* (1776), book I, chap xi
20 *Parliamentary Papers*, 1876, vols 335 and C.1492. Owners of land outside the metropolis total as follows (owners of one acre and over in brackets): England and Wales 972,836 (262,986); Scotland 132,131 (19,104); Ireland 68,758 (32,164). These total for the United Kingdom 1,173,725 (314,704), but allowance must be made for duplications. Deducting for these and for corporation, charity and glebe lands, George Shaw Lefevre arrived at totals of 1,153,816 (301,378) in a population (1871) of 27,431,000—*Freedom of Land* (1880), 10
21 Cf *Parliamentary Papers*, 1869, vol C.66: 'Reports . . . respecting the Tenures of Land in the Several Countries of Europe': the report on France (Part I, 59) gives an estimate of 5,300,000 owners, 5 million of whom average 6 acres each, in a population of 38 million; that on Prussia (Part I, 217) 1,111,117 proprietors, and only 60,739 tenants in a population of 19.7 million
22 Sir Arthur Arnold, *Free Land* (1880), 4
23 *Ibid*, 7; Brodrick, *op cit*, 165. Cf Joseph Kay, *Free Trade in Land* (1879), 14-17; Shaw Lefevre, *op cit*, 9-13
24 March, 1844, 'The Land Tax'
25 *Speeches on Questions of Public Policy* (1870), vol I, 344
26 Speech in House of Commons, 14 March 1842, reprinted as *The Land Tax Fraud* (1842)
27 T. E. Cliffe Leslie, 'The Land System of the Country a Reason for a Reform of Parliament', in *Fraser's Magazine*, February 1867. Cf *inter alia*, Anti-Corn Law League, *The Constitutional Right to a Revision of the Land Tax* (1842); *Westminster Review*, January 1870, 'Land Tenures and their Consequences', and October 1870, 'The Land Question in England'; Leslie, *The Land Systems and Industrial Economy of Ireland, England and Continental Countries* (1870), 207; Joseph Fisher, *History of Landholding in England* (1876)
28 *Free Trade in Land* (1876 ed), v
29 Ironically, the few spectacular examples of such behaviour, eg in the second Duke of Buckingham and Chandos or 'mad' George Wyndham, ended in sales of part or all of the land
30 Quoted by Beal, *op cit*, 24
31 'Ireland and the Land Act', in *The Nineteenth Century*, October 1881
32 Cf MacDonell, *op cit*, 118
33 Beal, *op cit*, vi
34 Cf Mill, *op cit*, vol IV, 239. 'Explanatory Statement of the Land Tenure Reform Association' (1870); Garvin, *op cit*, vol II, 191

35 Cf H. M. Lynd, *England in the 1880s* (New York, 1945), 124-32. For contemporary schemes for public ownership of land, see *inter alia*, George Odger, 'The Land Question', in *Contemporary Review*, August 1871; MacDonell, *op cit*, 72; G. B. Clark, MD, *A Please for the Nationalisation of Land* (1881); A. R. Wallace, *Land Nationalization* (1882); and the publications of the Land Nationalization Society, by Wallace, F. W. Newman, Rev W. R. Fletcher, F. L. Soper, and others. For attacks on such schemes by moderate land reformers, see Henry Fawcett, 'The Nationalisation of Land', in *Fortnightly Review*, December 1872; J. S. Nicholson, *Tenant's Gain not Landlord's Loss* (Edinburgh, 1883), 75; Samuel Smith, 'The Nationalisation of Land', in *Contemporary Review*, December 1883; Sir Frederick Pollock, *The Land Laws* (1883), 184. The special taxation of land was a familiar idea in Britain before the arrival of Henry George: cf the ideas of Spence, Paine and James Mill. MacDonell, *op cit*, 74, foreshadows the Georgist single tax in a scheme, alternative to nationalisation, for progressively confiscatory taxation of rent

36 Cf Joseph Hyder, *The Case for Land Nationalization* (1913)

37 Cf Lord Eversley, *Commons, Forests and Footpaths* (1910). Commons were not completely safe from encroachment by lords of manors until the virtual repeal of the Statute of Merton (1236) in 1893—*ibid*, 211

38 Cf James Howard, *The Tenant Farmer: Land Laws and Landlords* (1879); *Programme of the Farmer's Alliance* [Broadsheet, 1879]. The principal leaders of the movement were Howard, agricultural implements manufacturer and freehold farmer, J. W. Barclay, shipowner and freehold farmer, and W. E. Bear, agricultural journalist; they were all strong supporters of free trade in land, leasehold enfranchisement, and the campaign, led by P. A. Taylor and J. B. Grant, of the Anti-Game Law League

39 Cf MacDonell, 'Some New Aspects of the Land Question', in *Fortnightly Review*, May 1872; J. T. Emmett, 'The Ethics of Urban Leaseholds', in *British Quarterly Review*, April 1879; J. S. Rubinstein, *The Enfranchisement of Leaseholds* (1884); Henry Broadhurst, 'Leasehold Enfranchisement', in *The Nineteenth Century*, June 1885; *Reports, etc.*, of *Select Committees on Town Holdings*, 1886-92, and of *Royal Commission on Housing of Working Classes*, 1894. For a reasoned attack by an eminent lawyer, see Sir Arthur Underhill, *Leasehold Enfranchisement* (1887)

40 Cf Jesse Collings and Sir John L. Green, *Life of Collings* (1930, chaps xviiiff)

41 It was in no way a specifically Irish movement as might be inferred from W. L. Burn 'Free Trade in Land: An Aspect of the Irish Question', in *Transactions of Royal Historical Society*, 4th series, vol XXXI, 1949

42 Baxter, *op cit*, 4

43 Cf H. J. Habakkuk, 'Marriage Settlements in the 18th Century', *Transactions of Royal Historical Society*, 4th series, XXXII, 1950

44 Arnold, *op cit*, 126

45 'G.R.', article in *National Reformer*, May-June 1862, reprinted as *The Land Question* (1863)

46 March, 1846, 'Registration of Landed Property'

47 *Anti-Corn Law Tract No. 2: Sir Robert Peel's Burdens on Land* (1842)

48 Sir Edward Knatchbull, Paymaster of the Forces 1841-5—cf Fay, *op cit*, 93

49 *Anti-Corn Law Tract No. 2*, 103

50 Cf *Westminster Review*, March 1844, 'The Land Tax'

51 *Op cit*, viii

52 Cf Asa Briggs, *op cit*, 219

53 John Morley, *Life of Cobden* (1903 ed), 561

54 *Ibid*, 860 and 945

55 *Speeches on Questions of Public Policy* (1870), vol II, 367

56 Cf *National Reformer, loc cit; Morning Star*, December 1863 and January 1864, letters from Thorold Rogers and others; *Fraser's Magazine*, March 1864, 'The Land Tenure Question'; *Westminster Review*, July 1864, 'The Tenure of Land'

57 Cf my *Origins of Modern English Society, 1780-1880*, chap vii, section 4, 'The Forgotten Middle Class'

58 Of the 62 MPs mentioned in Dod's *Parliamentary Companion, 1880*, as land reformers or Radicals (excluding Irish members) 15 were primarily landowners or their relatives, 43 engaged in industry, commerce or finance, 15 professional men, 3 working-class representatives, and 2 army or naval officers. It should be noted that these figures do not exhaust the number of 'advanced' Liberals interested in some reform of the land laws

59 J. A. Thomas, *The House of Commons, 1832-1901* (Cardiff, 1939), 16

60 M. Beer, *A History of British Socialism* (1929 ed), vol II, 240

61 Other prominent members were the economists F. W. Newman and P. H. Wicksteed, and Mill's step-daughter Helen Taylor; Land Nationalization Society, *Annual Report, 1887*

62 Cf Henry George, jr, *Life of Henry George* (1900), 422

63 Other handbooks were Shaw Lefevre's *Freedom of Land* (1880), written at Chamberlain's suggestion and published by the National Liberal Federation; and Joseph Kay's *Free Trade in Land* (1879), a posthumous reprint of articles in *Manchester Examiner and Times*, December 1877-September 1878. After the founding in 1885 of the (Liberal) Free Land League (later the Land Law Reform Association), the Cobden Club itself concentrated on the defence of free trade against the 'fair trade' movement

64 'The Liberal Party and its Leaders', in *Fortnightly Review*, September 1873

65 *The Liberal Party, its Present Position and Future Work* (1880), 18; Mackay favoured universal adult suffrage and a United States of Europe

66 *Radicalism: its Effects on the English Constitution*, translated from *Journal des Débats* by T. L. Oxley (1880)

67 Garvin, *op cit*, vol II, 392

68 *Ibid*, vol II, 178

69 'The Aim of Reform', in *Fortnightly Review*, March 1872

70 Garvin, *op cit*, vol II, 67

71 *Daily News*, 5 May 1880; *Manchester Guardian*, 25 May 1880

72 It was replaced in 1925, but the principles remained unaltered

73 Garvin, *op cit*, vol II, 59

74 *Ibid*, 104

75 *Ibid*, 169

76 D. Lloyd George, *The Lords, the Land and the People* (1910). The taxes were a duty of 20 per cent on the enhanced value of land to be paid when it changed hands, and $\frac{1}{2}$d in £ on the capital value of undeveloped land and minerals. The root of the objection to them was not their size but

the fact that the valuation they involved could form the basis of indefinitely extended taxation or even nationalisation

77 Similar land taxes to Lloyd George's were, however, included by Snowden in his 1931 Budget, and repealed by the National Government of 1934

78 Smallholdings provided under the Liberal Acts up to the end of 1914 totalled 18,484, only about 2 per cent of which were purchased, and two-thirds of which were said to be taken by village tradesmen rather than full-time agriculturalists. In January 1949 the total stood at 22,449, of which 9,288 were part-time holdings—Board of Agriculture and Fisheries, *Annual Report of Proceedings under the Small Holdings and Allotments Acts of 1908 and 1910, etc., for 1914* (Cd. 7851 and 7892, 1915), 4, 22; W. H. R. Curtler, *The Enclosure and Redistribution of Our Land* (1920), 300, 304; Ministry of Agriculture and Fisheries, *Smallholdings* (1949), 50

79 R. C. K. Ensor, 'Some Political and Economic Interactions in later Victorian England', *Transactions Royal Historical Society*, 4th series, XXXI, 1949

80 'Liberalism and the Victorian Intelligentsia', in *Cambridge Historical Journal*, XIII, 1957

81 J. A. Thomas, *The House of Commons, 1832-1901* (Cardiff, 1939), 14-17, tables 1-6 (1868-1900), and *1906-1911* (Cardiff, 1958), 28-31, 44-5, tables IA, IIB, IVA

82 Cf Morley, *Life of Gladstone* (1903), vol III, 236

83 *Ibid*, 256

84 Cf H. D. Traill, 'The Allies: A Political Dialogue', in *The Nineteenth Century*, June 1882

85 Garvin, *op cit*, vol I, 462

86 October 1871, 'Essays on the Tenure of Land'

87 'The Radicals and Socialism', in *The Nineteenth Century*, November 1885

88 The 1892 Cabinet contained 6 landowners, 1 rentier, and 2 representatives of commerce and industry, as against 8 legal and professional men; that of 1906, 8 landowners and 1 from commerce and industry as against 9 legal and professional men and 1 trade unionist—of H. J. Laski, *Studies in Law and Politics* (1932), chap viii, and W. L. Guttsman, *The British Political Élite* (1963), chap iv

89 An equally illuminating test would be that of the railway directors who, beginning in 1886 with their opposition to Mundella's Bill to control railway freight rates, increasingly transferred their allegiance from the Liberal to the Conservative Party—cf W. H. G. Armytage, 'The Railway Rates Question and the Fall of the Third Gladstone Ministry', *English Historical Review*, LXV, 1950

INDEX